THE
PEOPLE'S WAR

Reader's Digest

THE PEOPLE'S WAR

RELIVING LIFE ON THE HOME FRONT IN WORLD WAR II

FELICITY GOODALL

This book is dedicated to my mother, who lost her youth to World War II.

Author's Note: Because most of these personal experiences were recorded either in letters or diaries, where words tumble on to the page in a rush to capture the thoughts and feelings of the moment, such documents are often typified by long sentences. Punctuation has therefore been added to these accounts to ensure clarity.

The People's War has been produced by David & Charles in association with The Reader's Digest Association Limited.

This edition © David & Charles Ltd, 2008
Text © Felicity Goodall
Images © see page 288
Reprinted 2008
David & Charles is an F+W Media, Inc. Company
4700 East Galbraith Road
Cincinnati, OH 45236

The text and first-hand accounts contained in this edition were first published as *Voices from the Home Front*, 2004, 2006.

A catalogue record for this book is available from the British Library.

ISBN: 978-0-276-44391-6

Printed in Italy by G. Canale & C S.p.A
For David & Charles Ltd
Brunel House, Newton Abbot,
Devon, TQ12 4PU

For David & Charles:

Head of Publishing: Alison Myer
Commissioning Editor: Neil Baber
Editorial Manager: Emily Pitcher
Senior Designer: Jodie Lystor
Picture Research: Tehmina Boman
Project Editor: Caroline Taggart
Proofreader: Susan Pitcher
Production: Beverley Richardson

"September 3, 1939: I am writing this while listening to Chamberlain at 11am. To have grown up for this!" (Mary Ross, 1939)

When Mary Ross wrote those words to her fiancé, little did she think that World War II would last for almost six years. She and the rest of her generation would have their lives overtaken by the machine of war. This book is an album of 'oral snapshots' from the lives of some of those who lived through the years 1939–45.

Contents

Take yourself back to the summer of 1939. A teenager picks flowers in a country garden, little dreaming that she will lose a cherished brother, or that she will nurse burnt airmen. A young woman works in a music shop, unaware that the handsome lifeguard she is walking out with will be shot down. A mother of four, who lost a fiancé in the Great War, will leave her comfortable home to run a canteen for troops resisting invasion. There are few cars; house doors are left unlocked in the countryside; and it is a matter of pride to men that their wives do not need to go out to work. Washing machines and refrigerators are only for the wealthy; children can leave school at 14; and there is as yet no vaccination against childhood diseases like polio and meningitis. There are few homeowners; the rent man, the bailiffs and the Means Test are the scourge of the majority; and the previous two decades have been dominated by recession. Gracie Fields, Deanna Durbin, Cary Grant and Errol Flynn are among the stars who entertain cinema audiences. Witty plays by Noel Coward entertain London theatregoers. Britain has an Empire and India is the gem in its crown, but the movement for independence is gaining momentum. King George VI has been on the throne for three years, Neville Chamberlain is Prime Minister, and Winston Churchill is waiting in the wings. Across the English Channel, ugly events have been brewing since Hitler rose to power in 1933. Germany has been re-arming; Britain has not. A war is about to erupt, though nobody wants to believe that it can, or will, happen.

ONCE MORE THE COUNTRY MUST MOBILISE. *With the experience of World War I fresh in people's memories, Britons knew that there was a bitter struggle ahead.*

A SEASIDE HOLIDAY IN SUMMER 1939 *was not as carefree as in previous years. Children paddling along the English Channel coast had to have their gas masks at the ready.*

1. From Peace to War

"I stood on the footway of Hungerford Bridge across the Thames, watching the lights of London go out. The whole great town was lit up like a fairyland, in a dazzle that reached into the sky and then, one by one, as a switch was pulled, each area went dark, the dazzle becoming a patchwork of lights being snuffed here and there until a last one remained, and it too went out. What was left us was more than just wartime blackout, it was a fearful portent of what war was to be. We had not thought we would have to fight it in darkness, or that light would be our enemy."

Mea Allan, September 1939

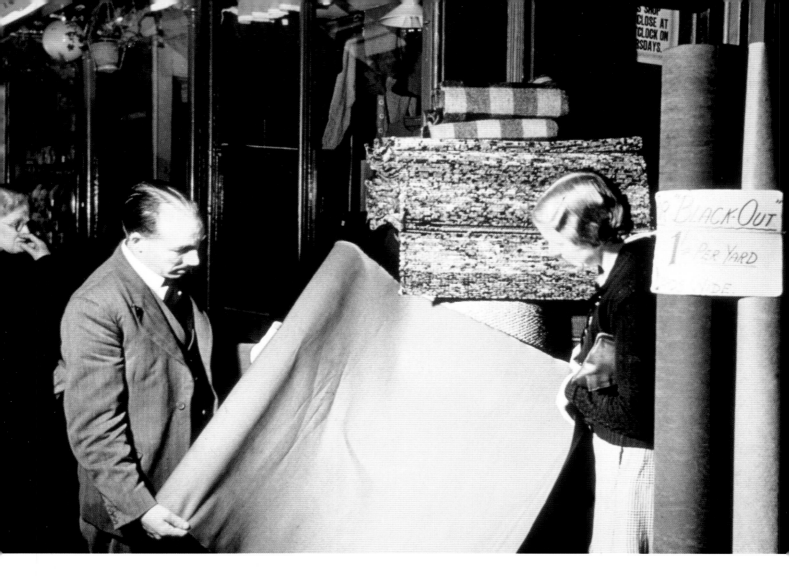

The world had watched and waited throughout the summer of 1939, as events unfolded on the continent of Europe. Some British families had gone away as usual, snatching the last seaside holiday for many years. But bags were soon packed, tent pegs pulled up, as families returned home to prepare for the civilian war. There was not the flag-waving enthusiasm witnessed when World War I was declared. Twenty-five years later, a new generation had grown up with the knowledge of the casualties and death toll of that Great War. As they listened to Chamberlain's announcement on the wireless, declaring that 'this country is at war', they knew what it would cost. They did not know that a year later Britain would stand as the last bastion of Western freedom, an isolated island on the fringes of Nazi-occupied Europe. They did not know that in this war thousands of civilians would be killed, as Hitler tried to batter the British into submission. They did not know that the demands of the Home Front would leave the British population exhausted, dressed in threadbare clothes and ill-fitting shoes. They did not know of the inner resources that would keep them soldiering on, giving rise to the legendary wartime spirit.

ONE IMMEDIATE CHANGE that the threat of war brought for civilians was the blackout. Drapers' shops supplied special material that people could use to make extra curtains.

For the first minute after going out of doors one is completely bewildered, then it is a matter of groping forward with nerves, as well as hands, outstretched.

Making and hanging blackout curtains was the first massive war effort by women all over Britain. Even before war was declared, yards and yards of dark blue, black and dark green material were being stitched by hand and machine. On 31 August 1939 Miss Andrews, living quietly in Tunbridge Wells, recorded in her diary:

Switch off that LIGHT!

LESS LIGHT – MORE PLANES

"We make curtains busily and finish ten minutes before the wireless order for universal blackout as from tonight, everyone rushing for curtain material, torches etc."

Those unable to buy cloth could use black card and secure it round the window frame with battens, sealing in the light and sealing out the fresh air. Blackout curtains could not be washed, as this was apt to let the light shine through. The Government issued instructions in a leaflet telling people to 'hoover, shake, brush then iron' – the latter to make them more light-proof. Nowadays light streams out into the streets and skies from shop windows, empty office buildings and traffic on the streets. Wartime buses and cars had their headlights covered to show only a crack of light, and they passed through empty streets like ghost vehicles. Phyllis Warner kept her diary as a basis for newspaper articles which she sent to American newspapers.

"The density of the blackout these cloudy moonless nights is beyond belief. No one in New York or Los Angeles can successfully imagine what it's like. For the first minute after going out of doors one is completely bewildered, then it is a matter of groping forward with nerves, as well as hands, outstretched."

GOVERNMENT PROPAGANDA *was vital throughout the war as a means of comminicating with Britons and boosting morale. The first of many campaigns encouraged people to turn off all of their lights in order to make life more difficult for the enemy bombers.*

TO SMALL CHILDREN *who remembered little of life before the war, closing the blackout curtains at the same time as the original ones seemed a perfectly normal procedure.*

were also subject to
blackout restrictions: only
the thinnest strip of light
was permitted.

Forces switchboard operator Mollie Wilson described finding her way out to the YMCA in the unfamiliar surroundings of Corsham, a military town in Wiltshire.

"It was pitch dark at about 8.40 when we set out, and it was pretty difficult to find the gate so Louie and I sort of crept along. We bumped into bushes and plenty of walls before we reached the road. Then we said, 'Oh, I'm beginning to see properly,' and walked bang into another wall. After that we weren't too bad 'cause we got on to the main street. We were walking gaily along the pavement, when suddenly bang!! – The two of us fell over a sandbag barricade. I nearly split my sides with laughter."

Broad white stripes were painted round doors of underground trains, as they were practically invisible in the dark, and railway carriages were blacked out. One Essex farmer even painted white stripes on his cattle so that they might be more visible in muted car headlights. Church bells were silenced; they would be rung only in the event of invasion. As the nation geared up for that anticipated event, milestones were boxed in, aeroplane-trapping poles were built alongside roads and in flat fields, and enormous barrage balloons appeared in the sky – gigantic fabric balloons filled with hydrogen and designed as visual and physical barriers to enemy bombers. In Glasgow, Dr JP McHutchison waxed lyrical about these strange objects.

> "I should record my impression of the strange beauty of the balloons over Glasgow – silver stars in the morning sunlight. Seen against a glowing western sky as dark shapes in a welter of colour, they make a picture to my mind somewhat more typical of our war landscape than even the long fingers of searchlights at night."

Urban streets became cluttered with green canvas sandbags piled round lampposts as a precaution against firebombs. Because of the perils of these sandbags, Londoner Lylie Eldergill accompanied her blind husband to work and back every day. Lylie had lived through World War I and was depressed at having to go through domestic preparations for a second war. She busied herself preserving her most precious possessions.

I should record my impression of the strange beauty of the balloons over Glasgow – silver stars in the morning sunlight.

> "I have packed my glass and china away – so really it looks like *Christmas Day in the Workhouse*. I am glad we had our holiday, I don't know when we shall have another. Eddie [her younger brother] is twenty-two years old today. I think that it will just about break my mother up when he goes to war."

BARRAGE BALLOONS *were used during daylight hours to confuse enemy bombers by making their targets more difficult to identify.*

But go to war he did, joining the RAF as a pilot. The dreadful screech of air raid sirens sounded across the country as their machinery was tested; searchlights probed the skies for enemy planes; and anti-aircraft batteries were installed in such incongruous places as Hyde Park. The population stepped into their new wartime roles.

The Home Front went to war, donning the uniforms, helmets and armbands of their new roles in Civil Defence, carrying identity cards and one vital piece of equipment: a gas mask. Carrying gas masks would become routine but first they had to fit properly. Peg Cotton noted that babies were catered for with special care.

> "Penny has a huge 'protective helmet' – a contrivance that covers her completely – then we pump oxygen into it."

Gas was one enemy weapon anticipated by the authorities, after its use with such brutal effect in the trenches during the Great War, and as a precaution Royal Mail pillar boxes were painted with pale green gas-detector paint that would turn red on contact with drops of mustard gas. According to a London County Council leaflet 'Anti-Gas Precautions for Civil Defence', mustard gas was the most difficult to detect but it smelt faintly of horseradish, onions or garlic.

Local authorities secretly stockpiled cardboard coffins, and the population responded to a huge campaign to donate blood in preparation for inevitable casualties. The Local Defence Volunteers (LDV) were formed in preparation for possible invasion and speedily acquired the soubriquet, the Home Guard. At the outbreak of war, journalist Leonard Marsland Gander had moved his family out of London to Angmering-on-Sea, in Sussex, where he applied to join the volunteers.

TWO YEARS BEFORE WAR was declared Britain had a standing army of 200,000 men. The introduction of compulsory military service early in 1939, and the volunteers who joined up as soon as war broke out, raised this number to 875,000 – still not enough to fight a war. In October 1939 the government announced that all men aged between 20 and 23 who were not working in a 'reserved occupation' such as farming must enlist in one of the forces.

GAS MASKS *were issued to young and old alike, along with instructions on how to use them.*

"I was asked if I would like to join the foot patrols but in view of the fact that the family are coming back to town I see no chance of getting down for duties. So I contented myself with typing out a list of phrases in German which I thought might be useful to the Home Guard, as Churchill calls them. Such as 'Hands up.' 'You are my prisoner.' 'You are surrounded by superior forces.' ' Surrender or you will be wiped out.'"

The Home Guard was taught to charge with bayonets, and took part in exercises with the regular army. Switchboard operator Mollie Wilson in Corsham found herself a bystander at a Home Guard practice.

"It was most exciting…The Home Guard and the 'Germans' kept taking pot shots at each other round the war memorial. Some of the 'Germans' climbed into Lady Methuen's garden and came down that way. I saw one shadowy figure creeping through the shrubbery and nearly had a fit, as there was a member of the Home Guard standing with his back to the railings. Then a rifle butt crept round the wheel of a van and someone was killed. I couldn't see who. Then some 'Germans', two all splattered with blood and bandaged up, came creeping down from the Priory, and were making fine

progress towards the capture of the Town Hall, but they became too sure of themselves. One of them, a corporal, had the bright idea to throw a bomb. While he was lighting it and the others were reloading, a lance corporal of the Home Guard made a sudden dash and machine-gunned them all. He even unintentionally held up and shot a Colonel who came up behind. So the day was won, and the Ambulance people carried out their task of collecting up the wounded and dead to be bandaged by the Red Cross nurses. One soldier I noticed was lying on the ground for about half an hour. Other soldiers kept coming up to look at his label (broken thigh or something) and going away again. It was so funny for us; but so sad for him. One of the men said that a large scale practice like this one is the best thing that could happen, for they find lots of remedies from every time. It won't be so funny when it really happens and there won't be so many spectators to get in the way."

This was 1940: Hitler's army was making aggressively for the English Channel and Mollie Wilson (like most people) used the preposition 'when' rather than 'if', when talking of invasion.

Journalist Leonard Marsland Gander was scornful of what he regarded as futile measures against invasion, spotted on the outskirts of London.

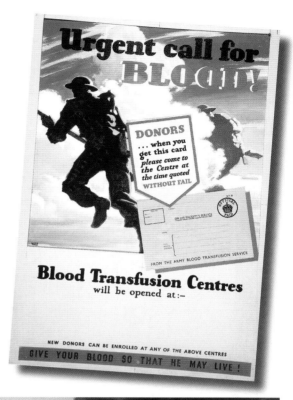

MANY APPEALS TO CIVILIANS' *patriotism were made, such as this one asking for the public to donate blood.*

LOCAL DEFENCE VOLUNTEERS *(LDV) – or Home Guard – consisted mainly of those too old or too young to join the forces. Their official role was to prepare to defend the country in the event of invasion. Although they were mockingly known as 'Look, Duck and Vanish', most of their members were brave and patriotic men. Here, the Birkenhead Home Guard round up 'looters' during an invasion exercise.*

"Near Chessington they seem to be building concrete tank obstacles of the superior sort right across countryside and roads. Are they making a sort of Siegfried Line as London's last defences? On the Kingston by-pass, added to the muck, are a large number of strange objects like galvanised iron chimney pots. Cannot imagine what they are for. But I am again dismayed by the sight of the derelict motor cars with baulks of timber thrust through the windows and the old carts standing by the road ready to be used for barricades. An ancient Morris car filled with earth seems a feeble, inefficient means of defence, incredibly crude and messy by comparison with a battleship or a Spitfire."

On the way to his office at the London headquarters of *The Daily Telegraph*, there was evidence of preparations for the desperate defence of the capital too.

"Pillboxes of various types have been constructed on the Embankment. One at the end of New Bridge Street is particularly ingenious as it is partly disguised to look like the entrance to a Tube subway and even has newspaper placards painted on one side. Numerous brick air raid shelters have been built on the pavements. The work on Waterloo Bridge goes on but there are also the beginnings of emergency pontoon bridges at several points."

GERMANY INVADES POLAND

Hitler became Chancellor of Germany in 1933 and promptly set about rearming the country. His avowed policy was to reclaim territories that had been conceded under the Treaty of Versailles at the end of World War I, to unite the German peoples across Europe and to give them more 'living space' or *Lebensraum*.

His first act of aggression was to occupy the demilitarised Rhineland zone in 1936. He followed this in 1938 by invading Austria and later the same year by annexing the Sudetenland (now part of the Czech Republic, at the time populated largely by ethnic Germans). This latter move was the one to which Britain and France – anxious to avoid the war that many now

saw as inevitable – acceded in the Munich Conference from which Prime Minister Neville Chamberlain returned declaring, 'I believe it is peace for our time.'

As part of that Munich Pact, France, Britain and Germany all agreed to respect the remaining Czech boundaries – an agreement which Hitler promptly violated. Finally realising that Hitler was not to be trusted, Britain guaranteed to defend Poland against a similar invasion. Germany duly invaded on September 1, 1939; Chamberlain's ultimatum was delivered and ignored, and on September 3 Britain and France declared war on Germany. The British people's last shred of hope vanished and they resigned themselves to a long struggle.

AN ANTI-TANK GUN
*is brought into position
(inset left) on the main
road outside Warsaw during
the Nazi invasion of Poland,
September 1939. The Germans
besieged Warsaw for three weeks
before the capital surrendered.*

A VICTORY PARADE IS HELD
*after the capture of Warsaw,
where Hitler admires his
successful troops (left).*

GERMAN TANKS ENTER
*a Polish village (top left),
September 1939.*

SOLDIERS REMOVE THE BORDER
*markers (top right) that had
been erected in 1923, showing
that this part of Upper Silesia
belonged to Poland.*

NAZI BOMBING REDUCED
*much of Warsaw to rubble on
September 25 (middle right).*

HITLER'S TRUCKS AND SOLDIERS
*occupy the centre of Warsaw
(bottom right) after the
surrender, October 1, 1939.*

The government had exhorted people to buy shelters in the summer of 1939. Some were given away to those on low incomes; many families pooled their resources. Dolly Howard in Liverpool described her family shelter: their reinforced garage.

"We filled hundreds of sandbags – I had blisters on my hands and Lillian's shoulders ached so much that she could not stand up straight for a week. Well now it is like a little refuge room, walls papered with waterproof paper, electric light (dim and bright), and beds. James has a camp bed at one side and there is a big double bed for Lillian and me. So after the nightly alerts, we just go to bed. Puss comes as well. We take supper and we knit if we do not want to go sleep. Lillian and James just put their heads down and sleep through everything but the guns keep me awake a bit. Jim goes on ARP duty, so I have put him a bed in the sitting room, and he pops in when there is a lull. If we feel cold in the winter we shall put a little radiator in the shelter but so far we have been too warm. We started with a lot of bedclothes but have been peeling off ever since."

As they prepared for siege, inevitably people's thoughts turned to food. Rationing had been introduced during World War I, as Britain struggled to feed its population. Those in the know began to stockpile. As an American, Peg Cotton had not experienced those shortages during 1914–18.

"Within a few months of the declaration of War people began to think of laying in a few stores of those commodities which, in time, were likely to become scarce. My grocer in London recommended tinned goods, sugar, candles, soap and toilet paper. The latter article made me smile. 'I remember the last War very well, Madam,' he admonished me, 'and there wasn't even a telephone directory to be had!'"

ANDERSON SHELTERS *were issued free to those on low incomes and sold for £7 to others. Measuring 6ft (1.8m) x 4ft 6in (1.4m) x 6ft 6in (2m), they were buried 4ft (1.2m) deep – mostly in people's back gardens – and covered with at least 15in (40cm) of soil. In the course of the war over two million such shelters were erected and they probably saved many thousands of lives.*

CAMOUFLAGING SHELTERS AND FORTIFICATIONS *required ingenuity and creativity, as with this pillbox in Felixstowe, Suffolk.*

ALTHOUGH THE SHELTERS *were 'standard issue', their owners were allowed to equip them as they wished. Some people managed to make them very comfortable.*

2. In the Line of Fire

"Once we thought of a frontline village as a heap of shattered ruins in a pockmarked earth bordering the tumbled wilderness of No Man's Land. Now there are hundreds of British front-line towns and villages along our coasts, in the shadow of a menace, but as yet preserved from the worst of war's ravages. No Man's Land is our own protecting element, the sea, where the Royal Navy rides and rules." Leonard Marsland Gander, *Daily Telegraph*, May 1940

Britain's coastline stretches for 11,232 miles. While the sea may act as a No Man's Land, this enormous coast with thousands of tiny bays and inlets required constant vigilance to counteract invasion attempts. Five days after war was declared Bessie Skea, a 15-year-old schoolgirl in the Orkney Islands, recorded in her diary some of the action in her small corner of the British Isles.

"Britain has caught two German ships and taken them into Kirkwall. They put both crews on one ship and sank the other one. Three Germans somehow got away in a motor boat and they spent the night in the Bay of Sandsgarth. Tommy Nicholson saw them and reported it. Tom Sinclair and Bill Nicholson (both first-war veterans) gave chase in Bill Nicholson's boat. A tug came from Kirkwall with armed men on it, touched here and set off too. The village people went into a 'steer' because the Germans were said to be armed and Bill and Tam weren't! They caught them near Stronsay. When the Shapinsay men came up to the Germans, they found them unresisting and friendly. They gave them cigarettes, and were about to make them a pot of tea when the tug-boat appeared, and unceremoniously ordered the Germans aboard at gun-point."

Hitler is sure to bomb Kirkwall; Orkney is a dangerous place to live in.

The Orkney Islands were in a vital strategic position, and the influx of service men and women boosted the islands' population to 60,000 – three times the peacetime population. Some of these troops were billeted on the local population.

WITH TEN 14-INCH GUNS *and capacity to carry two aircraft, HMS Howe (seen here off Scapa Flow) was a vital part of the home fleet. The brilliant flash from the guns which preceded the cordite smoke lasted for only a fraction of a second.*

WHILE SOUTHERN BRITAIN *was in the midst of the 'phoney war' northern Britain was beginning to suffer from Luftwaffe bombing campaigns.*

The first German bomb to land on Britain came down in Orkney, and the first civilian casualty of the war was also from the islands.

IMPORTANT NOTICE AIR RAID EXERCISE

An air raid exercise will be carried out in Orkney in the afternoon in a few days time. The object of this exercise is to test all departments of the defence, civil, naval and military.

The exercise will be made as realistic as possible, and all inhabitants are requested to act as they would do in the event of a real raid, and to comply with the instructions of the military.

The air raid warning sirens will sound the "All Clear" at 3 o'clock p.m. as a signal for the exercise to start, and the "All Clear" siren again at 4 o'clock. This period covers the time of the exercise as far as the civil population is concerned. The "All Clear" will be sounded again at 6 o'clock for the benefit of the military.

In the event of a real air raid occurring during the exercise, the air raid sirens will sound a warning in the usual way, and the exercise will cease automatically.

Aircraft will take part simulating attacks, and the A.R.P. services will be given tasks to perform.

Enemy troops are being represented by troops wearing distinguishing marks on their uniform. These may succeed in entering the towns, but the civil population should take no action against them beyond reporting their presence to the nearest police station. They will leave further action to the military and Local Defence Volunteers.

Road blocks will be placed on many roads, and cars will be required to stop and pass military sentries, the drivers proving their identity by showing their identity certificates.

It should be understood that no further notice of this exercise will be given. The next warning will be the siren giving "All Clear" at 3 p.m. on the day of the exercise. All concerned are requested to take this as the signal for the exercise to commence, and to act accordingly.

(Sgd.) **G. C. KEMP**, Major General,
Commander Orkney and Shetland Defences.

Stromness, Orkney,
3/6/40.

THE AIR RAID PRECAUTION SERVICE (ARP) *was ordered to mobilise by Chamberlain in August 1938, ahead of the first air raid on October 16, 1939. Regular blackout and air raid exercises were carried out to test all departments of the defence forces – civil, naval and military – as well as the British public.*

"We hear that Miss Balfour is making the private soldiers who are billeted with her eat their food outside in the cold. She even refused to let them put their stoves in the courts outside the kitchen door – the stoves are in the tennis court and the men must eat there in the rain! And the Lieutenant is treated like a gentleman, while he would prefer to be out with his men. They must take their boots off before coming indoors!"

From her coastal vantage point, Bessie watched with excitement as planes buzzed overhead, and great convoys of ships steamed past en route to Kirkwall.

"Hitler is sure to bomb Kirkwall; Orkney is a dangerous place to live in. The King was in Scapa Flow and Kirkwall last week; Churchill was here the week before. There are rumours that Churchill said Orkney was half-fortified – with the result that we are to have more coastal guns – one in Shapinsay too."

Her prediction was correct. Ten miles from Bessie's home in Shapinsay is Scapa Flow, a natural harbour deep enough for larger ships and encircled by islands. The German Navy scuttled its own fleet there during World War I. It was the British Navy that suffered there on October 14, 1939.

"There were two air raids over Kirkwall while I was in town. The Royal Oak was blown up in Scapa and about 800 lives lost – many young boys in training. The war is only beginning now."

Thousands of troops were billeted along Britain's south and east coast as defences were strengthened in the summer of 1939. A string of circular Martello towers, grim remnants of the last threat of invasion during the Napoleonic wars, found a new role as positions for anti-aircraft batteries. In 1940, as German troops roared victorious across the Continent, frontline towns became restricted areas, barbed wire appeared on sea fronts and beaches were mined. Until then the genteel seaside resort of Worthing, in Sussex, had been considered a safe destination for evacuees in 1939. On May 27, 1940 physiotherapist Joan Strange began to record the changes in her diary.

"Worthing is being prepared! All the bathing huts have been trundled off the beach, filled with stones and put to block roads leading up from the sea! All boats have been removed from the beach and no bathing is allowed.

May 28: Our pier has been closed by the military authorities and mined. No one is allowed to sit on the seats on the front in a given area round the shore end of pier.

May 30: Worthing looks different! The front is being cut up for 'pill-boxes', there's a lookout on top of County Café, soldiers and sailors abound. People are leaving the coast hotels very rapidly and some residents with small children are going too."

PART OF THE DEFENCES *to deter invaders on the south coast. All around Britain's coastline hundreds of miles of barbed wire was erected, defensive ditches dug and pill-boxes of varying designs built to protect against German invasion.*

NOTICE
SITTING ON RAILINGS
NOT ALLOWED
BY ORDER.

By May 1940 the German Army had reached the coast of France. Trapped on the beaches round Dunkirk were members of the British Expeditionary Force (BEF). At 11am on May 30 the crew of the Margate lifeboat was called out to help with the evacuation of troops. Equipped with steel helmets, cigarettes and rations, the crew launched the boat and set off. Ted Jordan had been on the crew for 18 years.

"The boat was launched at 5.20pm and put off into Margate Roads where we made fast to a naval craft. We proceeded in tow to Dunkirk, arriving there just before midnight. As we approached we could smell the fires which were raging in the town and about the docks, and the whole sea front was one mass of dense smoke and flame. We got in as close as possible, and saw masses of troops assembled at the water's edge, and we got about 80 aboard at first, and then got them aboard a nearby craft. A British officer swam to us, and came aboard, telling the coxswain that he had a large number of men further along the shore and guided us to the spot. He instructed his men how to make their way to us, telling them it was their last chance. Among them were several badly injured, and their mates were holding them shoulder high, on improvised litters."

A FLOTILLA OF SMALL CRAFT *is towed down the Thames on its way to France. Around 800 of these craft were used to evacuate Allied and British Expeditionary Force (BEF) troops.*

They ferried the wounded to a hospital ship with German planes buzzing overhead, then set off to look for survivors clinging to rafts and bits of wreckage closer to the shore.

"Everywhere around one could see sunken craft and hear the bursting of shells from German guns. Troops on the beach were frantically trying to dig out all sorts of small boats which had been left high and dry, cattle were wandering along the water edge bewildered and quite near to us were the charred remains of one of the popular pleasure steamers, *Crested Eagle*. The whole job was at times awe-inspiring."

Everywhere around one could see sunken craft, and could hear the bursting of shells from German guns.

THE LONDON-BASED TUG Sunvill, *seen here with her crew, took part in the evacuation. With the large vessels unable to reach the shallow shores at Dunkirk, the BBC broadcast an announcement for owners of 'self-propelled vessels between 30–100ft in length' to report to the Admiralty.*

GERMAN TANKS ARRIVING *at the Channel coast cornered the majority of the Allied forces near the Belgian border at Dunkirk. Many of these were injured and exhausted from fighting in Belgium, along the French border, and at Arras. The beaches they waited on for rescue were treacherous with enemy fire and strewn with the remains of men and horses, abandoned vehicles, weapons and muntions.*

The Margate lifeboat brought off 600 survivors. It was just one of around 100 civilian boats that crossed to Dunkirk. Sublieutenant A Carew Hunt RN described the actions of one man who was typical of the civilians who helped to make Dunkirk such a very British 'victory'.

> "I'd like to recommend highly the civilian cox of the *Thark* a man by the name of Ambler. This man who had only river experience succeeded in taking the boat to Dunkirk and back with no officer on the boat. He took the boat over again on Monday night and it was sunk, but I believe the crew was saved."

According to writer Noel Streatfeild, there would have been even more boats in the flotilla. On June 13, 1940 she wrote to her brother and sister-in-law in America:

> "The disgruntled who didn't go have appeared on the scenes. It seems to those hundred odd little ships that made up our Armada, there were countless hundreds more that were screaming to be allowed to go, and whose owners, presumably because they were already in useful jobs, were not allowed to take them. Whatever may happen to the owners of those boats for the rest of their lives, I don't think anything will ever compensate for them missing Dunkirk. They seem to feel like racehorses who should have run in the Grand National, and were not given the chance."

SPACE WAS AT A PREMIUM ON BOARD,
*so before leaving England the ships had
been stripped of all non-essential items
that could have added weight and taken
up valuable space. Troops were loaded
on by the hundreds (above) and had to
stand or lie in the same position until
reaching shore. Mercifully, the English
Channel stayed uncharacteristically
calm throughout the whole operation.*

THOUSANDS OF SOLDIERS LINE UP
*to be evacuated from Dunkirk (top
left). Many soldiers queued for hours
in chest-deep water to be rescued by
the little ships. Personnel took priority
over equipment and supplies, forcing
the costly abandonment of many guns,
vehicles, stores and ammunition.*

BRITISH REARGUARD SOLDIERS
*(middle left) were the last to be
evacuated from France. Of the men
rescued in Operation Dynamo,
98,780 had come from the beaches
and 239,446 from the harbour.
There were around 30,000 fatalities.*

THE AERIAL BOMBARDMENT
*of Dunkirk was unrelenting (bottom
left). More than 1,000 civilians were
killed on the first day of the
evacuation alone.*

THE WITHDRAWAL FROM DUNKIRK

Within a week of Neville Chamberlain declaring that Britain was at war against Nazi Germany the first elements of the British Expeditionary Force (BEF) disembarked in France. The battle of France did not begin in earnest however, until May 10, 1940, with the German troops invading the Netherlands and marching on through Belgium, continuing their rapid advance westward. A series of Allied counter-attacks, including the Battle of Arras, failed to stop the advancing army which had now turned north towards the English Channel in what was called the Manstein Plan, or 'sickle cut'.

The German spearhead reaching the French coast created a 50-mile divide in the Allied forces, and on May 25 General Lord Gort, Commander of the BEF, ordered the evacuation of the British, French and Belgian forces cornered at Dunkirk. On May 27 Operation Dynamo – the codename for the evacuation – swung into action. Nine days after the start of the operation some 338,226 soldiers had been rescued and the whole evacuation hailed a great success.

AFTER HITTING A MINE AND COMING UNDER ATTACK *from shore batteries off Nieuport on the way back from Dunkirk, the French destroyer Bourrasque started to sink. Of the 1,200 crew and troops on board many jumped to safety and 559 people were saved.*

A COOK HOUSE *set up on a London station platform served hot food to servicemen who passed through on their way home from northern France.*

As Dunkirk survivors arrived ashore, civilian workers of all sorts rose to the occasion. Arthur Mowbray, head postmaster at Dover, recorded how postal, telephone and telegram services coped.

"Foreign mails, labelled and unlabelled, outward and inward, sealed and unsealed were dumped in the Sorting Office as they were brought from France in anything that could float. Many bags were riddled and torn by bomb splinters while others, salved from the sea, were in a saturated condition, the contents like paper pulp, but with careful drying and a little imagination in deciphering addresses, the majority of items were sent off on a second journey. Special arrangements had to be made on the spot; as boats of every size imaginable were emptied of their human cargoes, hundreds of telegrams were handed in; 1,500 such messages were handed over in one day at a quayside office. The average daily traffic of 850 telegrams dealt with at the Head Office jumped to over 4,000. No appreciable delay occurred in disposing of the traffic, due to the wholehearted co-operation of the staff who worked long hours at high pressure. Teleprinter speeds of 109 and 110 messages per hour were obtained. Meal reliefs went by unheeded, for who could handle such messages and remain unmoved by the urgency of their appeal? The senders, somebody's father, somebody's son, were indeed straight from the jaws of Hell, back from the gates of Death, and the little we could do to assist them to relieve the anxiety at home was gladly undertaken."

The inn was swamped with troops, wet, wounded and exhausted; every chair, form, table, and available floor space was occupied; any place to rest was heaven.

Arthur Mowbray was particularly impressed by one post office worker: a 16-year-old Girl Guide, who volunteered to tend men in one of the town's pubs.

> "The inn was swamped with troops, wet, wounded and exhausted; every chair, form, table, and available floor space was occupied; any place to rest was heaven. This child stayed several nights, after her working hours, taking off men's boots and wet clothes and drying them. She did what she could. To some it may have been their last taste of human kindness."

Mrs Iris Phillips, from the WVS, was one of many who helped the wounded on to hospital trains, serving refreshments donated by shops and local inhabitants.

> "As soon as the patients were put down on the platform they began to look anxiously round, first for a cigarette, which we instantly provided, and secondly for their particular pal. It made all the difference to those pitifully wounded men to know that however painful and miserable the journey might be, their friends would be beside them to share it. Many of the patients were unable to sit up, and the nurses were all busy, so we knelt down where we were and supported the men with one arm and fed them with drinks with the other."

HOSPITAL OR AMBULANCE *trains were used throughout the war to transport the wounded soldiers to hospital. The walking wounded would sit in the normal seats of the specially adapted carriages which were also fitted with operating theatres and three-tiered bunk beds for the more seriously wounded. The trains would clearly display the Red Cross logo on the side and roof to avoid attack from the Luftwaffe.*

CIVILIANS RALLIED ROUND *as the troops disembarked from the boats, giving them a heroes' welcome of tea, sandwiches and other much needed refreshment.*

Kathleen Crawley had been on holiday when war broke out, and was evacuated from her home in London to Ashford in Kent.

"All the soldiers coming home from Dunkirk come through Ashford station. Crowds of people wait along the line for them to give them refreshments and to collect souvenirs. They throw lots of things out of the trains. When Doris was there one threw an old German Army boot and Doris claimed a buckle and a piece of leather off the sole."

This was evidence of the thrifty nature of wartime living even in June 1940. Farther along the railway line, Mrs A Radloff was nursing at a military hospital when the wards were suddenly emptied of patients. The hospital staff didn't have to wait for long.

"One lovely May Day they came – filthy, unshaven, tattered and verminous. Most slept as they walked, unless they groaned in agony in stretchers. They collapsed on the beds, some lying for 48 hours before waking. Time ceased to exist. The only means of sterilisation – the primus – must be lit and kept going and the blood-soaked, fly-ridden dressings removed."

HUNDREDS OF TRAINS *were laid on specially by operators to ferry the soldiers back from the south coast. They were taken to bases all over Britain to recover and be sorted, before being given a couple of days' leave. Some of the soldiers who lived on the south coast were fortunate enough to fleetingly see wives and girlfriends on their way through.*

THE BEF RETREAT
was a tactical victory for Germany, but 'the miracle at Dunkirk' was seized very effectively by the British government as morale-boosting propaganda. The 'Dunkirk spirit' – as seen here in one family's proud display of a Union Jack and Ensign – captured the hearts and minds of the public at a time when a German invasion seemed unavoidable.

Dunkirk was a military defeat but to the nation it became a cause célèbre as men returned to their families and home towns. On June 1, 1940, Joan Strange joyfully recorded in her diary the safe return of 'a number of Worthing men'. Captain Tommie Kerr described his welcome at a London railway station in a letter home.

"Somewhere about 8 o'clock we arrived at Victoria. There were crowds and crowds with policemen keeping open a lane. I toddled down in my tin hat and bedroom slippers, haversack and revolver still strapped round me. Someone shouted 'The good old Navy' and some woman kissed me and they cheered and I wanted to cry. Then a man got hold of me and said 'Where do you want to go? I will look after you'. He led me to a taxi and brought me to the Admiralty and paid the taxi off. I went up to see Claud and he led me off to his flat and gave me dinner, and I told him all about it and thanked him for the honour he had done me in sending me over, and so back here to get some clothes and bath. My stomach hasn't been too good, some filth I have eaten, and I have been sick a number of times. This morning I had a couple of boiled eggs and I won't eat any lunch but will now lie down and sleep again."

Dunkirk was a military defeat, but to the nation it became a cause célèbre.

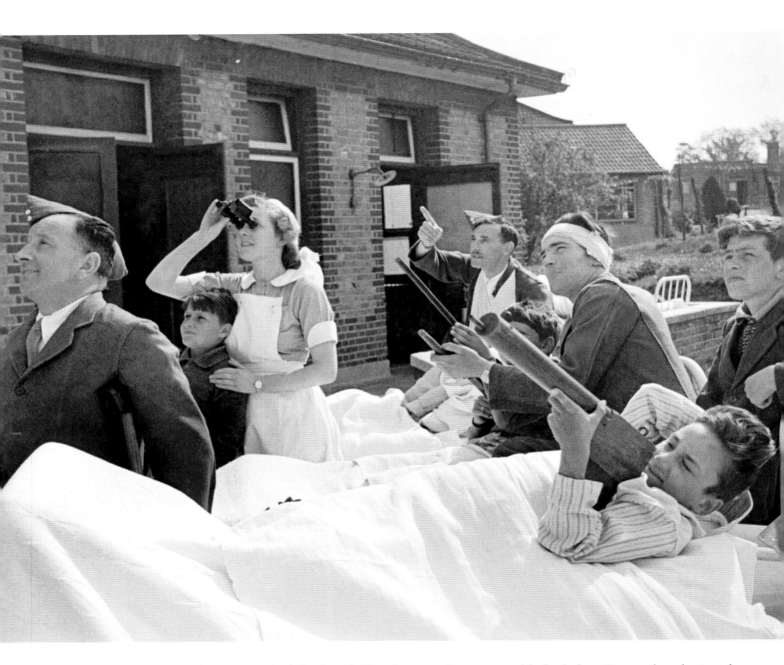

THE BATTLE OF BRITAIN *led to some spectacular dogfights over the country that were exciting viewing for spectators, as witnessed here by staff and patients at a country hospital. The tactical plan in a dogfight was to climb to a position above the enemy, descend out of the sun and shoot your opponent down from the rear, while the victim would try to turn out of the line of fire.*

What remained of the British Expeditionary Force was safely back from France, but the invader was still poised on the French coast. The government issued orders to all those in coastal areas to immobilise parked cars, in case they unwittingly offered transport to enemy parachutists. Removing the rotor arm from the engine of her car became routine for Joan Strange as she went on her physiotherapy rounds in the Worthing area. These coastal towns were packed with troops to defend British shores. Energetic Joan Strange was one of the many civilian volunteers who leapt into another wartime role.

"I drove the YMCA mobile canteen to Shoreham beach this evening. I felt a bit scared as it is all heavily land mined there and there have been a few fatal accidents. However all went well and we did brisk trade for about an hour. Bungalow Town is no more – the bungalows and houses proved troublesome to the gunners who fire into the sea from the Downs so they have all had to be demolished."

During the summer of 1940, people on the south coast watched dogfights in the skies above their homes as the 'ragged RAF' fought the Battle of Britain. In August, journalist Leonard Marsland Gander was astonished at the contrast between London and his Sussex home at Angmering-on-Sea.

A LUFTWAFFE DORNIER 17 *plummets to the ground after being shot down. In the unrelenting fight for control of British airspace the RAF lost around 800 planes, while the Luftwaffe lost more than 1,200. The Germans couldn't continue this kind of sustained battle and focus soon shifted to bombing British cities.*

"The atmosphere in London is unbelievable. The enemy is making mass raids on our coasts and here it is quiet. I heard yesterday that a German airman had baled out at Angmering and landed somewhere on the Willowhayne Estate. I made numerous inquiries by telephone and discovered that there had been a terrific fight over the village at about 6.30 in the morning, lasting roughly half an hour. About twenty Jerries came in at an immense height, invisible most of the time from the ground. Apparently they were intercepted right over the coast and, below, the locals could hear the continuous rattle of machine guns but see little except an occasional arching speck. Mrs Wells, the air raid warden, said that a German – badly wounded in the hip – landed in a cornfield. The air raid warden and the military captured him and Dr Ashby attended to his wound on the spot. He is said, apocryphally, to have given a weak Nazi salute. Mrs Wells said that he and another German pilot were taken to the institution for treatment. The second chap was truculent and threw off the British khaki greatcoat offered to him. Official reports showed that 78 German machines were brought down yesterday – a record."

WRECKAGE OF A BUNGALOW AND ADJOINING VILLA *on which a German Heinkel 111 fell as it burst into flames when shot down by anti-aircraft guns over southeast England. Its crew baled out and were captured. The main advantages the RAF had over the Luftwaffe in the Battle of Britain were that they had superior planes and that they were fighting over their own country, enabling them to fly for longer, refuel more quickly, and any crew who safely baled out could resume their duties quickly.*

Contemporary diaries and letters often include this day-by-day tally of the 'score' of the RAF versus the Luftwaffe, as the nation held its collective breath. The place in the vanguard of these frontline towns was Dover, only 26 miles from the French coast. Enormous German guns were positioned across the Straits of Dover at Cap Gris Nez, jutting out into the English Channel with their sights set on Dover. It was a matter of great pride to head postmaster Arthur Mowbray that even under this barrage his staff carried on working.

"Following a severe bombing attack on the harbour, barrage balloons were provided and these proved a comforting deterrent to the Luftwaffe tactics until August 31, when a determined attack was made by enemy aircraft on the balloons over the town and port. Twenty-three balloons were shot down between 8.30am and 9.00am, one of which fell in flames on the office roof and parapet near to the Telephone Exchange. It was somewhat alarming to the operators, to see the blazing balloon hanging over their window, and as the machine gunning and anti-aircraft barrage were very intense, the Switchroom was evacuated and work continued for twenty minutes on the Emergency Board. This was the first time the Dover Exchange had been abandoned since the outbreak of war. Prompt action by members of the male staff, who pushed the remaining portion of the burning balloon off the parapet into the street below, prevented further damage. In the evening a further attack was made and nine more balloons were shot down, one starting a fire at a house near to the office. In this attack one plane dived and machine-gunned the Post Office Garage and Mail Entrance. The Post Office Home Guard used their rifles with great relish. This day's five raid warnings lasted over nine hours, with hardly a dull moment."

Twenty-three balloons were shot down between 8.30am and 9.00am, one of which fell in flames on the office roof and parapet near to the Telephone Exchange.

THE GERMAN RAILWAY GUN *that was used to bombard the Kent coast. Advances in technology meant that similar loads of ammunition could be delivered more effectively from aircraft, or later V-1 and V-2 rockets, rendering these cumbersome, easy targets obsolete.*

Dover was bombarded with more than 1,700 shells from the Cap Gris Nez guns in the second half of 1940. Lookout posts on the cliff tops were manned night and day by wardens who watched the flash of guns on the French Coast. The coast line was marked out in sections on a map, and when a flash was spotted in that section, the control centre in Dover itself could alert ambulances and rescue workers to the section of town where the shells from that particular gun site would fall. Despite the intensity of the bombing, the post never failed to be delivered, though on one occasion it was 50 minutes late! Even when the railway line was bombed, lorries were on standby to replace the mail trains.

A NAZI PHOTOGRAPH of Dover harbour, taken with a long range camera. The entrance to the harbour, a patrol ship and its barrage balloon are clearly marked.

DOVER AND FOLKESTONE *were regularly bombarded by shells from the guns at Cap Gris Nez, and the Luftwaffe made regular bombing raids to Kentish towns and villages. People became accustomed to returning to the remains of their homes to retrieve belongings after a raid. Despite lookouts along the south coast, the low and swift approach of the attacking aircraft often resulted in no time for warnings. These 'tip and run' raids, as they were known, are believed to have been used as training missions for new recruits.*

*in many of the Kent coastal
towns were adapted to
become air raid shelters.
Previously used by the
Navy and railways,
additional entrances were
added along the network
so that they could be used
by as many of the town's
residents as possible.*

The Nazi flag and sword of the German Naval Commander of Cap Gris Nez were presented to the town after the Allied Invasion of Normandy, in commemoration of the courage and endurance of the inhabitants. Constance Logan Wright, an American, visited Dover in November 1944.

"During the five years of war the population had gradually dropped from 42,000 to 14,500. Many people left after the outbreak of war, but very many others did not leave till their homes were destroyed or made uninhabitable by the shelling."

She was particularly impressed by the tunnels in the famous and symbolic White Cliffs, which had originally been quarried to provide ballast for ships, then used as an arsenal during the Napoleonic Wars, and in this war used as air raid shelters by the people of Dover.

"On the outbreak of the present war, the tunnelled cliff-face was hurriedly extended into great long galleries radiating from a kind of central hall, and into these galleries were put three-tier sleeping bunks. The shelter we saw could accommodate 2,300 men, women and children and was wired with electricity throughout. It had a complete operating theatre and first aid post, independent water supply from deep springs within the cliff, kitchen, clothes and bedding space. With 100 feet of cliff towering above it, it gave its users a wonderful sense of security and these caves have literally saved many hundreds of lives."

A mass of tunnels was cut into the hill below the 19th-century Fort Southwick at Portsmouth, as an underground communications centre for the navy. Veronica Owen qualified as a coder in the WRNS (Women's Royal Navy Service – the women were known as Wrens) in December 1942 and was based there for the rest of the war.

"We only work 12 out of every 48 hours. We work in underground tunnels which have daylight lights and are air conditioned but it makes you feel rather sleepy until you get used to it. When you're on the long night watch, you sleep on double deckers near to the office but tonight we shall be sleeping in this Recreation hut which is outside and we'll get plenty of air."

MOST OF THE PERSONNEL
*at naval coding offices were
women. There were many
of these establishments built
throughout the war, such
as at Stanmore, Eastcote
and, most famously,
Bletchley Park, where
men and women worked
in underground tunnels
or Nissen huts coding
Allied naval messages and
deciphering Nazi signals.
Unlike the Luftwaffe code,
the German naval 'Enigma'
code was very hard to
break.*

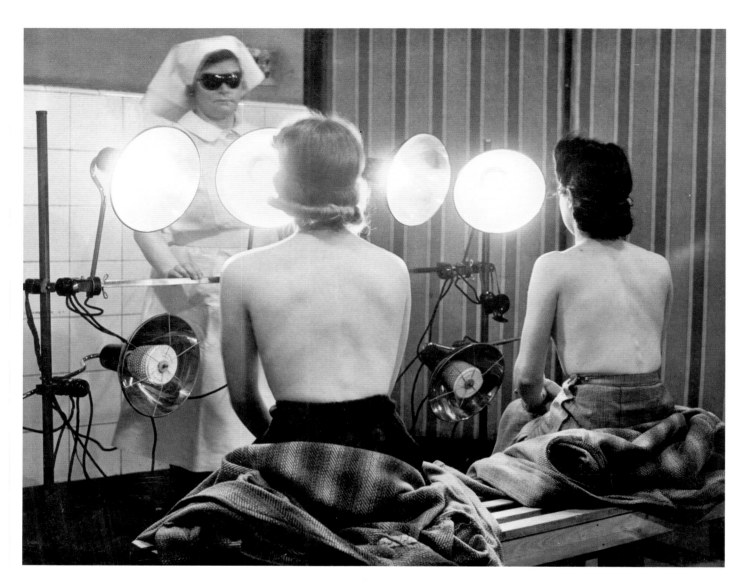

CIVIL DEFENCE WORKERS
*at the Finsbury Health
Centre in London, beating
the winter pallor with
free sun lamp treatments.
Designed by two
Czechoslovakian inventors,
it was called 'Mixray'.*

Veronica, daughter of a captain in the Royal Navy, described the work as 'dull and steady', coding and decoding signals that came in from all over the world. When there was an incident in the English Channel, Veronica and her fellow coders could be called into the plotting room – a scene familiar from wartime films, with gigantic maps where ships were pushed into position with a croupier's stick.

Most of those working in these tunnels – plotters, wireless telegraphists, messengers and cypher officers – were Wrens. Every watch meant a journey down 166 concrete steps into the ground to offices that looked like underground Nissen huts. To compensate for the conditions, the underground Wrens had three days of 'stand-off' a month, and a compulsory sunray treatment! When George VI visited in November 1944, Veronica recorded that the place was spruced up.

"He walked through the coding office looking in a glaze of exhaustion but spoke to two or three people. There were double the number of people below ground than normal, and the whole tunnel had been painted in glossy off-white paint a few days before. It was extremely hot, small and stuffy. The tunnel rumour was that the King had declared the place 'not fit for human habitation'. Whatever he had said, the number of air ventilators, certainly in the Coding Office and probably throughout, was doubled within two to three days – the improvement was noticeable."

Maureen Bolster, another naval daughter and fellow Wren, was thrilled to be selected as a naval despatch rider, as she wrote to her fiancé Eric Wells in July 1942.

THE WRNS, OR WRENS, *was formed in 1917 with 3,000 members, designed to take over the tasks of cooking, cleaning and other domestic duties from men in the Royal Navy. By the end of World War II their role had expanded to include over 200 jobs and 74,000 members.*

"There are very few despatch riders indeed, and we are a complete speciality – 'the darlings of the Navy'! You are attached with a couple of others to a port, and you run about all over the place. All traffic gives way to you. You don't have to work very long hours – 9–5 as a rule. The equipment provided is superb – breeches and shiny leather leggings and a tailored jacket, nipped in at the waist. Unfortunately, a crash helmet as well (Cor!) then for cold weather, a great big lined mackintosh, windproofed etc. One gets two ordinary Wren outfits, with special markings, to show your superiority over the rank and file. When you've been qualified three months you get wings. One can be reasonably assured of a good time socially. It all sounds so wonderful, I can't wait to go...I pray nothing will happen to stop me!"

BOTH WORLD WARS FORCED WOMEN *out of their traditional roles. Propaganda encouraged them to take on the jobs that men traditionally did, from farming to working in munitions factories, enabling the men to go to the front. Women's organisations included the Land Girls, WAAF (Women's Auxillary Air Force), the Wrens and the Women's Voluntary Service (WVS).*

When she wrote that, Maureen had been eager to leave her current job as a billeting officer for a factory. In October 1942 she became a woman in uniform, and began her probationary period with the WRNS. The glamour wore off pretty quickly, as she wrote to her fiancé in November.

"Am in a cabin with 14 others – all couriers. Except for this other girl who's 25 none are under 30!!! Six are over 40! Some of them are ladies but queer, their conversation is dreadful – lots of them use their job as a means to another end – if you get me! They're all as dull as dishwater and so ugly. I'm as lonely as hell."

As a despatch rider she had to travel all over the country, by plane, train and ship.

"You don't know what it was like that particular kind of mental strain – taking things that cost vast sums of money – taking things that you were told a ship was waiting for before it could sail: new inventions, highly secret dispatches, having to have things in a certain place by a certain hour. Taking enormous quantities of gear, coping with porters, working parties, transport."

I adore this life. I love the water – the sea – the boats, the dockyard, the old salts and the yarns they spin – the movement and colour.

WRENS WERE NOT ALLOWED *to go into combat but were involved in the planning and organisation of naval operations, as well as maintenance. Thousands of women served overseas and large numbers served in other branches of the Navy, such as the Fleet Air Arm, Coastal Forces, Combined Operations and the Royal Marines. The Wrens suffered 303 fatalities during World War II.*

Rail travellers were plagued by delays: trains travelled at speeds of 15mph over parts of the line in case of bomb craters; carriages and corridors were crammed with people; and there was always the possibility of air raids. Maureen's fiancé was a squadron leader in the Middle East, and her own experiences as a courier during those ten months were a close parallel to those of men fighting abroad in at least one respect.

"The lack of sleep. Have you known what it's like to keep on going without it and never making it up? Sitting up through the night, maybe several nights running – having travelled all day your eyelids red and sore, the muscles of your face all strained – probably hungry because you hadn't the money to get yourself a decent meal. And then – when back in quarters, unable to get rest, being in a noisy dormitory – no companionship, as the others were so old and ugly, and forever quarrelling and fighting."

Maureen Bolster was eventually transferred from the courier service and became a stoker. In the dust and heat of RAF Headquarters in the Middle East, her squadron leader husband must have felt refreshed reading these exuberant words.

"I've had a wonderful day. I've spent it driving round Portsmouth Harbour in a speed boat! Whizzing along the water and a long wash of foam behind. There's nothing to it – clutch, rudder wheel and throttle. Easy! Crew of three sailors – Coxswain (instructor), stoker and deckhand. I took them to Gosport and nearly to Spithead. The exhilaration was terrific. This morning we went over the water to get the rum ration for our establishment but I wasn't allowed even a smell! I adore this life. I love the water – the sea – the boats, the dockyard, the old salts and the yarns they spin – the movement and colour. I like sitting on the gunwale, swinging my legs and talking to the tough seamen in the little boats."

Finally Maureen had found her niche!

As homes to ships of the merchant and Royal navies, ports were constant targets for Luftwaffe pilots. Dolly Howard lived in West Derby, a suburb of Liverpool – the destination for many convoys. After one raid she wrote to a friend:

"Most people's water systems 'went west' here. In fact we have been waiting for a plumber for four weeks. I heard of one plumber with 500 names on his list and he was taking them in strict rotation. We were so tired of waiting that yesterday Jim borrowed a blow lamp and solder, begged petrol (as we have no coupons) and set to work himself. He finished a short while ago after repairing three broken pipes, and looks gorgeous – as black as a sweep. So now we can have a fire downstairs again, and can pull the lavatory chain. It has been a procession of buckets."

Low water pressure was a recurring problem for the fire service in many towns and cities, particularly during a massive raid on the east coast in 1943. In the early hours of June 14, 101 people were killed and 300 seriously injured in Grimsby and Cleethorpes, in Lincolnshire. An anonymous diarist in Grimsby recorded the damage, as high explosives, incendiary bombs and anti-personnel bombs fell for an hour.

"Most damage in the docks by fire, portion of two pontoons burned out. Waly Road Hospital gutted. In town anti personnel bombs caused deaths through people kicking or moving them. For several days afterwards anti-bomb squads were exploding bombs found in offices and private houses. The NFS [National Fire Service] and Civil Defence people were

GRIMSBY SUFFERED HEAVILY *from aerial bombardment throughout the war. Due to its close proximity to the strategically important docks at Hull and the many airfields of Lincolnshire, it was an easy and major target for the Luftwaffe.*

VOLUNTEER SERVICES, *such as the Auxillary Fire Service (AFS) and the Air Raid Patrol (ARP) were generally the first to arrive and help in the aftermath of a raid. The AFS – seen here having a joke at Hitler's expense – was created in 1938 to support the London Fire Brigade.*

overmatched and much of the theoretical organisation went 'phut'. Fire brigades came from Mansfield, Lincoln and Leicester. There was much criticism of the NFS, but low water pressure contributed to the comparative failure in some cases. After the raid notices were posted about touching strange objects. If they had been posted before, many lives would have been saved. The Chief Constable had received notice about them but instead of giving the matter publicity treated it as all very hush hush and secret – the fool."

A few days after the raid this anonymous observer discovered an unexpected hero among the Cleethorpes citizenry.

"Mr AA Beardsall, well known chartered accountant and a leading man in Cleethorpes Civil Defence, was one of a party of ARP men, soldiers and police, who swept fields at Stallingborough for anti-personnel bombs, and also the sands at Cleethorpes. Through growing corn they searched for bombs with sticks and found about 100 in two fields. The bomb squad exploded them by fastening long lengths of string to each. Beardsall made light of it, although he admitted he got the wind up. While on the sands he found his foot on something hard which had sunk in soft sand. It turned out to be a bomb, but luckily it didn't go off."

THE FIRST ANTI-PERSONNEL BOMB *fell on Grimbsy on the morning of June 14, 1943. Butterfly bombs were so named because of the hinged outer shell which opened as two half-cylinders when it was dropped and spring-loaded vanes at the ends would flip out. These rotated the spindle as the bomblet fell and armed the fuse.*

A month later Grimsby and Cleethorpes were hit again, making 3,000 people homeless, killing 65 and leaving 173 injured. Schools, churches, the fish docks and numerous residential streets were hit, as the area was dive-bombed. British bombers limping back from raids on Germany were also a danger as they crash landed in the surrounding countryside.

On Christmas Day 1941 the same observer noted that 80 men were rescued from three ships sunk off the Humber, but most seamen did not survive in the North Sea for long. His brief notes catalogue a trail of casualties at sea which brought the dreaded telegram, 'The Admiralty regrets . . .', to so many wives and families.

> "Trawler *Lord Shrewsbury* given up with crew of ten hands. Skipper IH Noble and son IJ Noble lost; Charles Perritt (mate) married; John C Elliott (third hand) married, two children; Leonard Sparkes (trimmer); Sidney Allan Rodgers (trimmer); William Judge (deckie); Henry V Gerwaney (cook), wife two children; George Robertson (chief engineer); Thomas Jobson (second engineer)."

Many fishermen joined the merchant navy, their trawlers converted into minesweepers and coastal patrol boats. The years 1939–45 brought some of the coldest weather on record and led to teams of women knitting for victory. Mollie Blake was one of the many women who formed knitting groups for 'adopted' ships of the merchant navy. Seamen were delighted with the supplies of sweaters, balaclavas, gloves and socks that were sent to them. Sam Gibbs, gunner on His Majesty's Trawler *John Stephen*, was a former deep-water fisherman used to the icy waters round Bear Island, Greenland and Iceland. He was 'adopted' by Mollie Baker in September 1940.

"I want to thank you for the woollens you sent for the boys. I hope this finds you and your two children in the best of health also your lady friends, if any of them care to write I will always be pleased to answer these letters. I'm married with five children, three have been evacuated to Gainsborough, my home is in Grimsby, I was a fisherman before this bit of bother started. You asked if we would like to be adopted, I'll say we would, then we could say that John Stephen has a few sweethearts. The lads and myself will always be thankful for a few woollens and books. I had to smile when I saw the stocking without heels, but one cannot look a gift horse in the mouth. I hope I'm the lucky one to get that sweater you wrote about. I know what the winter is like at sea after spending the last 20 Christmases in the North regions."

WOOL WAS IN SHORT SUPPLY *throughout the war, but the public on the home front were encouraged by the Ministry of Information to 'knit for victory' or 'make do and mend'. Knitting groups (such as this WI one below) sprang up all over the country as women of all ages got together to knit for the men at the front.*

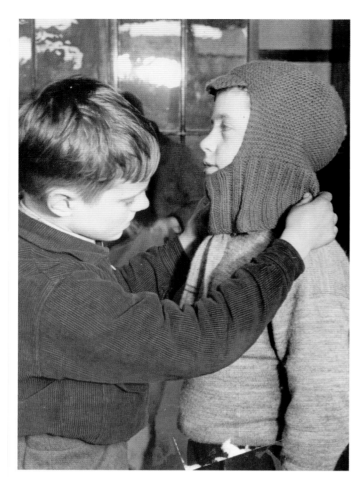

In November Mollie and her knitting group knitted woolly hats for the crew.

"Thank you for the caps etc they were just what we needed, I shared them out to the lads and told them you sent them, they said thank you. I dare say it comes hard on you people knitting things you're not accustomed to but you're doing well keep it up but don't tire yourselves you need your rest the same as other people.

We have been working a different sweeping system this last day or two, the lads called it the suicide squad, how would you fancy cooking dinner with a life belt round you but I was taking no risks. I didn't want to have to walk back to shields [North Shields]. I can swim but there are times when one may be hurt and not able to, so safety first."

In December Sam wished Mollie 'a Jolly Time' at Christmas, and told her things were getting 'a bit warmer' out in the North Sea.

I thank you for promising me the sweater, I want to tell you I'm not very fat.

ALL OF THE ARMED FORCES received items knitted in their set colours – blue wool for the RAF, black for the Navy and khaki for the Army. There were also some interesting new designs, including a balaclava with an ear hole for using the telephone and mittens with an index finger fitting for pulling a trigger.

"We left harbour this morning and about five minutes after we left there was a nasty crack just behind us, towards where we had left but we didn't see anything and when we got back this afternoon we found two big ships had struck a mine each, but luckily only one killed and four injured on one ship which was a large two funnelled passenger [liner] carrying a lot of passengers, and on the other four were killed, six injured, but both vessels have been brought to land. We have to go to ships that are in trouble through enemy action – the last one we went to had lost 65 men, previous to that we went to one that had been bombed, we had to blow them up and it wasent very nice seeing the bodies after the explosions, but I suppose it's all in a days work."

The dirt and danger of his job played only a small part in these letters. Instead Sam told anecdotes of drunken shipmates, wrote poetry and showed concern for the welfare of Mollie and her family, all tinged with the humour and affectionate intimacy of an old friend.

"Well Dear, regards the stocking, I should say the men would prefer them with heels and if you make the foot, say to fit a man taking nine in shoes I don't think you'll be far wrong. I'v worn them all my life being a fisherman in peace time so I hope you don't get offinded at me telling you how to knit them. I thank you for promising me the sweater, I want to tell you I'm not very fat. I stand 5ft 8, and weigh 10 stone, so I'll leave you to guess the size but whatever size it is I shall be proud to wear it because you made it for me. I'm very proud to have someone like you to write to. I hope you feel that way about mine. A letter always cheers one up and if you have someone you can rely on to write to you well you something to look forward to."

William Lind was a merchant seaman on the MV *Angularity* on her way to Newcastle with a cargo of phosphate. The ship was torpedoed between Harwich and Lowestoft on a freezing cold evening in February 1941.

"It was a bitterly cold night and a snowstorm was raging with a heavy sea on. At 20:30 hours GMT there was a muffled explosion. I opened my cabin door to see what had happened, but no sooner I did this when a solid wall of water drove me back into the cabin. The next thing I knew was I was trapped in my cabin under water. Fortunately, my cabin got air locked through the vessel going down bow first. I reckoned the whole thing happened within ten seconds . Strange enough I did not panic. I was swimming in circles in my waterlogged cabin with just enough air space to keep the water below my nose. My head was bumping the bulkhead. I took one deep breath and dived through the open doorway. It seemed ages before I broke surface. The seas were high and the water was bitterly cold. When I came to the surface I could see the stern of the doomed ship sticking out above water, the strong tide was carrying me away from her and suddenly she disappeared. There was nothing in sight except the dim outline of the Suffolk coast. I kept swimming without a life belt. Sooner or later I too would come to an end, nothing but a miracle could save me. Just when things began to look black for me a hatch from the doomed ship came floating towards me. I grabbed at it and hung on for dear life. . . . I thought of my wife and children, very soon I would be leaving them for ever."

As he recited stanzas from The Rubaiyat of Omar Khayyam, he saw two shapes 50 yards away in the gloom.

"I shouted, they heard me, and one of the dark forms came in my direction. With some difficulty they hauled me on board, I could not help myself owing to my numbed legs. They bundled me in blankets when they got me below. I was laid in one of the crew's bunks. Then three sailors sat on top of me to impart the warmth of their bodies. The offered me a bowl of hot soup, and a glass of schnapps."

A MERCHANT SHIP *of the Elder Dempster Line,* Apapa, *ablaze after being hit by a German bomber off Anglesey, 1941. The Battle of the Atlantic began in September 1939 when a U-boat off Ireland torpedoed the SS Athenia – a cruise liner of the Donaldson line en route to Canada from Britain. It had more than 1,000 passengers on board, 118 of whom died. The majority of the fatalities came when one of the lifeboats was sucked into the propellers of a rescue craft.*

After his rescue by the German E-boat (a torpedo boat), William discovered that he and the Second Engineer were the only survivors. He spent 4 years as a German prisoner of war.

The years 1940 and 1941 saw a horrifying loss of life and ships, as convoys bridged the gulf between Britain and her transatlantic cousins, Canada and the USA. Ships carrying munitions, oil and food travelled in convoy at the speed of the slowest vessel. Out in the vast Atlantic wilderness they were hunted by U-boats (submarines). Rough seas were another danger, but mountainous waves also brought a degree of camouflage. One eyewitness described a direct hit on a ship carrying aviation spirit.

> "A sheet of flame, a roar as the blaze spreads across the water and no chance of saving either life or the ship."

Convoys were ordered not to stop or make detours to pick up survivors. Merchant ships and escorts were supplied with snowflake rockets, which illuminated the sea in a burst of white light in a bid to hunt the hunters but with the risk that the rest of the convoy became more visible and more vulnerable. Warwick Brookes was a trimmer on the SS *Beaverford* on the transatlantic run to Canada. A month after war broke out he married his 21-year-old fiancée, Mary, and for a year the couple shared the brief shore leaves and frequent partings common to maritime marriages. On November 18, 1940, Mary Brookes received the dreaded telegram saying that the *Beaverford* had been sunk, and her husband was reported 'missing believed killed'. In March 1941 the General Register and Record Office of Shipping and Seamen sent her notification that 'Warwick T Brookes is supposed to have died on November 5, 1940'.

> "That word 'supposed' sustained my hopes, for never at any time had I been informed that, quite categorically, all the crew had perished."

She was unable to come to terms with her husband's death until in 1944 a friend sent her an eyewitness account of the sinking published in the *Evening Standard*. The captain of the last ship in the convoy had watched from his bridge as he steamed away.

"At 5pm on November 5, 1940, in the North Atlantic, the enemy raider encountered the British convoy. Instantly the *Jervis Bay* (the escort ship from the Royal Navy) headed for the foe, her guns blazing. The whole weight of the raider's guns was concentrated upon her, but the desperate twenty minutes of her noble effort to draw the raider's fire gave the convoy time to disperse."

Within 20 minutes the *Jervis Bay* went down, and the enemy's focus shifted to the *Beaverford*.

"Vengefully, the foe singled out the *Beaverford* for concentrated attack. So it fell to her to take the place of the *Jervis Bay* and to carry on the delaying action against the enemy by which so many of the convoy were saved."

The *Beaverford* and a neighbouring ship gave the rest of the convoy a chance to run for saftey.

"For more than five hours the *Beaverford* stayed afloat firing and fighting to the last, pursued by the raider. Using the big reserve of engine power for speed, and steering and manoeuvring to baffle and evade the enemy's aim, she held her own, hit by shells but hitting back, delaying the raider while the rest of the convoy made its escape into the rapidly gathering gloom. The unequal engagement lasted until 10.45pm when there was a burst of flame from the *Beaverford*."

On Christmas Eve, 1940, Mary Brookes received a parcel: a bundle of her letters, returned by the shipping company. They had never reached her husband.

RESCUED SAILORS WATCH *the* MV Dunbar Castle *going down after hitting a mine in the English Channel. Britain was dependent on its merchant fleet for the import of food, fuel, equipment and raw materials, as well as the movement of troops. While Germany mobilised U-boats, battleships and mines in an attempt to sever Britain's supply lines, merchant ships faced the perils of the Atlantic without adequate protection. More than 30,000 merchant seamen lost their lives during the Battle of the Atlantic.*

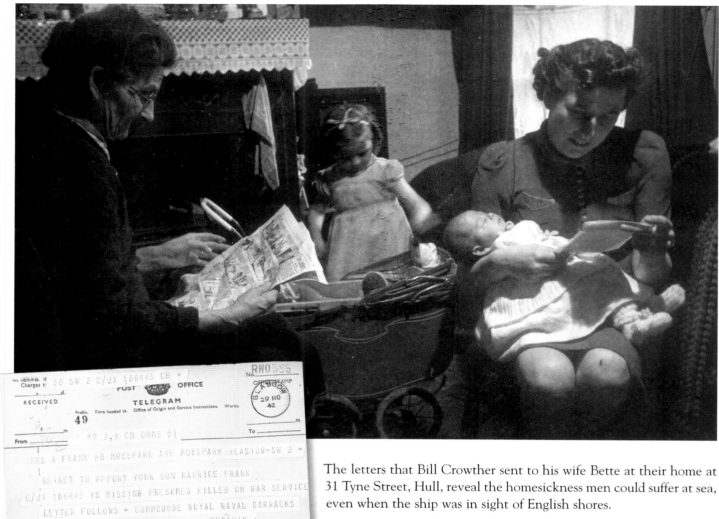

The letters that Bill Crowther sent to his wife Bette at their home at 31 Tyne Street, Hull, reveal the homesickness men could suffer at sea, even when the ship was in sight of English shores.

"There was a doleful figure of a man on the poop as we slipped through the locks and headed out to sea. His head was bent and the look on the poor man's face would have put Dismal Desmond [a cartoon Dalmatian dog] to shame. His heart was left in 31 Tyne Street and his actions in giving orders were those of a robot. Well, such is life in the merchant navy."

Bill had married his sweetheart Bette only two months earlier, in September 1941. Throughout the next 15 months he travelled back and forth across the Atlantic.

"Easter Sunday, somewhere at sea [1942]
Time marches on and here we are rolling along like an ocean greyhound, homeward bound and feeling quite pleased about it. The sun is shining and if it wasn't for our escort nosing around the convoy, one would hardly believe there was a war on. I didn't send any letters to you over on yon side [the USA], as we weren't in port very long, and we would have arrived

His heart was left in 31 Tyne Street and his actions in giving orders were those of a robot. Well such is life in the merchant navy.

home before them but I hope you received my cable OK. I received some letters from you over on the other side, they were old ones posted last December but I enjoyed them just the same. I often get them out and read them over again, they are as good as a tonic to me and my hair sort of takes on another curl."

Bill was at sea when his wife gave birth to their first child.

"I only wish I could have stayed at home for our happy event, to comfort you and welcome the new arrival to the home, but such is life. No one knows the heartache which a sailor has to silently bear in missing such times which are normal in the ordinary man's life."

In September that year his ship was torpedoed and sunk by a German U-boat on its way back from America. He and the rest of the crew were rescued and he returned home on 'survivor's leave' to meet his baby daughter, Carol, for the first time. They celebrated the Christmas of 1942 together. Bette joined him aboard ship while it was in dock at Birkenhead. It sailed on January 11, 1943 and spent the next 14 months in the waters off South Africa, India, Egypt and Australia. In November 1943 Bette gave birth to their second daughter. At noon on February 29, 1944 Bill Crowther's ship, the SS *Ascot*, was torpedoed by a Japanese submarine in the middle of the Indian Ocean. Four of the crew were killed instantly, 52 boarded the ship's life rafts. The submarine's captain ordered the survivors be machine-gunned. Eight survived, but Bill Crowther was not among them.

3. Occupation

"Today we have the dreadful news that all wireless sets have to be given up. It has shocked us all, as it was the greatest comfort we possess to be able to link ourselves with England. How eagerly we listen to the familiar announcers' voices; and the good news they have at times is like a tonic, to the dreary and hard times which we are going through now. We love to hear of the assurances given to the occupied that we shall be delivered from this awful tyranny." Iris Bullen, September 1940

A shocking photograph appeared in the *Daily Express* on April 28, 1942. It depicted the familiar British bobby standing next to a jackbooted officer of the German army in a British street. This was not propaganda designed to make British hearts skip a beat. This picture had been smuggled out of Jersey and was a sight familiar to Channel Islanders – loyal British subjects since the 13th century. The Channel Islands were occupied in a fashion that can only be called ignominious. The British government decided that the islands would be too costly to defend, lying only 15 miles from the French coast, and declared them a demilitarised zone.

Iris Bullen was 25 years old, and a mother of two young children, when she heard the British government's statement at five o'clock on June 19, 1940. She wrote in her diary, as boats were being readied for evacuation:

"It was a very unsettled evening for everyone, we couldn't make up our minds, and also the difficulty was that in some families all did not wish to leave, therefore many had the chance to go, and yet felt they could not leave some of those dear to them behind, which also meant leaving homes and animals etc behind."

Leaving beds unmade and tables uncleared, they made a dash for the boats.

A SHOCKING IMAGE *for* Daily Express *readers in April 1942: a German officer and a British policeman in conversation on a Jersey street. It was a rare piece of publicity for the plight of the islanders who had been abandoned by their own government.*

MORE JERSEY RESIDENTS *wanted to leave than there were boats available to take them. These hopeful residents (below) sat patiently on their suitcases waiting to hear whether they would be among the lucky ones.*

Like many Channel Islanders, her husband John was serving in the British Forces. On June 25 he returned to Jersey on special leave to see his family.

"We were still undecided as to whether we should go back with him to England. John had a strong view that the Germans were coming to pay us a visit soon which meant that, if they occupied the island, I should be cut off from the mainland. After much thought over it, we both decided it would yet be safer for the children and myself to remain behind."

On the Island of Guernsey, a few miles closer to the advancing Germans, Methodist Minister Douglas Ord recorded the arrival of French evacuees, followed by people from the tiny island of Alderney. But, simultaneously,

". . . in the opposite direction an unceasing stream of women and children went down to the harbour to embark. Beasts have been left in some fields tethered in Guernsey fashion but without arrangements for milking. The vets have put so many pets to sleep that they have run out of the wherewithal to continue this unhappy task. Many took swift decisions. Leaving beds unmade and tables uncleared, they made a dash for the boats. Among these were some who will one day have regrets."

About half the population left Guernsey in that exodus. Among them was Mr E Hamel, a telephone engineer from the island's capital, St Peter Port.

"I needed no telling that to abandon everything we possessed was almost too terrible to contemplate; but what was the alternative?"

German troops landed first on Alderney, then Guernsey, where Douglas Ord saw them arrive on July 1, 1940.

"All day long planes and troop carriers have been coming over from France, flying very low with deafening din to impress us. As we went to town car after car went by, packed with officers and NCOs. The men were fetched in local buses as they arrived and stared open-mouthed at the well-dressed civilians, the clean, freshly-painted houses and at the shops with their windows invitingly full of good things. Germans are everywhere – eating, eating, eating. They prove their prowess as trenchermen, ordering omelettes made with eight eggs. From time to time they go out into the street to be sick and then valiantly resume their place at the festive board unless ousted by others. It was instructive to see Germans eating butter in half-pound packets without bread as they went about the streets."

IRIS BULLEN'S HUSBAND was serving with the British forces in England, but after much anxious thought the couple decided that it would be safer for Iris and the children (pictured above) to remain in Jersey.

THE OCCUPATION BEGINS: German Kommandant Lanz arrives at his new headquarters in Guernsey, the former Channel Islands Hotel in St Peter Port. A British policeman holds open the door of his car while a German sentry guards the entrance to the Kommandantur.

RENAULT TANKS *commandeered by the Germans from the French Army arrive in St Martin's Guernsey, following Hitler's decision to fortify the islands in 1941.*

On July 1, when news of Guernsey's occupation reached her, Iris Bullen managed to send a final telegram from the Post Office to her husband in England. Moments later, communications with the mainland were severed.

"The most tragic time of the day, was when we were all informed that we had to have a white flag of surrender flying from every house in the island, by 7am on Tuesday morning [July 2], the time when the Germans were to occupy the island, so we were all busy making and erecting this unhappy flag. We also thought it best to take away any pictures of Royalty or Military origin as we did not know what our invaders were going to do, many papers etc we burnt."

Channel Islanders were quickly subjected to curfew; their clocks had to be moved an hour forward to German time, and their wireless sets tuned to German stations. Iris Bullen thought these restrictions 'very lenient'. But, as the occupation progressed, the Germans announced that anyone caught in possession of British propaganda pamphlets would be imprisoned for 15 years; and they confiscated cars and lorries. Iris wrote in September 1940:

"What absurd robbery. We are all very upset, especially those concerned, some have worked very hard to have a car, though a written receipt is given for each one, we know it is a dud bargain."

I needed no telling that to abandon everything we possessed was almost too terrible to contemplate.

Iris' main concern was feeding her two children, Roy and Monica. Long queues were forming outside shops where people were taking more than their fair share and the basics were soon unavailable.

THE GAUMONT PALACE *cinema in St Peter Port was also occupied. Here, it is showing* Sieg im Westen *(Victory in the West), a 1941 propaganda film about Hitler's greatest military victory – the conquest of Holland, Belgium and France.*

Flyers from the German Luftwaffe bragged in streets and shops of the imminent invasion of the mainland. Douglas Ord was woken by the roar of enemy planes flying north towards England on 9 July.

"Could this really be confirmation of the boast of those Luftwaffe fellows? I lay balancing arguments for and against in my mind. With some anxiety I awaited the early news on the wireless. Nothing to report!"

On August 14 he wrote:

"Our confidence in the futility of invasion grows. Several damaged planes have gone down round our shores while occasionally, as yesterday, a plane limps back to the airport. Many Germans, like the cranks who foretell the world's end from Daniel and Revelation, are now betting on August 15th when London will be entered. Hotels here have been booked for dinners and dances to celebrate."

But they had underrated the RAF as opponents. As the Battle of Britain continued over the Home Counties, Channel Islanders had pressing domestic concerns: food was becoming increasingly scarce. In September Douglas Ord was warned that:

"Germans were likely to make domiciliary visits to check on private food stores. We therefore hid some of our precious tinned stuffs bought before the Occupation, as people

GERMAN SOLDIERS DISPERSE AFTER A PARADE
*celebrating their occupation of Jersey. Many local residents
had their cars and trucks confiscated, so they were reduced
to cycling or walking.*

were advised to do, in the lower part of the piano!! In the garden I also constructed a rockery with such plants as summer snow, arabis, etc trailing attractively over. But inside was a fairly strong metal deed box, quite three feet in length. It was a useful cache."

Morale was boosted as a boat-load of people escaped from Guernsey to the mainland, landing at Start Point in South Devon. The news was brought to the islanders by one of the forbidden pamphlets, dropped by the RAF. Morale dipped when wireless sets were confiscated in November; but ordinary islanders braved informers and German reprisals to hang on to their sets and listen secretly to the BBC. This is what Douglas Ord heard as he tuned in on New Year's day 1942:

"At the end of the news last night the Secretary of State for Scotland referred to us in passing. It is puzzling that so little mention is made of the Channel Islands and that we never get any more leaflets via the RAF. We try to imagine this is owing to policy and that we are an infinitesimal pin-point in the map of world affairs. Still, we are a loyal folk and would welcome a chance of defying orders in picking up anything the RAF might drop, from daily newspapers to a side of bacon, though, greedily, we would expect them to drop the latter in the bounds of our garden."

WIRELESS RECEIVING SETS

The public are reminded that all declaration forms concerning Wireless Receiving Sets must be delivered to the office of the Department of Essential Services, 10/12 Beresford St., not later than noon to-morrow (Sat.) November 16th.

W. S. LE MASURIER,
President,
Department of Essential Services

An evacuated islander kept a scrapbook of articles that did appear in English newspapers. Most appeared in the Methodist Church press and, naturally, more column inches were devoted to dramatic escapes in tiny boats. But as one correspondent wrote to the Daily Express in 1941:

"I'm still waiting for some of our leaders to remember the Channel Islands when they speak of the various oppressed peoples. Even the Archbishop of Canterbury, on the Day of National Prayer, when he expressed sympathy with the invaded countries and mentioned several by name, omitted them. So did the Prime Minister in his last broadcast. The Channel Islanders have given their men to the forces, and have always been loyal to the British Empire. Now they are under the Nazi heel, yet we never hear of anything being done for them."

An octogenarian Guernsey peer, Lord Portsea, managed to get limited publicity by offering to parachute into the Islands. But diarists and letter writers on the mainland rarely even mentioned the occupation. In fact, publication of newsworthy stories of escapees was likely to bring reprisals on those left on the Islands. On September 16, 1941, two Guernsey men and two French girls had escaped. Douglas Ord heard them on his wireless.

"A wretched blunder on the part of the BBC will assuredly have its effect on us. Two men and two French girls were allowed to tell the story of their experiences of their escaping by boat to England a fortnight ago. One of the girls said the Germans were permitting civilians in billets to listen to London. Muller will know just what to do to stop that leak. But why mention the escape at all? Surely London will know this may bring reprisals on us all, while any information the party took would probably not add greatly to the stock of knowledge in the Intelligence. It is not very long since they issued menaces against escapers, and the probability of their being put into operation against innocent folk is enough to deter all but the utterly selfish."

The Germans subsequently demanded a deposit on all boats from fishermen in the islands.

NOTICE:

LOUIS BERRIER,
a resident of Ernes
is charged with having
released a pigeon with
a message for England.
He was, therefore, sentenced

TO DEATH

for espionage by the
Court Martial and

SHOT

on the 2nd of August.

August 3rd, 1941.   Court Martial

SEVERE PUNISHMENT *faced those who were caught acting in defiance or protest of the occupation. Some residents were also imprisoned in the islands' jails, or transported to concentration camps. Notices would be put up around the islands to serve as a warning to others.*

THE TOWN HALL *in St Helier (right), flying the flag that indicates it has become a German headquarters.*

PETROL SHORTAGES *meant that even those whose vehicles were not confiscated had to adapt to their new circumstances. The baker's van from La Rocque, Jersey, was one of many that became horse drawn for the duration.*

The terror, daily uncertainty and anxiety of occupation was increased as lists of deportations were announced through the Evening Post, which had been taken over as the main arm of German propaganda. People deported as 'undesirables' included Jews and ex-officers, but those who contravened German regulations were also sent to the camps. Iris Bullen was great friends with Eddie and Olive Muels. At the end of the war she felt able to record what had happened to Eddie.

As I was so friendly with Olive, his wife, I became mixed up as a suspect of hiding the soldier.

"Tried and accused of giving civilian clothing to a German soldier, December 43/January 44. In prison in Jersey, taken to concentration camp just prior to D-Day. As I was so friendly with Olive, his wife, I became mixed up as a suspect of hiding the soldier, and had visits by the Germans and cross-questioned by the Gestapo, even though I could swear that I had never had anything to do with the soldier whatsoever."

Eddie Muels died in a concentration camp. A total of nearly 570 Channel Islanders were deported to camps such as Auschwitz and Ravensbruck and 31 were murdered or died as a result of the ill treatment they suffered.

There were many deaths among Channel Islanders under the occupation. Douglas Ord regularly officiated at funerals.

"Dr Revell, Medical Officer of Health, has sent me a copy of his printed Report for 1940. Although the population fell from 43,000 to 24,000, deaths in the second six months were more than double the number recorded in the first six. Deaths among the elderly were naturally more numerous."

Food shortages were part of the problem. German troops had the lion's share of supplies shipped from the French mainland. By May 1941, Ord heard of a breeding rabbit being sold for £16.

"A man, barefoot, clad only in pyjamas, was found wandering about at two in the morning in St Peter Port, utterly exhausted, he told the policeman, one of ours – that he was cold and his feet ached. He was taken to the hospital and a brief examination showed that he was an extreme case of undernourishment. Many others who are in a like condition do not appear before the public. Many say they feel as if they had been beaten with truncheons all over them. I find it extremely difficult to lift my head from the pillow in the mornings. Falla the florist confessed to having lost four stones and to being racked with pain. Some have shrunk so much that their clothes hang loose about them."

EDDIE MUELS, A RESIDENT *of Jersey (inset and left with his wife Olive and son David), was accused of sheltering a deserting German soldier. As a result he was deported to a concentration camp, where he died.*

DEPORTATION LISTS DETAILING *the registered Jews in Jersey, 1943. Anyone with more than two Jewish grandparents was required to register with the authorities. One woman later recorded that she spent a year and a half in fear, not knowing whether the Germans would arrest her, her husband or their baby daughter. In the end they were all deported.*

GIRLS WHO FRATERNISED *with German soldiers were nicknamed 'greenfly'. At the end of the occupation many were publicly tarred and feathered as retribution for collaborating with the enemy.*

GERMAN TROOPS MARCH PAST
one of Paris's most iconic monuments
(top right), the Arc de Triomphe.

HITLER'S ARMY TOOK CONTROL
of Paris on June 14, 1940 (top
left). Eleven days later, an armistice
between the two countries was signed
at Compiègne – a symbolic site
chosen by Hitler, as the armistice that
signalled Germany's defeat in World
War I had also been signed here.
Paris was not liberated from German
occupation until August 1944, two
months after the D-Day landings.

WENCESLAS SQUARE IN PRAGUE,
dominated by German tanks (middle
left). Hitler's troops had penetrated
further into Czechoslovakia
shortly after the Munich Pact
which permitted him to occupy the
Sudetenland.

PARIS BECAME AN ATTRACTIVE
posting for the German military after
the armistice. Here (bottom left),
officers and men mingle with locals
in the ironically named Café de la
Paix in the Place de l'Opéra.

NAZI TANKS AND TROOPS PARADE
through the centre of Amsterdam
(right), on a route which takes them
past the queen's palace.

HITLER TAKES CHARGE OF EUROPE

Hitler had signed a non-aggression pact with Stalin in August 1939 and after the fall of Warsaw, Germany and Russia divided Poland between them. The Führer was now able to turn his attention to the west and north, invading Denmark, Norway, Holland, Belgium and France in quick succession. In Norway, a puppet government was established under Vidkun Quisling, who had collaborated with Hitler before the Nazi invasion of his country and whose name passed into English as a synonym for traitor. After an armistice agreed with the French Premier Marshal Pétain, almost two-thirds of France was occupied by the Germans; the remainder was disarmed and established as a neutral state administered by another puppet government, based at Vichy.

It was Hitler's plan to invade Britain and had he succeeded there would no doubt have been scenes of German soldiers marching up Whitehall and lounging in London's pubs and restaurants just as there were such scenes in cities such as Paris, Prague and Amsterdam.

By 1941, Hitler was also at war with Russia and had invaded Romania, Yugoslavia and Greece, extending his influence to the gates of Moscow and as far south as North Africa.

Iris heard nothing from her husband John for a year. Then on June 20, 1941 there was a summons.

"This morning I had a shock when the postman brought me a red cross envelope with an enclosed slip of paper asking me to go to the Bureau, as there was a request for information there. As I had not heard of anyone previously having such a request, I became alarmed, as I thought that if it were a message to me from John I should have had it handed to me at home, and so I imagined that all was not right with John, and was rather upset. I went to town on the 2pm bus. I had to go to an office over Burton's. My legs were shaking when I went up the stairs, but was soon relieved when told that it was an enquiry from John concerning his family."

Iris composed a suitable reply to be sent via the Red Cross in Geneva but sometimes these messages could take two years to reach the recipient. In July 1942 Douglas Ord sent a Red Cross message, ingeniously using biblical verses as a sort of code.

"Last two verses Acts, Moffatt's version. 'Now this reads: for two full years he remained in his private lodging welcoming any who came to visit him. He preached the reign of God and taught about the Lord Jesus Christ, quite openly and unmolested.' Some of these passages seem designed for the conveyance of messages, if only they are not censored!"

THE D-DAY LANDINGS *by Allied forces in Normandy in June 1944 cut off German supply lines from France to the islands, so the occupying forces began to suffer the same food shortages that the locals had endured for four years. Six months later they finally allowed the Red Cross to send food, medicine and other necessities to the starving islanders.*

GERMAN SOLDIERS INSPECT *parcels as they are unloaded from the Red Cross ship SS Vega, which made six relief trips to the islands in the last six months of the war.*

Two months later his 'unmolested' status was threatened.

"An evil day for Guernsey. I was doing my best to prune the fruit bushes in the garden, feeling very tired and unlike effort, when I became aware of G coming down the path with a grave face. Someone had just rung up to ask if I knew anything about the Order for the Deportation of the English-born people. We had heard nothing."

This morning I had a shock when the postman brought me a red cross envelope with an enclosed slip of paper asking me to go to the Bureau.

English-born Douglas Ord had been a German prisoner of war in the closing stages of World War I in 1918.

"I confess I did not sleep all night. Memories of the imprisonment in 1918 and of the dreadful train journey to Germany haunted me, tired out though I was, and feeling far from well. The shock together with the thought of all G would now face, what I had once been through, weighed me down. And now this morning the rain is coming down in sheets and all seems black."

*from the roof of Fort
Regent, the eighteenth-
century fortress that towers
above St Helier harbour.*

Thanks to the duties of his ministry, Douglas Ord won a last-minute reprieve, but the deportation included some of Iris Bullen's friends and neighbours.

"They have lost no time in mustering the people they want. They sent constables, along with a soldier late last night, waking up people to be ready to go this afternoon. We are very distressed at these inhuman actions. Vera Whiting, her husband and little girl have gone today. In town there were people in groups looking very sad, some crying, and nearly crazy with anxiety. All families of English men have to go."

Iris was one of those who went to St Helier, the Jersey capital, to watch the exodus.

THE RESIDENTS OF JERSEY
*continued to defy Nazi
occupation. The painter
of this piece of graffiti
would certainly have been
imprisoned if caught.*

"Observed a very distressing sight of people making their way down to the pier with their little luggage, including a blanket. We gave them some hearty cheers as a send off from Library Place as we couldn't get any nearer to the pier, the Germans had barred us off. How the Germans must have observed our unbroken spirit in that pilgrimage to the boats. I heard that on last Wednesday's boat, as it left the pier heads, they struck up as loud as they could the song 'There will always be an England' and 'God save the King'."

Over 2,000 British-born Channel Islanders were deported to internment camps, and more than 40 died.

For those left behind, conditions grew worse. The Germans requisitioned homes at a few hours' notice to accommodate troops; gas and electricity supplies became increasingly intermittent; and firewood was in short supply. It was sometimes a choice of getting warm or having a hot meal. One anonymous 70-year-old woman left a diary for the year 1944. It is a pathetic record of her loneliness (she received few visitors, thanks to the lack of petrol and lack of transport), misery (as her family was in

England) and cold and hunger (she went to bed in the late afternoons and remained there till the next morning in order to keep warm).

"I generally feel starved about 3:30pm and have some thick gruel (flour, milk and water). How I long for a good rump steak."

Guernsey and Jersey have highly fertile agricultural land, but the occupying forces were busy fortifying the islands at the expense of agriculture. Douglas Ord watched in horror.

"Tractors are busy hauling long-range artillery to points of vantage all over the island, without regard to crops. In one place they cut across a field of standing corn and in another right through a whole field of cauliflower. Anxious however, for the production of food, the German authorities issue an order most obligingly permitting the cultivation of gardens by their dispossessed owners, though the troops are occupying the dwellings. Who will reap the harvest? Already thieving is taking place on a wide scale and civilians cannot keep watch after curfew."

GERMAN TROOPS *overlooking St Helier harbour, Elizabeth Castle and St Aubin's Bay – one of a series of photographs taken for propaganda purposes.*

Slave labourers of many nationalities were brought in by the Germans for these fortification works and thousands died. Iris Bullen and others treated them with astonishing compassion, especially as the islanders were hungry themselves.

"We have lots of Spanish and French men which have been brought here by the Germans – for what reason is not quite clear. When I went to the shop today to get my bare weekly rations there was a negro and another man also going into the shop. They looked pitiful, Miss Vanberg had previously met them, and taken them to her home and given each a slice of bread, They had not had anything to eat since 6 pm the day before and have only soup and ¼ loaf a day. They are half starved, and in camps guarded by soldiers. They could not get anything from the shop as everything is rationed on coupons."

SLAVE LABOURERS
imported by the Germans
to help with the fortifying of
the islands.

THE GRAVES OF SLAVE *labourers on Longy Common, Alderney. The exact number of slave labourers – most of whom were brought to the island from Eastern Europe – who perished will never be known. At the peak of the fortification work there were some 5,500 slave workers on the island.*

A STATES OF JERSEY *ration book belonging to one Jack du Feu of St Helier. Although the Channel Islands are rich agricultural land, there were not enough people to farm it after the great evacuation that preceded the German invasion. Food was soon in short supply.*

During her trips to the market by the end of 1942, Iris Bullen was only able to buy swedes. These were desperate times.

> "There are a lot of robberies going on in the island. In the west of the island last week, a man was killed and his sister injured, when they were attacked by two men (believed to be Russians, as they have brought a lot here to work). They were after the fowls. It is not money they are after but food, as some of them are starving. It is not always the foreigners that rob, the German soldiers often do themselves as they are on small rations, and after curfew are at liberty to scour the fields and farms. Shops and stores also have robberies."

Iris's children both suffered from frequent bouts of diarrhoea. On Guernsey, Douglas Ord recorded frequent gastritis. He also witnessed a harrowing sight.

> "How serious the food shortage has become was rudely illustrated this morning when I saw two bricklayers trying to haul a handcart with some bricks and cement. The men were just skin and bone, their facial bones protruded and their legs wobbled with sheer weakness. As they struggled uphill cars filled with officers and NCOs flashed past – men in prime condition, fed on the best that can be plundered in fair France before they come here to do the like. It isn't good for one to feel the intense resentment within at such contrasts. The wet season is producing potato disease and the outlook for winter is none too good."

News of D-Day brought muted feelings of excitement. This was a double-edged sword: liberation could be at hand but German supply ships from France were cut off. Rations were cut; morale was high but Iris had to go gleaning to put food on the table. On September 1, 1944, she wrote:

"The gas supply of the Island failed at 7:30am on Aug 4. This means a great hardship on the population with practically no fuel available. We are registered to have one meal a day cooked at the bakehouse in a container without handles for 3d. We have only an open grate, and what we can get hold of for fuel, such as sticks and peelings, we use to warm up some porridge for breakfast, boil milk etc."

Could things possibly get worse? Six weeks later:

"Everything is in a critical state, no leather for shoe repairs and no boots or shoes available. Clothing very scarce. People get what they can from second hand shops. Also a lot of bartering is going on, including black market. Some unpatriotic people have been watched during the occupation years, and had their houses daubed with tar and swastikas just to remind them their day of payment is coming for their black marketing and co-operation with the Germans."

THE FIRST BRITISH *landing craft, laden with supplies, arrives at Creux Harbour, Sark, following the German surrender.*

Our emotion was overwhelmed when he mentioned the dear Channel Islands would be freed today.

AFTER THE LIBERATION *food supplies are restored. For the first time in five years the Channel Islanders are able to buy as much food as they need.*

Relief ships carrying food, tea and other basics signalled that liberation was at hand. On May 8, 1945, Iris was able to write:

CROWDS OF PEOPLE WAVE *for the camera in the streets of St Peter Port as they prepare to welcome the liberating British Task Force on May 9, 1945.*

"Truly this is the greatest day of our lives, for most of us in these islands. Wireless sets opening up from everywhere. And we heard Mr Churchill's speech. Our emotion was overwhelmed when he mentioned the dear Channel Islands would be freed today. After the speech which was just after 3pm, we all put up our Union Jacks, and flags of the Allies. Any one that has not had the experience of occupation such as we have had, can not realise what it meant to us, to hoist our flags once again. For five years we had our patriotism suppressed, we could only show our faith in the future by our acts and forbearance."

The following day the Channel Islands of Jersey, Guernsey, Alderney and Sark were liberated.

"As the soldiers landed they were simply mobbed, and could hardly move, and I was jammed in the crush complete with cart, children, and a dog – which I had difficulty to control. We heard that there were six Jersey men on board, so all who had loved ones in the Forces were eagerly looking if they could spot one. I saw a touching scene of a mother who found her son. We all cried, it was a touching episode."

However, as excited islanders returned from exile on the British mainland, they found that many of their homes had been looted and wrecked by the occupation forces. It was a poor homecoming.

4. Out of Harm's Way

"We were slowly let down into the stormy Atlantic alongside of the now rapidly sinking *City of Benares* and then the sailors tried to row away. But the boat was sadly overloaded with the children and passengers from the smashed lifeboats, and it soon became waterlogged. We were sitting in water up to our chests. The poor little children hadn't a dog's chance. It was awful."
Bess Walder, September 1940

Suitcase and teddy bear in hand, wearing labels with their name and age, scores of British children were taken from their homes and evacuated to the homes of strangers. The plan was well intentioned: to safeguard the rising generation from the worst of war. During World War I, 1,400 people had been killed in air raids, and 18 children were killed when Upper North Street School in the East End of London was demolished by a bomb in 1917. So at the start of World War II, entire schools were evacuated to places like Cornwall and Wales. Most children were sent to rural areas but others took long risky sea voyages to America, Australia, South Africa and Canada.

About 11.30 (at night) we were literally shaken out of our beds by the explosion in the engine room.

Twelve-year-old Bess Walder and her little brother were among the passengers on the *City of Benares* steaming for safety in Canada. The ship sailed in convoy from the River Mersey on Friday, September 13, 1940. It was torpedoed four days later, 500 miles from land. Safely back on British soil, she wrote a letter to her teacher and school friends. 'How I managed to escape what so many of my fellow seavacs had to go through.'

THE CITY OF BENARES *had been built as a passenger liner, travelling between Liverpool and what was then Bombay. The great loss of life when she was torpedoed brought to an end the programme of evacuating children from the war zone by sea.*

CONFUSED AND UNHAPPY *children, identification labels round their necks, await evacuation.*

"About 11.30 (at night) we were literally shaken out of our beds by the explosion in the engine room where the U-boat torpedo had cleaved the power engine in two. This was followed by louder and terrifying detonations. I jumped up and put on my dressing gown, and fumbled for my life jacket (as we were completely in the dark as the lights were out) and grabbed hold of my mac. Then I fished the other two that were in my cabin, got their lifebelts and got one little girl onto the boat deck. Then I went back for the other little girl, Ailsa. I found that our wardrobe had blocked the cabin door, I grabbed hold of something, (to this day I don't know what it was) and hacked at the wardrobe. I managed to squeeze through a hole, into our cabin, I found that Ailsa had fallen over something and was bleeding to death. I wrapped her in my coat that I wasn't wearing and tried to get her out. The cabin was fast filling up with water and I found to my horror that I couldn't get past the wardrobe."

One of the adults escorting the evacuees heard her frantic cries, and helped Bess and Ailsa towards the stairs leading to the boat deck.

"As we rushed along the passage the stairs that led to our boat deck collapsed and so we had to rush back again and use the other stairs to the lifeboat we were allotted and found that it had been smashed to smithereens. By this time Ailsa had fainted and was nearly dead. But she was such a brave little kid and game to the end, which mercifully came while she was unconscious. The escort lowered her into the sea and said a prayer for her, and then hustled me into another lifeboat that was being lowered."

The overloaded lifeboat descended into the freezing Atlantic waters but it soon became waterlogged. Those with nothing to hang on to were washed out of the boat. Finally the boat capsized, throwing the remaining 20 passengers into the sea.

"I decided to swim for it. It was really surprising how strong I felt when I swam against the waves, I suppose I knew it depended on me to keep myself alive. I swam until I reached the upturned lifeboat, when I tried to scramble on to it I found I had sprained my ankle, so I had to use my arms and only one leg. When I had regained my breath I saw my pal Beth Cummins trying to get on. I held out one hand and by hanging on with the other I fished her up on top of the boat, where we both hung onto the keel with all our might. At last the waves calmed a bit and we were able to see by moonlight the other people on the boat. Two Indian seamen, one was dead and the other was half-alive."

The two girls clung on all night in increasingly rough seas.

"When dawn broke, there was just us and the Atlantic. Perhaps you know that creepy feeling that comes over you when you are in a lonely field at night with nothing but fields in sight."

Four hours later the two girls were picked up by a British destroyer.

"I saw my brother on the destroyer. He had been picked up later. I was so relieved, as I was wondering what I should tell mother if he was lost. I came out of hospital yesterday and am staying with my brother and mother at this very beautiful mansion house. I think we are staying for some time, as my nerves have gone to pot but it won't take me long to pull myself together again. If the occasion arises that I feel I should like to go to Canada, mother will let me go by plane if I still want to go."

AFTER BEING TORPEDOED *in rough waters, the* City of Benares *sank very quickly. The survivors suffered severe exposure, shock and exhaustion, and some spent up to eight days on lifeboats awaiting rescue. Of the 90 children on board the boat when it set sail, only 13 survived.*

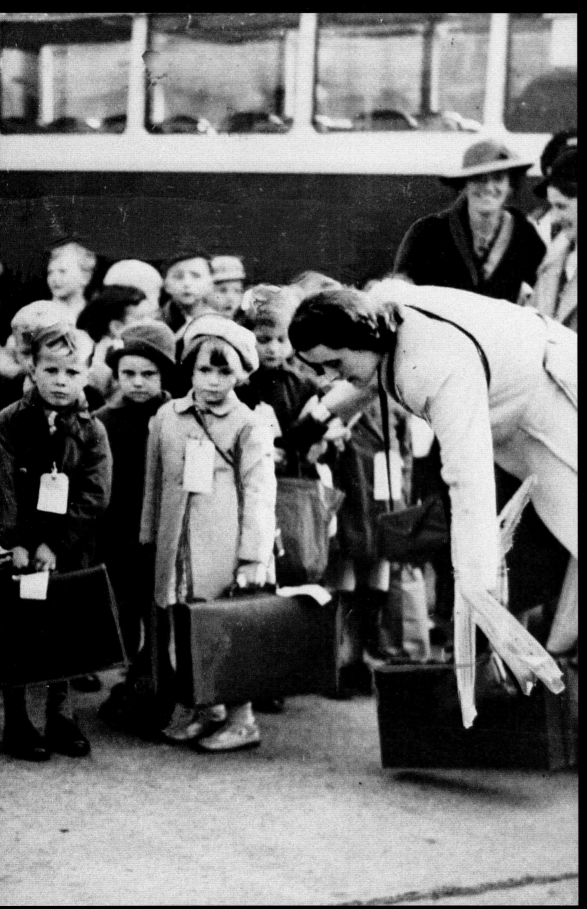

OPERATION PIED PIPER
in 1939 was the biggest and
most concentrated mass
movement of people in
Britain's history. After the
fears of bombing weren't
realised, many of the
evacuees were returned
home, until France fell to
Germany in 1940, and
bombing campaigns started
with a vengeance in Britain.
The evacuation plan started
again, and whole classes
of schoolchildren would
be rounded up, with adult
guardians for the journey,
have a label attached to them
and loaded onto a waiting
bus or train. When they
arrived at their destinations,
tired, confused and hungry,
they were lined up ready
to be selected by their
prospective hosts.

CANADA BOUND
*evacuees arrive at their
assembly point for
registration before joining
their ship.*

The *City of Benares* was one of several ships taking 'seavacs' to Canada and America as war in Europe began to hot up. Veronica Owen was 15 and reluctant to leave Britain. Her mother wrote to her stressing that the younger generation needed to be saved for postwar roles.

"Your object in life must be to fit yourself for the future – you may feel you can do all sorts of things here which are of direct help – like you are doing now in weeding, washing up etc – but you will be able to do that just as much in Canada, as Canada will put, in fact is doing so already, every ounce she has into helping the mother country – You will be spared the immediate horrors of war, such as air raids etc. I know you will say 'I don't want to run away', but you are not – the world of the future is going to depend on your generation, therefore we want you to have every advantage. Purely from the practical reason of defending this country it is better that there should be as few people as possible who cannot by reason of their age be directly helpful – your duty, darling, lies in the future, ours is in the present."

Not all evacuees were sent overseas. Mollie Dineen accompanied her son Bryan and the rest of his Streatham primary school to Eastbourne. She wrote a vivid account of her experiences in her diary.

"The great evacuation of schoolchildren from London began for us at 7.30am on September 1, 1939. We all arrived at school fully equipped with clothing, gas masks and food for the great unknown journey. Children were very excited, the older ones perhaps a little scared, helpers and teachers worried and mothers with sad eyes but brave smiles."

As a journalist on the *Daily Herald*, Mea Allan covered the evacuation for her newspaper and wrote about it in notes for her unpublished autobiography.

"Trains ran all day from the main stations. I covered this wonderful exodus, rising early in the morning in the grey summer haze to see the first train out and returning to the office in the stifling heat of evening, hoarse with cheering the last train off on its journey. Parents were not allowed on the platforms. 'No fuss, no tears,' was the motto of the London County Council. And it certainly worked for the children went away singing. It was all rather like a glorified school treat. Some of those mothers who had made the brave sacrifice of loosening loving Cockney apron strings, came for a last peep at their departing Tommy or Violet or Billy. Pressed behind the barriers they saw little more than the rear-lamp of the guard's van."

NOTICES AT RAILWAY STATIONS *in September 1939 (right) announce the 'alteration of the railway schedule owing to the vast evacuation plan that is being put into operation'. Passengers are warned that certain trains will not be available for normal use as they are required for the evacuation of children.*

PARENTS AND AN INFANT *sibling wave goodbye to evacuee children (left), not knowing when they will see each other again.*

Mollie Dineen and her charges had no idea of their destination as the train pulled out of the station.

"From the window we watched London fade away and the green fields of Surrey and later on the hills of Sussex came into view. We realised we must be going to the sea as the stations flashed by, and presently we heard the cry, 'All change, Eastbourne'. We marched from the station in our lines of five again, with crowds looking on, we might have been film stars arriving, the attention we received."

The child won't eat at table because she had always taken her meals sitting on the doorstep.

Volunteers provided a welcome cup of tea, and settled the children for a rest, before putting them through a medical examination – checking for head lice. First aider Miss Andrews was a volunteer who met two trains of evacuees at the station in sleepy Tunbridge Wells in Kent at 5.30 on the morning of September 1. Among them were expectant mothers and mothers with babies.

"The mothers are naturally far more bewildered and 'difficult' than the children – homesick as they felt the country was 'more unsafe' than London, being so empty."

BEFORE BEING SENT ABROAD
*all children had to have a
preliminary medical check.*

The Government paid a billeting allowance to those who opened their homes to evacuees, but it barely covered a child's keep. In Tunbridge Wells Miss Andrews recorded in her diary how billeting brought out the worst in some people.

"A rich woman first refused to have anyone billeted in her mansion; then when billeting powers were used (in the form of the village constable) grudgingly agreed to four staff (eight were sent) but decreed that 'those women' should be quartered with the servants, provided no beds and threatened to turn them out if she was made aware of their existence."

The behaviour of some of the evacuees brought a smile to her face.

"The family quartered on Mrs Leonard preferred to sleep on the floor, and the child won't eat at table because she had always taken her meals sitting on the doorstep."

A LONDON FAMILY LEAVES *the billeting office in Janary 1941, after registering for the latest phase of the evacuation scheme.*

CHILDREN EVACUATED *from London to a country house in Surrey line up for their daily dose of 'medicine' – probably cod-liver oil, to combat the widespread childhood disease of rickets.*

In 1939, before German troops had overrun Belgium and France, children were still being sent to towns on the south coast. Doreen and Sheila Manwaring were sent to Deal in Kent. Doreen was a feisty young communist sympathiser.

"I was billeted in the Rectory. The house and food was all right but the people were snobbish blue-blooded Tories. The Rectory is the biggest house in Deal, yet they only took in four children. There were seven large rooms in the house which were not used. Yet the lady of the house complained that four children were too much for her to manage (her maid did all the work) and said that Sheila and I would have to move to another billet."

There was no school for the girls in Deal, so they were shunted off to Folkestone.

"The billeting authorities moved us into a large hotel. Directly we were in, they started moving us out into private billets. I was in a lovely hotel, Barrelle House. We were treated exactly as guests; we had the same meals as the hotel visitors. Mrs Godefroy, the proprietress, treated us so well that she went bankrupt and had to close the hotel."

Constant changes of billet were one of the themes of the Home Front, as officials tried to match billet and billetees. With hindsight, billeting officer George Whiteman felt that the authorities had failed in many ways when the great exodus was planned.

"They made little allowance for the essential difference between billeting schoolchildren and billeting mothers and children together. There was apparently no allowance for the different character of different reception areas, so that people from the dirtiest evacuation areas were quite possibly directed into the cleanest reception areas; or cities with a known preponderance of, say, Irish Catholics in their danger areas, allocated to country areas of rigid protestantism. I even suspect that Whitehall, in planning the reception of evacuees, never contemplated that they would need to be transferred from one billet to another. Transfers are of course inevitable. The record in my district was held by one boy whom we tried out in eleven different billets. In fairness to him, it should be said the parents were chief cause of his billets being upset. Four or five changes of billet before the right one has been found have not been uncommon."

BILLETING OFFICERS *were responsible for finding accommodation for the evacuees, which was particularly difficult when families wanted to stay together. Here the billeting officer in High Wycombe, Buckinghamshire, checks that a London family have everything they need in their new cottage.*

TAKE THEM BACK!
TAKE THEM BACK!
TAKE THEM BACK!..

DON'T do it,
mother —

LEAVE YOUR CHILDREN
IN THE SAFER AREAS

ISSUED BY THE MINISTRY OF HEALTH

MOTHERS STRUGGLED
*with the enforced separation
of evacuation, and missed
their children desperately.
The government issued
propaganda posters, such
as this one above, trying to
persuade them that bringing
their children back would be
playing into Hitler's hands.*

A FOSTER MOTHER
*in Haywards Heath,
Sussex, welcomes the
parents of some of
her charges for a visit.
Evacuation wasn't always
an unhappy experience.*

Parents visited, despite the difficulties of wartime travel on overcrowded trains and buses. One London parent wrote to thank George Whiteman for their son's home from home.

"I came away on Sunday afternoon with the grandest feeling of content and I feel like a feather this week. The people the boy is with, made us most welcome and are extremely kind to him. I only hope he will appreciate it all his life. I sincerely believe he does because he asked if we would mind him coming back to Mum and Dad for weekends when the time comes for him to come home altogether. To me it is the most wonderful thing in the world to hear him call the people he is living with Mum and Dad. People here say I wouldn't care for my child to call a stranger Mum and Dad but I tell them Saffron Walden people are not strangers (somehow they make one feel that way) and it just proves that they really are Mums and Dads."

There were many others who were not so happy. This mother had been billeted 'on the southern side of London'.

"We have been billeted the last place on God's earth that working class mothers and children should have been. Ninety five per cent of the mothers and children have returned home. The residents

EVACUEES AT THE BARRIER
at Ipswich station in
Suffolk. The incoming train
brought parents, relatives
and friends on special
excursion fares to visit their
loved ones.

here are snobs who never wanted us here in the first place but thought it was their duty, the few modern shops are beyond our purse, and while the weather was fine we were able to walk about, but now it's damp and cold the householder doesnt even like the idea of us sitting in the cold kitchen. We are in the way, so it's better to go home to danger, but have our nice fires and comfort. They have tired of us and our children already. One can't blame any mother or child for returning home to a home and welcome, where our children aren't looked down on and untrue nasty stories aren't told."

Some children started to trickle back to their homes and parents, particularly as the phoney war dragged into 1940. Mrs Doreen Manwaring expressed the heartache of all wartime mothers.

"It has been such a wrench for us to part with our children, but the press and wireless are forever begging us not to bring them home, so we do what we hope is for the best and let them stay. We can only keep hoping that it won't be for long."

THE RAF WINS THE BATTLE OF BRITAIN

The home population could do little but watch the gallant 'few' involved in defending Britain's skies. The German air force or Luftwaffe, which had been tried and tested in the Spanish Civil War and more recently destroyed the Polish air force in a matter of weeks, was much feared. When Germany set its sights on invading England, Hermann Goering, Luftwaffe Commander-in-Chief, understandably boasted, 'My Luftwaffe is invincible... And so now we turn to England. How long will this one last – two, three weeks?' He was in for a rude awakening.

British victory owed much to superior aircraft, ingenious tactics and the technological advantage of radar. Most significant and most fondly remembered of the

aircraft was the Spitfire, the brainchild of the brilliant RJ Mitchell, who died tragically young in 1935. The design of the Spitfire's wings in particular was revolutionary, providing the smallest possible turning circle and withstanding high speed better than some early jet aircraft designed ten years later.

Radar – Radio Detection and Ranging – had been developed in the 1930s as a means of detecting enemy aircraft via microwaves. Picking up radar signals and plotting the information they provided was one of the most important tactical jobs that WAAFs – members of the Women's Auxiliary Air Force – performed during the war.

A CROWD GATHERS ROUND THE WRECKAGE *of a German bomber brought down by RAF fighters, March 1940.*

RAF PILOTS 'SCRAMBLE' *towards their Spitfires at the start of a mission (top left). Spitfires were the only British fighter to be produced throughout the war, with over 22,000 built between 1938 and 1948.*

THE POPULAR SINGLE-SEATER SPITFIRE *(top right) was a favourite with pilots because of its speed and the superb handling qualities that enabled it to turn quickly and avoid counter-attack.*

SIR ROBERT WATSON-WATT, *(above) the pioneer of radar, which provided a key tactical advantage during the Battle of Britain.*

A CHAIN OF RADAR STATIONS *– known as 'Chain Home' stations – was established across Britain to pick up radar signals and monitor the movements of pilots in the air. Pictured here (middle right) is the Receiver Hut at Ventnor, Isle of Wight.*

PLOTTERS OBTAINED AND COLLATED *information from signals staff, who picked up signs of raids and indicated whether they were friendly or hostile. Like coding offices the staff were mainly women, as seen here (bottom right) at Bentley Priory, the headquarters of Fighter Command.*

By the summer of 1940 the south coast was deemed unsafe and children were re-evacuated. Doreen and Sheila were sent to Abertillery in Wales.

> "It is a mining town in Monmouthshire, lying in a valley between very high mountains. It is one of the distressed areas and has a high death rate from TB. But apart from these failings it is reckoned to be a safety area. The girls are living in a miner's home and are being very kindly treated. These people have had very hard times, and know what trouble is."

Despite the disruption of two evacuations, Doreen's elder daughter (also Doreen) passed her exams and went on to university. Her younger sister Sheila remained, safe but homesick.

> "She wants to come home, as indeed they all do. Most of the girls in her school are heartily sick of evacuation. I feel rather sorry for poor old Sheila. She wanted to be a ballet dancer, and as she said, she ought to be having the training now, but that's out of the question. She has her toe shoes with her, and she and two other girls practise each Saturday, but it's not enough of course. She seems to have given up the idea now of ballet as a career, and wants me to let her come home and take a commercial course and then get a clerical job."

Their home is a heap of rubble – but he's got no sense of bitterness.

PARENTS ARE REUNITED with their evacuated children in Saffron Walden, Essex, after six weeks apart in October 1939. Nearly one thousand London parents attended a reunion party, hosted by the mayor of the town.

LONDON'S DOCKLANDS were a major target for the Luftwaffe, which meant that the whole of the East End suffered severe destruction. Residents were evacuated by the truckload, with many families separated as priority was given to the youngest.

Bryan Dineen and his mother, Mollie, were also re-evacuated to Wales. The children had their school friends to socialise with but Mollie was lonely, as she expressed in the diary she kept for the five years she was there.

"At home my friends are many and almost every evening someone would drop in for a cup of tea and a chat. Now my time in the evenings is spent alone mending or reading in bed, but it's my job to be here."

Mollie was in for a culture shock. The Welsh village of Llandovery was so small that there was no radio, no newspaper, no cinema or theatre. She threw herself into the job, offering a prize for the tidiest child, becoming cub leader, and enjoying the simple pleasures of country life, like blackberry picking and the May Queen celebrations. She settled into village life so well that her return to London in 1945 was as much of a wrench as it had been to leave – she was homesick for Wales!

A year after the major evacuation of schoolchildren, a new evacuation was called for. Thousands were made homeless by the Blitz in 1940, and entire families arrived in Saffron Walden to be billeted by George Whiteman and his colleagues.

A FAMILY REST ON THEIR SUITCASES *while waiting for a bus to take them to safety in the country.*

"The refugees had been travelling for four or five days, and many had slept on the ground in Epping Forest. Ours were the first Rest Centres, they said, where they were able to sleep on camp beds and not on the floor. Now in the midst of this problem of trying to billet families, nearly all large, averaging about seven or eight, another problem was forced on us. We found men appearing who were chasing their families, trying to get re-united. In the last three days we have had literally dozens of men and some women, who have been trailing from village to village, sleeping under hedgerows, determined to find their families at all costs. They're absolutely worn out, and when we've been able to put them on to where their families are their faces light up. The real difficulty has been that Canning Town and Silvertown seem to have been completely evacuated during the day while the men were at work, or looking for work. One man with his wife and six children, including one baby of four weeks, has just got what he and his family stand up in. Their home is a heap of rubble – but he's got no sense of bitterness."

Two years later George recorded that a third to a half of those homeless evacuees were still in villages round Saffron Walden.

"Those who found their way into billets stayed but a short time of course. It was the expedient of putting them in quarters on their own, which enabled them to 'settle in'. Condemned cottages were used in a good many areas."

Kathleen Crawley had been evacuated to Ashford in Kent at the beginning of the war, but as Kent came under fire she was sent to Llanelly.

EVACUATION WAS NEVER *compulsory but receiving evacuees was. This home in the Midlands (right) was already crowded when three more children were billeted here.*

BY THE MID 1940S *the authorities were concerned that the south-eastern and eastern counties of England, to which hundreds of thousands of London children had been evacuated, were no longer safe from the threat of bombing. A further wave of evacuation moved many of these children further afield to South Wales.*

"It really is ridiculous sending us to Llanelly. We are surrounded by factories etc (careless talk may give away vital secrets) which the Germans are having a go at. They've stopped sounding the air raid sirens too and we never know whether the planes are British or not. We keep hearing thuds, which are mostly caused by some queer process in the steel works Don't get alarmed will you, but some bombs were dropped round the docks etc. Thank goodness we are the other side of town. The people here are very jittery and the children won't go to bed at nights. Have you had any air raid warnings lately? They've had lots at Ashford I hear. I don't think there is a safe place anywhere in England now."

Phyllis Higgins, writing to her son Stephen in the Forces, described the evacuees she took into her large house in Hale, Cheshire, in August 1944, as the pilotless planes (V-1 rockets) were dropping on south east England.

Mr Churchill came round in his car on the hilltop, they wanted a training ground for the army. And he just said move all those people out and that was that.

"I have five evacuees, a mother and her three children and the grannie who is only 54 but oh terribly bomb-shocked. She is shaking all the time. They are an exceedingly respectable nice family so I have sent for another daughter and her 14-month-old son. They are having a ghastly time down in Kent where they come from. They love being here and the children are wonderfully good. The grandpa came last Sunday and returns tomorrow. The husband of their youngest daughter is here for his 48 hours. He is stationed at Chester so comes over every Saturday and Sunday. The flying bombs are coming over pretty frequently so it would be stupid for them to return home."

PRACTISING FOR D-DAY: *a group of English children and an American guard watch from a distant fence as American troops stage a mock invasion of a cove near Slapton Sands, Devon.*

THE PEACEFUL VILLAGES *around Slapton were turned topsy-turvy by the American 'invasion'. This picture was taken in September 1944, after the GIs had moved on. Piles of their camp beds await collection. Many of the houses pictured lost the glass from their windows during the training exercises.*

It was not just children who were evacuated. Whole villages gave up their homes in 1943 as plans for the Second Front became concrete. People living in farms, hamlets and villages round Slapton Sands, on the South Devon coast, were given six weeks' notice of evacuation. On December 20, 1943 the area was 'occupied' by American troops, who used the beach, countryside and buildings as a training ground for D-Day. Some farmers who returned to their land the following year found it impossible to restore their fields to their previous productivity. Further eastwards along the south coast, villagers at Tyneham in Dorset had to leave their homes as the British Army moved in to practise manoeuvres. Miss Lillian Taylor was the village Sunday school teacher.

"Mr Churchill came round in his car on the hilltop, they wanted a training ground for the army. And he just said move all those people out and that was that. We had to be out by December 19, just a few days before Christmas. We had a job to find a place for our family because my father had arthritis and had sticks, so we had to be careful. The thing was that anywhere with stairs and he would be housebound. It was depressing leaving home and coming to live among strangers, but we lost three brothers in the First World War. They hadn't had adequate training in England before they were sent abroad, better for men to be trained on their own ground then to go abroad to be trained."

Villagers evacuated from Tyneham were given compensation. Most did not own their cottages, which belonged to the big estate.

"We got about £12 compensation for the garden, things we had left in the vegetable garden. Twelve pounds was quite a bit. We left several things behind, but we could go back and get anything we wanted the following week. So we went back to get a few cabbage plants and things that we had coming on in. Somebody 'd been there before us! Even the doors in our bedrooms were gone, we'd only been gone a week, and the copper – for doing the washing. Local builders went in. The soldiers told us, 'People came with horses and carts and took things."

The evacuated Tyneham villagers never returned to their homes, and this quintessential English village is still used as a training ground for the British Army.

5. Bombs

"The planes are very determined. One comes along and slows up, gyrating down and down, lower and lower, and slower and slower, the engine gets louder and nearer and nearer. You are just expecting a bomb when suddenly the guns let fly with a resounding crack like the world blowing up. And all of us in the shelter – stiffening suddenly in fright and then relaxing as suddenly, till the next volley. Of course one can do interesting things – one can time the shells, from the moment of firing until they burst into the sky. Meanwhile one would like to be doing anything else – making a cup of tea, going to the lavatory." Mea Allan, September 1940

Sporadic air raids were launched on Britain in June, July and August 1940, but Hitler's blitzkrieg (literally, lightning war) began in earnest with a massive raid on London on September 7, 1940. What had been called the phoney war was over. Throughout the next five years there would be eerie lulls in the bombing, sometimes more difficult to cope with than the terror of the Blitz itself. It begged the question: when would it start again? It was far easier to go through the nightly routine of sleeping in an air raid shelter. Civilians soon learnt to distinguish between the 'alert' and the 'all clear' as the sirens shrieked their chilling tunes. Pupils at the Kneller Senior Boys School in Twickenham had something new to write about in the autumn term of 1940, and, from their essays, it is clear that these 11-year-olds relished the adventure of war, but it did disrupt their education.

"Since 'Goering's Blitzkrieg in the air' began we have found school life rather messed up. For one thing if there is an air raid between 12pm and 6am we do not come to school until 10.30am. We hardly have a whole lesson without it being interrupted but we will have to put up with it for the 'duration'."

Sadly their essays also record the death toll in the streets around their homes, particularly that of a schoolfriend, Gordon Morgan, who died in the raid of November 29, 1940.

"His mother died on the same night. He is the first boy of Kneller school to be killed in this war because of enemy action. His father died in the last war. Kneller boys subscribed over £2 and bought him a wreath. Each day before he went into school he would play on the swings in the Recreation Park in Kneller Gardens."

Older pupils were drafted in to help to dig their school air raid shelters. Shelters were constructed at factories and offices, and many streets had their own shelter. Mr Piper was one of those running a church shelter in Hamilton Road, Everton, a poor area where few shelters had been erected and most of these 'had been captured by groups of people determined to keep them to themselves.'

"This selfish monopolising of shelters was, partly at least, broken up by a group of young men, composed of Catholics and Unitarians, armed with short staves not unlike policemen's batons. They visited shelters which had the reputation of refusing admission to the stranger. Many a bully received a cracked head; some of the crusaders did not escape injury but this selfish monopolising of shelters by small gangs came to an end."

The legendary wartime spirit fortified these city dwellers in crisis. But under such stress friction was inevitable. In the shelter diary, Mr Piper recorded typical examples:

"Men fighting in bunks, several instances of gross dishonesty ie people coming in for tea and beating it before the collection is taken."

Kathleen Church-Bliss and her friend Elsie Whiteman had given up their cottage and country teashop to volunteer for work in a Croydon munitions factory. After sleepless nights running up and down stairs from their rooms to the basement shelter, they decided to try a public shelter.

"Our trench is occupied exclusively with the highly middle class owners from Duppas Hill. It is very amusing to hear all the various families arriving and bedding themselves out. Torches and hurricane lamps light up the gloom and husbands and wives argue and fuss according to temperament, and the chorus of snores!"

BOMB CRATERS BIG ENOUGH *to hold a double decker bus became a regular feature of the London streets, when entire terraces of houses might be demolished in a single night. By the end of the Blitz over 20,000 London civilians – and 40,000 in the rest of the country – had been killed.*

Despite raids, the pair managed a restful night's sleep and started to use the shelter regularly. But class is no barrier to friction in stressful times.

"Last night there was the most almighty row in our shelter. Mr and Mrs Bellwood returned from their week's annual holiday to find that one of their bunks had been given away to another man by Mr Harvey (in charge of the shelter). They naturally felt rather aggrieved about this...and now all he would say was that the Bellwood family must separate and one of them go into the upper shelter. Altogether there was a row royal and high words on all sides."

Teacher and voluntary social worker Phyllis Warner recorded in her diary the trauma of going on a London bus when the sirens went.

"We all fell flat on the floor of the bus. I remember thinking, 'My God, what did I come here for? I'm going to be blown to bits with this lousy crowd of strangers, and I haven't even got an identity disc on.' Then the bomb dropped a few streets away, but we still had to remain with our faces amongst other people's feet until the plane was a suitable distance away. I shall always detest the smell of shoe polish now."

We all fell flat on the floor of the bus. I remember thinking, 'My God, what did I come here for. I'm going to be blown to bits.

SOME TOWNS BUILT PUBLIC *shelters designed to protect up to 50 people. Despite many having canteens and bunk beds, they were unpopular, dark and squalid places, which in reality offered little protection.*

Department stores had shelters for customers. Peg Cotton, the American, still living in London, found the John Lewis shelter in Oxford Street a delight.

"I was buying some cretonne when the Banshee howl drove me into the sub-basement. There in the shelter below Oxford Street were hundreds of people, mostly women shoppers, crowded on wooden benches set back to back in close rows across the basement rooms. I found a place among them and settled down to read. Almost everyone carries a book nowadays as well as a gas mask. Certain of the store staff wore armbands reading Head of Personnel, Shelter Warden or First Aid. Salesgirls circulated through the rooms selling candy, biscuits, soft drinks, small sixpenny books, embroidery patterns and silks and even offering free wool in navy, khaki and Air Force blue, complete with needles and directions. 'Won't you please knit for the forces at John Lewis' expense?' Music was furnished by gramophone and, every so often, an attendant sprayed the air with disinfectant. An hour and a half spent thus is not too bad. But still it is an aggravation and a waste of time. I got a perm a few days ago. One less thing to bother with if one's hair is manageable. Of course the sirens went while I was still crowned with wet hair-pinned snails! I had plenty of company – lots of other women in various states of presentableness or rather, unpresentableness. I can see that inhibitions will soon be 'Gone with the Wind' – or the bombs!"

One thoughtful daughter bought her ageing mother a dressing gown to throw over her nightclothes as she scurried to the shelter. No one wanted to be caught in the bath, or scantily clad, during a raid.

Survivors who emerged into the streets found familiar landmarks had disappeared and gaping holes where neighbours' houses had stood the day before. Lylie Eldergill was a garment-machinist living in the East End of London. Her husband, Tom, had been blind since the age of six, and his handicap brought added danger.

"Tom and I don't go to a shelter. We have never been to one. We stay in the flat and chance it. If I had my way I should have gone to a shelter, but Tom didn't want to go. He was afraid of panic if a bomb hit the place. What I am afraid of is being buried alive underneath these buildings."

THE BASEMENTS of department stores also provided makeshift shelters where customers could take refuge if the sirens sounded.

BOMBED-OUT householders saved what possessions they could, with nowhere to put them but the street.

Tom's fears were justified. On March 11, 1941, Bank underground station was hit, killing 68 people. Mea Allan, the ambitious journalist on the *Daily Herald*, was the first reporter on the scene. In a letter to a close friend, she wrote an account that would not have got past the censor and on to the pages of her newspaper.

"One usually verbally measures bomb craters by the number of buses they would accommodate: but this one would take a depot. It stretches from pavement to pavement across the length and width of the roads. When I saw it, it was a jumble of thousands of tons of roadway, twisted steel girders and huge chunks of concrete. Beneath were dead shelterers whose bodies were one by one being brought out. The high explosive had fallen through the roadway, exploded underneath, thrown the whole thing up, and then it had all dropped back again. The blast was as bad as the actual bombing. You know the terrific gale that can be caused by the ordinary approach of a tube train – multiply that gale by a terrific and horrible velocity – so that people were picked up like pieces of paper and hurled along passages and on to the line – every bone in their body smashed…I went down to the platforms, by way of steps plentifully covered with sawdust. Blood, brown and slippery was still oozing through. Talked to the 'regulars' who were taking up their positions for the night in passages that had not been damaged. They told me – ' the worst thing was getting breath, we were choked with fumes and dust'. A shaft of grey daylight pouring down from the shattered ceiling, a barrier up, and beyond it the machine gun roar of dozens of drills breaking up the debris. Chaos noise and death – and amid it all the regulars are sitting down to sleep – not thinking they are brave, just Londoners carrying on in the good old wartime style."

THE AFTERMATH OF A RAID *was often as dangerous as the bombing itself. Firefighters fought a constant battle to keep flames under control.*

CRASH TENDER VEHICLES *were equipped with pumps capable of producing several thousand litres of foam or water per minute. Here a firefighting crew in Ilford, Essex, practises with the latest piece of equipment at a simulated air crash.*

While many civilians took cover underground, a network of civil defence workers above ground coped with the aftermath. Frank Hurd, London firefighter, volunteered for the Auxiliary Fire Service in April 1939 and was called up in September. He wrote an account of the first major raid on September 7, 1940, when his unit was called to Becton Gasworks.

"Chaos met our eyes. Gasometers were punctured and were blazing away, a power house had been struck, rendering useless the hydraulic hydrant supply – the only source of water there. And then over head we heard Jerry. The searchlights were searching the sky in a vain attempt to locate him. Guns started firing, and then I had my first experience of a bomb explosion. A weird whistling sound and I ducked beside the pump. Then a weird flash of flame, a column of earth and debris flying into the air, and the ground heaved. I was thrown violently against the side of the appliance."

FIREFIGHTERS AND RESCUE WORKERS *often reached the scene of a raid too late to do anything other than fight the blaze.*

Reaching an alleyway only 20ft (6m) wide, lined with warehouses, Frank confronted every fireman's worst nightmare: a fractured gas main was on fire.

"The flames issued from wide cracks in the road surface. Gas main fires must not be put out, as this would leave escaping gas with great risk of explosion. We were working with our backs against one side of the street, aiming our jets into the warehouse, with the street alight in front of us. The top floor of the building against which we had our backs, kept bursting into flame. On top of this, we were warned not to let our jets strike the brickwork of the warehouse wall, as this was very shaky and the impact would probably cause it to fall. An eighty foot high wall collapsing into a twenty foot road – not a pleasant prospect."

A fortnight later, Frank Hurd was one of 14 firefighters killed during the great City raid on the night of December 29, 1940. Records show that he was off duty and probably on his way home.

Bill Regan had been a builder in peacetime, but 'for the duration' was a member of a Heavy Rescue Squad on the Isle of Dogs. These men dug through bombed-out buildings with sticks and hands, searching for survivors. At Christmas 1940 they were still searching through the debris that had been Saunderness School, which had been bombed three months earlier. Rescuers found the bodies of two girls, members of the Auxiliary Fire Service.

AN ENTIRE LONDON PUB *was blown into the street on October 19, 1940. The rescuers shown here are searching for survivors among the devastation.*

SOME BOMBING VICTIMS *were lucky. The elderly woman in this house was trapped but unhurt by the rubble; rescue workers were able to dig her out.*

A DIRECT HIT ON A HOUSE could reduce it to a pile of debris within seconds, while its neighbours were practically unscathed.

"I know that none of us are very happy having to handle corpses and it shows. They have uncovered two young girls, about 18 years of age, quite unmarked, and they looked as if they were asleep. I looked around at the other men, and most of them looked shocked and a bit sick; we had usually found bodies mutilated, and they were usually lifted out by hands and feet and quickly got away. Feeling a bit angry at the prospect of these girls being lugged out by their arms and legs, so I got down beside them, and they have obviously been in bed for the night. Dry weather we have had and the rubble packed round them had preserved them. Their limbs were not even rigid. They were lifelike; I could not let them be handled like the usual corpses."

Bill called for a stretcher and blankets.

"Then I put my right arm under her shoulders, with her head resting against me, and the left arm under her knees, and so carried her up. I laid her on the stretcher, 'You'll be comfortable now my dear.' I did exactly the same for the other one."

Once rescue squads had pulled the survivors clear, first aid workers helped the injured to casualty clearing stations. Constance Logan Wright described such a station at Great Ormond Street Hospital, which dealt with children and adults.

"In the first room, the injuries are diagnosed by the doctor and each patient is labelled according to his or her requirements. The staff work in absolute silence – a method found to be excellent since the first need, when rescued from the blazing shattered streets, was a sense of peace and quiet. They have a special device for keeping the patient warm if suffering from severe shock. It is a wooden cradle containing three very powerful electric bulbs, and the stretcher is put on top of this so that the patient is examined and kept warm at the same time. This casualty clearing station has an operating theatre specially prepared for the Blitz; it can be cut off from the London electricity and water mains and could be entirely self-providing for 24 hours in case of need. With gas proof ventilation, it is as well protected as it is possible for any place to be and the architects say that it might even resist a direct hit."

A BOMB VICTIM ASKS
*rescue workers to give her a
cloth to wipe her face before
they continue to dig her out
of the remains of her home.*

Luftwaffe bombers did not just target London, they raided towns and cities across the country – from Cardiff to Canterbury, Newcastle to Norwich. The raid on Coventry and the destruction of its ancient cathedral on November 14, 1940 horrified the nation. PG Bridgstock, a former pupil of Kneller Boys School in Twickenham, wrote to one of his teachers afterwards.

"Coventry looks a complete mess but the papers did not give a very good account of the damage done. The town centre was so unsafe that the military had to dynamite parts of it, and there is not a street in Coventry which hasn't at least one bomb crater in it. Austin Reed's Shop, where my father works, was very lucky and the only damage done was all the windows blown out. There is still no gas, electric or clean water, so we cook our food by fire, sit at night with candles and all the water must be boiled before using."

Coventry looks a complete mess but the papers did not give a very good account of the damage.

Attached to the letter is a diagram showing five bomb craters a few yards from his home. The morning after a particularly bad raid, anxious relatives would jam telephone exchanges, sending telegrams and booking long-distance calls to get news. Phyllis Warner, in London, would generally have to wait for around 15 minutes for her long-distance trunk call to be put through to her family on the outskirts of Coventry.

FIRST AID CENTRES
*were often run in the
basements of department
stores, some of which were
also being used as shelters.
Red Cross volunteers could
offer tea, sympathy and
bandages to those in need.*

WITH FACTORIES DEDICATED
*to the production of
aeroplanes, engines and
other wartime necessities,
Coventry was among
the cities worst hit by the
bombing, outside London.
Two massive raids – in
November 1940 and April
1941 – killed hundreds of
civilians and forced the city
to organise mass funerals.*

THE CATHEDRAL OF ST MICHAEL
*was hit very early in the evening
of November 14, 1940. Within 15
minutes of the first strike the roof was
ablaze, and every firefighting appliance
in the city was battling the ferocious flames
and explosions. By the end of the evening
26 fire-fighters were dead and 200 were
injured. Here, the ceremony to enthrone
the new Bishop of Coventry, Dr. Neville
Vincent Gorton is taking place in the ruins,
February 1943.*

In October 1940 journalist Mea Allan, who spent her daylight hours reporting on the horrors of the Blitz, was bombed out herself. Anxious to recover her belongings, particularly the typescript of her first novel, she returned to what remained of her flat.

I just don't know where to go! Someone suggests Kensington, and next day you hear of a landmine in the very vicinity one would have been in, and so it goes on.

"I'm quite sick with fatigue tonight. It was awful tramping through the flat, picking up an object, tapping the dirt and broken glass off it and then recognising it – 'Oh yes, that was the green cushion.' What filth, and dust and chaos. You could hardly believe blast could do such damage, but when I tell you it was a thousand pound heavy explosive, and an aerial torpedo – well, perhaps that accounts for it! The carpets are like earthy plots. You could have ploughed them. Inches of brick dust and lime, plus macaroni, flour, rice and the contents of my hall store cupboard, the side of which blew off and spewed the contents – including marmalade. It feels very queer having no home. I just don't know where to go! Someone suggests Kensington, and next day you hear of a landmine in the very vicinity one would have been in, and so it goes on."

BARRIERS WERE ERECTED *to keep the public away while the police dealt with an unexploded bomb. The signs displayed on this barrier across Fleet Street in London give the temporary addresses of businesses forced to move after their premises were destroyed.*

THE VIEW FROM ST PAUL'S *Cathedral, London showed the scale of the destruction, at the height of the Blitz. The surrounding area was almost entirely destroyed, while the cathedral itself miraculously escaped serious damage.*

Phyllis Warner also had to move out in October 1940, because of an unexploded bomb. It was part of the ARP warden's job to record the whereabouts of unexploded bombs and evacuate nearby houses. A small suitcase stood ready at the door in every home for just such an emergency. Phyllis Warner heard 'her' bomb land one Tuesday evening.

"The door bell rang at 9:30 last night. The police, to say that the bang we had just heard was a time bomb in the garden next door but one, and would we please evacuate. We hastily picked up the thick coats and the suitcases we had brought to the shelter every night for just this emergency. It was an unpleasant walk through the streets, with the guns thudding and an occasional piece of shrapnel coming down with a terrific whang – in fact we finished at a sharp run. We were taken to a Government shelter beneath many floors of reinforced concrete, where noises came but faintly, and we settled down to a real night's slumber, feeling secure at last.

It was bewildering to wake up in that bare stone room, amongst a crowd of strangers, and to remember what had happened, and to realise that we couldn't go home to bath or change. We adjourned to a neighbouring hotel where we took a couple of rooms between a dozen of us to use for leaving our suitcases, dressing etc, and then we had breakfast. It's no good taking rooms to sleep in, because we couldn't use them for that purpose anyway, and as long as we're 'time bombed' we shall be able to use the Government shelter."

As well as her day job as a teacher, Phyllis worked as a volunteer at a feeding centre in the mornings, where she encountered those less fortunate than herself.

> "We had about 700 of the homeless poor crowding out the Feeding Centre this morning. We worked madly from the time the All Clear went at six, until after ten. I could have wept as I put mugs of tea and slices of bread and butter into the trembling hands of old men dug out of the debris in their nightshirts, old women with blood on their white hair, little children covered with the dust of falling homes, fathers whose children are still beneath the ruins. It's their pathetic gratitude for the little we do that gets me by the throat."

Light was another enemy of those on the ground, and a friend to enemy bombers. ARP wardens patrolled the streets looking for chinks showing through the blackout. They are famously remembered for the phrase 'Put Out That Light!' Every factory and office had teams of fire-watchers perched on the roof to raise the alarm when incendiary bombs sparked fires. Equipped with stirrup pumps ARP wardens worked to put out these fires, which lit up the streets and enabled the next wave of bombers to pinpoint targets on which to drop high explosives (HE).

Charity Bick was a 15-year-old bicycle messenger during the first major raid on West Bromwich, in the Midlands. Her father was an ARP warden and her mother a Red Cross nurse. Charity told the local newspaper:

> "I was out on my bike, when I was blown off into the gutter by a bomb. I got up and carried on. Then I saw an incendiary drop on the roof of a pawnbroker's shop. I climbed up and put it out."

WITH ITS BUSY DOCKS, *Liverpool was another major target. Here, wardens help an injured woman from a first-aid post to a reception centre after her home has been bombed.*

What the newspaper did not recount was cited in her recommendation for the George Medal.

"The occupier's stirrup pump proved to be out of order, but they were able to extinguish the bomb by splashing water onto it with their hands. Mr Bick turned to make for the entrance to the roof, but put his foot through the false ceiling. He turned to warn his daughter and as he did so, she fell through the ceiling into the bedroom below."

Injured, Charity went back to the Warden's Post.

"A High Explosive bomb fell immediately opposite the Warden's Post at which she was doing duty and she was instructed to take a message to the Control Room asking for assistance. The girl borrowed a bicycle and started off but on five occasions she had to get off and lie in the gutter because of bombs falling near her. She was the only despatch rider to this Post, and therefore the only means of communicating with the Control Room. She made three journeys from her Post to the Control Room, a distance of one and a quarter miles during the height of the raid. The town was lit up by four very large fires and she had to pass in close vicinity to all these fires on her way to the control room. There was a continual rain of High Explosive bombs and shrapnel and anyone out of doors was incurring a very serious risk of injury."

A B-17 FLYING FORTRESS PASSES *over Berlin on February 3, 1945 (far left), one of a force of 1,000 Allied planes that dropped 2,500 tonnes of bombs on the German capital in a single night.*

THE REICHSTAG IN BERLIN DESTROYED *by an Allied bomb (left).*

THE TOTAL NUMBER OF CASUALTIES *is still disputed, but the single night's bombing of Dresden probably killed upwards of 30,000 people (below left).*

BOMB VICTIMS TAKE TO THE STREETS *with their few remaining belongings (left). Overall, the Allied bombing of the capital is estimated to have killed up to 50,000 people and made hundreds of thousands homeless.*

A STILL FROM FILM SHOT BY THE RAF *over Dresden, showing the city in flames (bottom). The high concentration of buildings in the city meant that fires spread rapidly. Some 30,000 buildings were destroyed as a result of just one raid.*

BOMBING GERMANY

The Blitz ravaged many British cities but the Allies' retaliation, devastating German cities such as Cologne and Dresden, undoubtedly exceeded it. In 1942, British Bomber Command's new leader, Air Marshal 'Bomber' Harris, conceived a plan to increase the number of aircraft at his disposal to 1,000 and then to unleash the fleet's full force on a single city. The idea was that the effects would be so demoralising that the German people would demand that its government seek peace. After some dispute in which Hamburg and Essen were lucky to escape, Cologne was selected as Harris's first objective.

Berlin, as the German capital, was naturally also a target,

notably during the disastrous 'Battle of Berlin' in 1943–44, when the Allies lost some 500 aircraft and over 2,500 men, and then again in early 1945.

The bombing of Dresden on the night of February 13, 1945 is widely regarded as the most shameful Allied act of the entire war. Dresden – a beautiful medieval city – became strategically important when Allied Commander-in-Chief General Eisenhower wanted to link up with the Red Army advancing through southern Germany. The city was known to be crowded with refugees retreating from the Russians, and the Allies knowingly calculated that the high number of casualties would ultimately shorten the war.

THE RUINS OF COLOGNE *after the first of Bomber Harris's 'thousand bomber raids' on the night of May 30, 1942. Cologne had already been bombed over 100 times in the course of the war. In this raid over 100 hectares of the city centre were destroyed, 469 people were killed and 45,000 made homeless.*

German bombers launched a massive attack on factories on Glasgow's Clydebank on Thursday, March 13, 1941. As Director of Education for Dumbartonshire, Dr JP McHutchison toured the damage with the local MP.

"In the bus in the morning I heard that Clydebank 'was in ruins', though I was inclined to doubt that, since from our house no sign of conflagration was visible. A visit to Clydebank proved there was not much overstatement in the remark. Not a single school escaped, so thoroughly had HE and incendiary bombs been showered all over the town, and it was a heartbreak to see as gaunt ruins splendid buildings which the same week I had visited to discuss fire-watching. But the real tragedy of the indiscriminate bombing was the gutted tenements and ruined and blasted council houses in the poorest working class areas – in which streets the miles of four storey tenements had been completely gutted by fire. Some parts were still blazing and hundreds of the tenants watching from piles of saved furniture the holocaust of their homes. Long queues of now homeless folks awaited the buses that would take them away, and Drumry Road was black with men women and children waiting at the Church Rest Centre for food and guidance."

FOLLOWING THE RAID *in March 1941, Clydebank, Glasgow was left in ruins. Here, a civil defence worker directs traffic away from a bombed-out street.*

On Friday, March 14, continuous waves of German bombers bombarded the town for another five hours.

"Houses that had escaped on Thursday night did not escape this time, and over all, the huge columns of black smoke from the oil tanks which were on fire. It was a great mercy that the weather was fair and fine, as otherwise the appalling situation, with practically the whole town homeless, would have been unbearable."

CIRCUS

Mrs Paroutaud was at teacher training college in Bristol when Bath was bombed in 1942. This was one of the Baedeker raids, so called because the targets were historic or culturally important cities listed in the famous Baedeker guide books. Mrs Paroutaud volunteered as a bicycle courier taking telegrams to city homes from anxious relatives.

> "In the case of Bath it was systematic terror raids to break morale. It was totally unexpected, no military targets only cultural ones. I saw Bath the next day. We were taken over on a bus with our bicycles so that we could act as emergency message carriers. Bath was inundated with telegrams and who could deliver them? Call out the students. We cycled all over Bath carrying messages and bringing back reports. It was heartbreaking. We would go to one address only to find that it wasn't there any more. I shall never forget the streets of Bath all crunchy with broken glass and rubble. The shocked, tense faces of the people, and this stiff upper lip thing that kept them from crying and raging over the loss and the desolation. Why didn't they weep and mourn and lament? It would have been much better for everybody."

SOME 800 PEOPLE DIED
*and a further 800 were
injured when this Clydeside
tenement was destroyed.
The local shipyards, which
were refitting vessels to
serve in the war, had been
the target.*

By the end of the war 2,379 civil defence workers had been killed in the line of duty and 4,459 seriously injured. In all, 60,000 British civilians were killed, and 85,000 seriously injured during the German bombing of the British mainland in World War II.

6. Struggling On

"Much is said about medals for troops, but I'm sure most housewives have earned a row of 'em. Theirs is a job and a half, and when there is an outside job to do in addition, it's very hard going." Ernie Britton, October 1940

HORSE FLESH
NO COUPONS REQUIRED.

Ernie Britton summed up the lot of British women as they soldiered on through the war. Women went out to work to release men for the Forces, just as their mothers had done during World War I. They worked in factories and in the London underground; they became postwomen and bus conductors. Normal domestic life was completely disrupted during the Blitz, but washing still had to be done in an era when few had washing machines. Long queues formed outside shops rumoured to have a supply of precious oranges or some other rarity. Cooking meals required ingenuity and clothes were mended and altered to last longer. On top of all this, women in the ranks of the Women's Institute and the Women's Voluntary Service collected salvage, helped to billet evacuees and collected hedgerow fruits to make jam. If they were not already exhausted by the daily grind, they worked at feeding centres, or made munitions in their 'spare time' and dug for victory in gardens and allotments to supplement the family's rations.

Ernie Britton's wife May took great pride in her home, and combined housework with her job as shop assistant in a North London department store, where he felt that conditions were less than ideal.

"Having to have her lunch at 11.30 and nothing to eat or drink until six in the evening (after she has got it ready!), it's much too long as she works very hard while she is there."

In October 1940, a stray bomb landed 80 yards (73m) from Ernie and May Britton's house.

"May and I were in the kitchen, making tea before the next lot of planes, and May was just leaving the kitchen with the tray, when the front door and kitchen door blew open and for what seemed minutes there was nothing but falling bricks, tiles, glass and the Lord knows what. May didn't drop the tray! We both laughed at our safety and she said 'Drink this tea I've just made!' So we did."

Leaving their blitzed home, Ernie and May took the car and ventured out into the night, to find temporary shelter with friends.

"We couldn't go left so we went right. That was a bit troublesome owing to various fires, with roads stopped but we got there amid a few more bombs and gunfire. We didn't care a damn anyway."

After a sleepless night the couple returned to assess the damage.

"May worked on the inside cleaning up plaster and glass. May has always been such a one for her home, it was a sad day for her to have everything so upset. The affair shook her up badly."

Ernie's concerns for his wife, voiced in letters to his sister Florrie Elkus in the States, are echoed by another sibling, Ethel Mattison. Her turn was to come when husband Jack was called up in January 1941. Ethel found the separation hard, but even harder was her first visit to Jack, now Gunner Mattison.

THE ONLY RELIABLE WAY *to obtain fresh food was to produce your own. Here, a London woman tends vegetables on her allotment on Hampstead Heath.*

WOMEN HAD TO LEARN *how to operate machinery in addition to spades, as in this factory manufacturing smoke bombs.*

"I was nearly sick with excitement. I felt full of beans right up until the train got to around Salisbury, which is about two-thirds of the way and then suddenly I knew that I was going to be terribly upset by seeing him. I was furious with myself because the one thing I wanted was to look happy. I had been preparing myself for the shock of the uniform all the way in the train but it was a shock all the same. The hat was the worst part. You know he's never worn any sort of hat since I've known him, and there he was in this cap with practically a convict's crop. I just didn't feel he was the same person until I saw him in pyjamas and a dressing gown."

Ethel longed for a baby, but she postponed starting a family because of the daily dangers and uncertainties of wartime life. In the spring of 1941, she wrote:

"Perhaps the war will be over next year and I'll be able to have a baby in April 1943, only two years later than I had planned. Two years isn't long in a lifetime, but I feel I shall burst."

Ethel kept her spirits up by doing physical training to the radio every morning for ten minutes. In April 1943, the month she had hoped to be a mother, the war news was better, but her desire was still unfulfilled.

"I wasn't at all convinced in the early stages that we shall win the war, but now I am, to the extent that if Jack is still in this country in June I will start to have a baby. The desire is becoming an obsession, like wanting a lover when you're adolescent, and it isn't made easier by the fact that since I've been in my present job, four women have left to have babies and two of them in my room. They bring all the things up to show us."

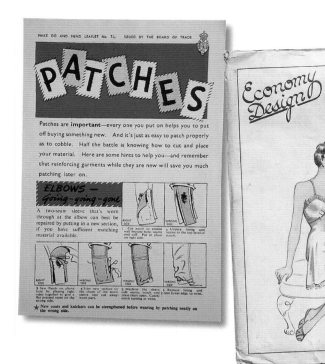

The uncertainty of what the morrow might bring had made many couples leap into wartime marriages, snatching at happiness (however temporary). Ethel wrote to her sister about the impact on her own gunner husband.

"The pay bombardier has just left to return to his civilian job for six months, so Jack has stepped into his shoes. This bloke was a solicitor's clerk, and the number of divorces have reached such proportions that the firm can't cope without him!"

As the prospect of victory seemed more likely, Ethel finally achieved her dream and gave birth to a daughter, Patricia, in 1944. Her sister Florrie sent her nappies from America, and Ethel made a pram cover from a fur coat sent across the Atlantic at the beginning of the war – a rarity in England as many women had donated their furs to the Finns in the winter of 1939–40. Her ingenuity was helped by a sewing machine, which she bought at auction in October 1944.

"Already I've done lots of odd jobs, like making oven cloths out of old nurses aprons, hemming towel ends, making a sleeping bag for Patricia out of an old blanket-cloth dressing gown – things that I could never have tackled by hand."

Devon bus conductor Mavis Bunyan was also a canny needlewoman and made clothes for her daughter. When she went Christmas shopping in Torquay in 1944 she was outraged at the prices.

"I bought a tablecloth for George and Lillian, it was £2.18.10 and the pre-war price was 22s 6d. It is heartbreaking to go shopping, especially now it is Christmas. A box of four hankies that was 1s 11d is now 6s 10d. Some binding that was 3d now cost 1s 8d. Second hand jewellery is fetching atrocious prices. One necklace marked £6 was awful, honestly I have seen better in Woolworths for sixpence."

Clothes rationing was introduced in June 1941 and even the humble hankie was on the ration (this is the era before the use of tissues). By 1944 hankies were 'priceless'. Florrie Elkus in California sent over scores of handkerchiefs to her friends and family during the war. She was a one-woman transatlantic supply line, sending a warm coat for her father (which he wore for fire-watching) and a powder compact and underwear for her sister Ethel.

FABRIC WAS IN SHORT *supply and clothing manufacturers were instructed to concentrate on uniforms rather than fashions. Women became experts at repairing or altering clothes, or making their own. Leaflets bearing the government slogan 'Make Do and Mend' were issued to help those who had not had to do this before. For those making their own clothes, old parachute silk was a much-prized luxury. Necessity also dictated changes in fashion – shorter skirts saved precious material.*

Already I've done lots of odd jobs, like making oven cloths out of old nurses aprons, hemming towel ends.

"I must thank you for that beautiful slip-and-knicker set you sent me, which must have been nearly new. I was urgently in need of a slip, but the coupon situation had prevented me from lashing out in one so far. If I had bought one it wouldn't have been nearly so beautiful and

would certainly have been too long, whereas this one is just right. I couldn't have had a more delightful surprise."

In July 1942 Mrs E Walsh (Miss Williams had by now married Kenneth Walsh) wrote optimistically to her brother Ellis Williams in British Somaliland, hoping for similar bounty.

"By the way everyone seems to be getting silk stockings sent them by their relations in the Dominions. I suppose you couldn't do anything in the line. It's an absolutely crying need. The stockings are now all rayon and don't cling (you wouldn't know but this is an essential) to the legs. They look horrid and undermine one's self confidence."

It was no accident that the postwar New Look featured feminine skirts flowing with an abundance of material. By 1943, even turn-ups on men's trousers were banned, in a drive to simplify garments and use less material.

STOCKINGS WERE HARD *to come by during wartime, and many women resorted to painting seams down the backs of their bare legs to give the impression that they were wearing 'nylons'. This shoe store went one better, offering a unique stocking-painting service.*

CRACKING THE ENIGMA CODE

The activities of German U-boats in the Atlantic severely hampered crucial supply lines and forced the British people to use all their resourcefulness to cope with the shortages. Unknown to them, however, code-breakers at Bletchley Park were using the first computer to break the German naval codes and give the Allies the upper hand in the Atlantic.

The codes were transmitted using the Enigma cipher machine, an electro-mechanical device that had been available commercially since the 1920s and whose potential for wartime communication had been quickly realised. It operated by a system of rotors which meant that each letter could be encrypted as any other letter except itself, giving literally billions of possible combinations. The key to the code lay in knowing the way the machine had been set up, but as the settings were changed on a daily basis, the code had to be broken afresh every day – a seemingly impossible task.

The Bletchley team were greatly aided by a group of Polish mathematicians who had been working on unscrambling Enigma messages since before the war. They passed their research on to Alan Turing and Gordon Welchman, two brilliant mathematicians employed at Bletchley, who used it to develop the Bombe machine which eventually enabled them to translate 3,000 enemy messages a day.

BLETCHLEY PARK
Station X, an innocent-looking Buckinghamshire mansion which housed the most important code-breaking operation of the war. The site – conveniently situated halfway between Oxford and Cambridge, where many of the code-breaking experts came from – was bought personally by Sir Hugh Sinclair, head of MI6, because no government department would fund it. It is estimated that the work of the thousands of cryptographers at Bletchley, and particularly the cracking of the Enigma code, shortened the war by two years, saving many thousands of lives.

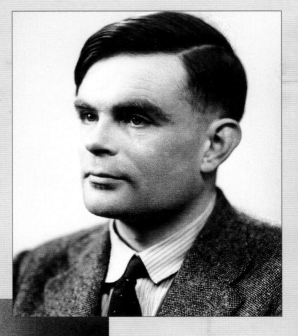

ALAN TURING, TROUBLED GENIUS
(top left), who was the single
most important brain behind the
cracking of Enigma. He eventually
committed suicide in 1954.

THE WORLD'S FIRST ELECTRONIC
programmable computer,
Colussus, developed at Bletchley
and in operation from 1943 (top
right). After Enigma had been
deciphered, Colossus went on to
break the even more sophisticated
Lorenz code, thus making a
significant contribution to the
Allied victory.

THE MACHINE ROOM IN HUT 6
at Bletchley, centre of code-
breaking activities (middle right).
One of the keys to Enigma was
educated guesswork, assuming that
a pattern of letters that recurred
in a message was likely to be a
common word or phrase, such as
a general's name or the weather
forecast. From there the code-
breakers could work out what a
short section meant and use the
letters involved as a 'crib' for the
rest of the message.

A RADIO OPERATOR ON A GERMAN
U-boat uses the Enigma machine
to decode a message (bottom right).
German technicians made frequent
small refinements to the Enigma
machines, making deciphering the
codes even more difficult.

CRACKING THE ENIGMA CODE | 135

Shoes were another scarce commodity. Crepe-soled shoes became popular, because the soles lasted longer, and wooden soles were introduced. People made shoes last by strengthening them with pieces of cardboard. Women painted lines down the backs of their bare legs in imitation of stocking seams; they remodelled clothes by adding new buttons and changing the cut; and they bought what clothes were available with the limited supply of coupons.

Newspapers were thin because paper was scarce, so the shortage described by American Peg Cotton (by then living in Devon) is remembered by many. It was the hot topic of conversation at a drinks party in early 1945.

EVEN TOILET PAPER *was in short supply: women who were in the habit of making their own clothes were sometimes reduced to using old tissue-paper dress patterns instead of Bronco.*

"Making small talk over glasses of sherry, Mrs Russell suddenly said, 'Have you been able to buy any toilet paper, Mrs Cotton? I haven't. There doesn't seem to be a roll, or packet, in all Devon!' As a topic of conversation this may seem odd to the uninitiated – and the unrationed. But to the housewife in Britain, this sixth year of War, it was simply the introduction to a serious discussion of a very urgent problem. Just another 'one of those things' that have added to the intricacies of wartime life."

Peg Cotton had bought several dozen rolls of toilet paper at the beginning of the war on the advice of a friendly London grocer, but this had run out by 1944. She had been forced to buy blocks of writing paper and this was also in short supply.

"Until an article becomes very scarce, and later quite unobtainable, one rarely attaches a full value to it. Before the summer of 1944, TP was no particular problem, and certainly one never spoke of it in ordinary conversation. TP was one of those things found only upon household lists, or on the shelves of Grocer's and Chemist's Shops, or quite unobtrusively displayed in its proper habitat in homes, hotels, stations, etc. TP was an uncounted blessing that one accepted without thought or thanks. But suddenly, in mid-1944, the British Public became 'TP-conscious' and began to realise how very unappreciative it had been of TP's important contribution to the Nation's comfort and morale."

Thousands of women joined the Women's Voluntary Service, which was started in 1938. The WVS provided essential household services for women who had been bombed out. Children were kitted out from their clothing exchange; pots and pans, china and glass were available. All these practical items helped women to maintain some semblance of normal life.

Those in the Forces had one advantage over the ordinary population: better and more abundant food. Letters and diaries are packed with references to food. Londoner Phyllis Warner summed it up in her diary in August 1941.

"We all think and talk about food eternally, not because we are hungry, but because our meals are boring and expensive and difficult to come by. How browned off I am with vegetable pie and savoury butter and inferior sausage and boiled potatoes, what wouldn't I give for orange juice or steak and onions or chocolate or apples or cream! People take most aspects of rationing philosophically but the great egg muddle makes them vitriolic. In London I haven't seen an egg for months, but many parts of the country had a reasonable

THE GOVERNMENT DID *its best to provide for those who needed more than the usual meagre rations, and that included ensuring children had plenty of vitamins. Oranges were never plentiful, but when they were available they were strictly for children only.*

THE NAVY, ARMY AND AIR FORCE INSTITUTES (*NAAFI*) *provided canteens for service people at home and abroad. On Christmas Day 1942, every member of the forces who ate in a NAAFI canteen was to have a fresh egg as a special treat. The eggs were tested for freshness (above) in a NAAFI depot.*

supply until the control scheme came in a few weeks ago. Since then millions of eggs have been immobilised in packing stations until they have gone rotten. Poultry keepers forced to yield up every one of their own supply, have been allowed to buy two or three Canadian eggs which also turn out to have been held up until they are rotten."

Anne Lee Mitchell kept hens on an allotment in Somerset. In May 1942 she had a mishap.

"Dropped all of my egg ration on to the back path! Scraped them up into a bowl and we shall have to live on scrambled eggs."

FRESH FOOD WAS READILY *available in the country, but in towns even such basics as milk and eggs were hard to come by. These ARP wardens in Hackney (top) are nurturing their own supply of fresh eggs at their post. The alternative was much less appetising (above).*

Scrambled eggs could also be made with dried eggs. In 1943 the Women's Institute gave useful tips on the 'essentials for success in making scrambled eggs with dried eggs – thorough blending of dried egg and water and slow cooking'. Leaflets were produced encouraging people to use a hay box – a box insulated with hay for cooking casseroles slowly, thus saving fuel. Rationing had been planned in 1936 and ration books were issued in January 1940. The postwar consensus is that the wartime population was healthier as a result of a diet rich in vegetables and low in sugar and dairy products (a familiar regime today).

Lord Woolton was the much maligned Minister of Food. After five years of war, Londoner Ernie Britton was filled with admiration for him.

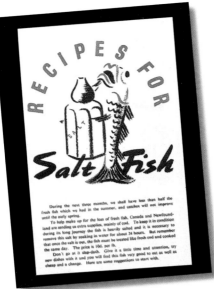

THE BENEFITS OF EATING *fish were widely proclaimed, but with fishing a hazardous activity in mine-strewed waters, fresh fish was a rare luxury. What little there was available was often salted to make it last longer.*

"Lord Woolton and his staff make a good job of rationing and nobody goes hungry. Naturally we don't consume the amount of dairy produce we did before the war and we lack the infinite variety of pre-war days. Perhaps we lived too well before 1939."

Writing in the same year, as victory looked likely, Peg Cotton commented on the effect of the British wartime diet on the population.

"Although the English people have had enough to eat in quantity, throughout this war, the nutritional value of food has been so reduced that the average diet here has undermined people's vitality."

People were urged to eat things that were normally alien to the British diet (soya-link sausages are remembered with horror by many). Recipe tips were published in an article in a Daily Telegraph column, 'Women in Wartime'. Joan Strange, living in Worthing with her elderly mother, recorded in her wartime diary the government's attempt to persuade people to eat salt-cod.

"I thought I would mention food today, it is the most talked about subject now that Hess is stale! I actually brought Mother some salt-cod from Godalming, but she wasn't very keen. I was lucky today and bought ½lb of currants quite by chance. I had posted a parcel of flowers to one of Kit's bombed tenants and the man who also has a grocer's shop asked if I'd care to have some! I was lucky last Sunday too as Frammie gave me six ripe tomatoes, and they are about 5s a lb in the shops."

RESTAURANTS ALSO TURNED *to growing their own produce. Here, waitresses at the Quality Inn in Regent Street harvest the tomatoes they will serve to their customers later in the day.*

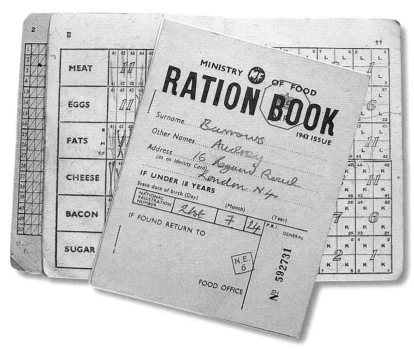

THE RATION POINTS SYSTEM *was complicated because some foods were put 'on the ration' earlier than others, and the permitted quantities varied from time to time. There were concessions for small children, pregnant women, invalids or those with special dietary needs: a vegetarian, for example, was allowed to forgo the meat ration and perhaps have extra cheese instead.*

FOOD RATIONING
involved an enormous amount of administration. Innumerable clerks at the Food Executive Office prepared the ration books from the National Registration returns.

Transport problems often made the supply of food unreliable, even goods 'on the ration'. In 1941 Worthing featured in the national newspapers because the town was so short of meat. Later that year, Joan Strange recorded how inventive wartime cooks had to be.

"Although our food position is remarkably good considering all things, yet mother finds it difficult thinking out meals – our meat ration is still 1s 2d worth each per week (we're sure we had horse last week) and it's difficult to get any offal. We did have half a calf's head last week, which made some excellent brawn. Milk is rationed now and we get one quart a day. Sugar is 6oz per week, butter 2oz and margarine 4oz, cheese 4oz, 3 eggs a month! It's very difficult thinking out puddings or having visitors in to meals."

Wartime scarcities did not prevent Joan and her mother using all their ingenuity and contacts to raise money for charity. In the summer of 1941:

"Mother and I gave a bridge drive today for Council of Social Service and raised £7.7.0. Eight tables and tea and raffles. For raffles we had strawberries (a terrific treat given by Mrs Claff from her father's nurseries) Two lots of eggs and a rubber hot water bottle! For tea we had white bread and butter (mother had saved some white flour). The butter came from Canada last Christmas. Tea from Australia and we saved milk from the ration."

No purely white bread was allowed after the spring of 1943. Even the sugar coating on pills was stopped in 1943. Wartime recipes were broadcast on the wireless, so that people could sample the delights of 'mock goose' and 'Victory Sponge' (which capitalised on the natural sweetness of carrots instead of using sugar) and there was that wartime staple, 'Woolton Pie'. Mrs E Walsh wrote to her brother Ellis wondering if he had sampled this novelty, named after Lord Woolton, the much maligned Minister of Food, and comprising root vegetables, cauliflower, onions, parsley and oatmeal, topped with mashed potato sprinkled with grated cheese.

"Have you had a Woolton Pie? They are for the pig pail. Nothing is wasted nowadays. Have you seen all the Ministry of Food appeals – jam out of the jar, cut don't break your bread, jam straight on to the bread and not on the plate etc."

Lack of variety, and an endless diet of swede and turnip, irked people. Bill Regan, on the Isle of Dogs, summed up the joy of tracking down wartime rarities.

"Bought a jar of mustard pickle on the way home, they are very scarce now. They are good, no carrot or turnip to spoil it. The war-time abortion contains about 50% carrot and turnip. Horrible concoction. Winkles for tea, a great change, not had them for about a year."

Those lucky enough to have relatives and friends in Canada or the USA received frequent food parcels. Florrie Elkus sent delicacies from her California home to her family and friends: California raisins, tinned butter, tinned cheese and even cakes and cookies made their way across the Atlantic. People had been encouraged to dig up their gardens to grow fruit and vegetables. Dolly Howard described with pleasure the abundant produce that she bartered with her neighbours in Liverpool.

SOME RATIONING RULES required customers to surrender coupons before they were allowed to buy restricted goods, rather than using points. Coupons were used to ensure that everyone got their fair share of a rationed item, rather than 'stockpiling' and unfairly using their points on just one product.

AMONG THE COMMODITIES
*supplied by the USA were
powdered milk, dried eggs
and tinned meat.*

"Food is dearer, but we are fortunate in having a vegetable and fruit garden, besides a small allotment. We had a bumper crop of raspberries besides black and red currants so I was able to claim extra sugar for jam."

Hedgerows were plundered for blackberries. Rosehips were gathered to make a syrup rich in Vitamin C for children. But as the war drew on, more and more foodstuffs were rationed. In March 1941 Phyllis Warner wrote:

"A nasty shock today. Jam, including marmalade, treacle etc is to be rationed at half a pound a month, starting tomorrow. We're going to mind this meagre allowance more than any rationing yet. They must have let the stocks get very low to be so drastic."

No wonder she was upset. Jam had pepped up that wartime staple, bread and margarine – a combination that was anathema to the British, with their love of butter. American flyer Bob Raymond had joined the RAF, abandoning plentiful food in the United States, for the wartime fare on offer in Britain. He wrote in his diary in November 1941:

"Food situation – very plain and tasteless, but sufficient. Too much cold corn beef. No wonder the English are so fond of using spiced sauces for their meals. It's the only way to change the taste of this diet."

As an American, Peg Cotton found it difficult to understand the English devotion to one precious staple: tea. She noted its particular importance on journeys by train.

"After some time in England, I came to the conclusion that the English when thirsty think in terms of tea, not water. Tea is what the Englishman drinks, consistently and in quantity as we Americans drink water. This 8:30am train from Instow to London makes two 'long' stops – Exeter Central, and Salisbury. At these stations practically every compartment door bangs open and figures, male and female, leap out upon the platform and hurriedly zig-zag through the traffic of people and porters milling about there. The platform tea-trolley or the Station Buffet is 'the objective of this race. The prize – mugs of hot tea. The return from this sortie for refreshment is like a triumphal procession. With a large white china mug of steaming tea in either hand, or a mug of tea in one hand and a couple of saffron colored buns in the other, the returning contingent surges back in groups – one eye on the slopping tea, the other on the open door of a particular compartment, both ears cocked for the Guard's whistle. At its shrill screech there is a frantic dash of late stragglers. Cups in hand they leap into the nearest open door on the train. Bang – clap – bang – clap! Here in the compartment is a fresh stir, a lively bit of chat, a stimulus in the air. Tea! Opposite me sit four people – with four mugs of tea. Two of the people cuddle the mugs in both hands, as though the mugs were brandy inhalers. But each of the four faces above those four mugs of tea has the serene, concentrated expression of the connoisseur of fine wine. Tea! It satisfies and stimulates."

THE BRITISH FAITH IN *the restorative power of tea never dwindled, even though the taste became less pleasant. Leaf tea was reused as often as possible to eke out shortages.*

VOLUNTEER ORGANISATIONS *were supplied with tea to hand out to those who had been bombed out and moved to public shelters.*

ALLOTMENT HOLDERS MADE GOOD USE
of their plots, growing fruit and vegetables to
bolster their rations. Any available land was
turned over to food production, including Clapham
Common, shown here. Everyone was encouraged
to transform even the smallest of gardens into
mini-allotments. The government issued a 'Dig for
Victory' leaflet providing guidance on what to grow
including required plot sizes, when and how to
plant the vegetables and how to achieve year-round
productivity.

Peg Cotton led a relatively privileged existence, with a large home and a 'daily'. Up in the Highlands of Scotland, May Chalmers was another of the privileged class. In a large house with servants, and with her husband Archie's status as the Sheriff of Oban, May Chalmers had not had to cook.

"Archie says I've been threatening to cook for 20 years and it has taken a war to make me! But I am finding it fun and am getting to know how to work the Triplex and am on very matey terms with three Primus stoves. Cooked bacon and eggs on one last night. I find that the rations – salt butter, margarine etc are ample. In fact last week I put coffee butter icing on a cake to use it up and had to dispose of 4 ounces of bacon, and the Sunday roast lasted for the whole week! I'm only getting half ration of cheese, as we simply can't use it."

Her husband augmented their rations with a spot of shooting for the pot.

"We did rather well 'off the land' last week as we had nothing from either butcher or fishmonger having lived on twelve rabbits (sure I'm growing a wee white tail!) and this week should be equally good as there is a whole roe deer hanging in the larder. I gather that we are worse off for food here as the convoys requisition just what they want. If things go on like this and the forces can get what they like from the Naafi there will be a revolution. The munition workers will say either Naafi for us too or no munitions. After all the Naafi was only intended to supply an army abroad and certainly not in the home country."

ANYONE WHO HAD ACCESS *to a shotgun and some farm land could supplement the meat ration by their own efforts (right).*

SWEETS AND CHOCOLATE *were rationed to 2oz (50g) per person per week, and ice cream and imported fruits such as bananas and grapes were simply not available. These children are making do with a carrot on a stick for a snack.*

The Naafi (Navy, Army, Air Force Institute – a supermarket for the British Forces) was the source of many luxuries. In May 1942, an old friend in London sent May Chalmers a wartime luxury.

"Goodness where did you get the sherry? I haven't tasted it for over a year. The only drink I have now is Bass and it is most unsatisfactory and very loosening to the bowels. We are allowed one bottle of whisky per week, which is gone after one visit from the Home Guard forces, so I never get any."

Food shortages were not a nationwide problem. Phyllis Warner was shocked when she spent a weekend with friends in Hampshire in October 1941.

"My hosts have a large garden and their own shoot, so there's no shortage of pheasant, partridge, vegetables and fruit, nor for that matter of wines and liquor. I went out with the guns today, not a pastime I particularly approve, but it does mean that you see parts of the country you would never reach normally. It was heart-achingly beautiful today with the leaves just yellowing under a washed blue sky. The evening mist drifted across countryside unchanged, except that there was no nostalgic sound of church bells lingering over the fields. The lives of these people haven't changed either – it's quite a shock to find how little some of us have been affected by the war."

One activity that every woman, regardless of class and age, started once war was declared was knitting. Telephone operators knitted at slack moments on their shift; shelterers in the Blitz kept their needles clicking away; when their housework, war work and vegetable garden had been attended to, women sat down to listen to the wireless with their knitting. At Christmas in 1942 Mrs Walsh unpicked old jumpers to remake as Christmas presents for her family.

IN THE EARLY DAYS *of the war, there were no branded fuels, only rationed 'pool' petrol.*

Petrol was rationed from the early weeks of war, to ensure a supply for those in essential jobs or on war work, and some people took to cutting lawns and even tennis courts with shears. The use of private cars was later banned, and cars were stored in garages on blocks, but other vehicles, reminiscent of more peaceful times, were rolled out of outbuildings and stables. Mrs Walsh lived in Rickmansworth – a far more rural spot then than it is today. Nevertheless she was still amazed at the action of one of her neighbours.

"To counter the petrol shortage Mr Needham has bought Mrs Needham a pony and trap. Brian is driving it up from Dorset this coming week and I suppose we shall see it next weekend. It should cause quite a stir at first. More trouble than it's worth, I should imagine."

As the women of Britain soldiered on, they also had to cope with the loss of loved ones. Louie White, whose husband Jack was a gunner in the RAF, was a first aider at the munitions factory where she worked in Leeds. Her husband often came home on leave at short notice and her employers gave her the week off when he unexpectedly turned up in June 1943. The couple went to Scarborough for a week. On June 21 he went missing during a raid over the industrial city of Krefeld. Two days later, she wrote in her diary:

"June 23: At 10.00 Mother brought a telegram to say that Jack was missing. I got a pass out and went up to his mother's. Came home for my dinner and then went back to work. Rather be doing something than think."

PETROL WAS RATIONED *from the day war broke out, allowing about 200 miles of motoring per month for each owner. Then in 1942, when the Japanese had occupied Malaya and German U-boats were destroying supply convoys in the Atlantic, the British government banned private motorists from buying petrol at all, with only those individuals and organisations deemed as priority users allowed fuel. Everyone else had to rely on public transport or their bicycles – or just stay at home.*

THE ROYAL MAIL *reverted to horse-drawn vehicles in order to save fuel. These 'vans' are lined up at a sorting office for loading.*

There followed several weeks of uncertainty as Louie filed her husband's details with the Red Cross, in case he had been taken prisoner. Air crews were known to reappear months after being listed as missing, making their way back to Britain via the Resistance in occupied countries, and so there was hope. Two months after he went missing, the telegram came.

"Aug 24: Cold. Usual all day. Stayed for First Aid. Was very depressed. Got home at 9.00 and found a telegram to say that Jack is believed to have lost his life. It upset me very much and I went to bed immediately.

Aug 25: Showers. Did not go to work as I didn't feel I could stand it. Went into town with Mother, then went to see Jack's mother. We had a chat then I came home. Spent the afternoon knitting. After tea I had to go out so I went to the Astoria."

She was back at work the next day. Even at the end of May, she was reluctant to believe that her husband was dead – until she received an eyewitness account.

"A letter from Richard Quigley, Jack's pilot. He tells me everything that had happened on that night of June 21–22, 1943. There is no doubt that Jack was killed in his gun turret, at approx 1.30 am June 22, 1943. Today I have been so heartbroken. I cannot think that I shall never see Jack again – not on this earth anyway."

War memorials and cemeteries at home and abroad bear the names of those who died. But the forbearance of the population who bore those losses is not commemorated.

The notebook of PC Walter Atkins, a Sheffield beat bobby, reveals another problem faced by society during these dark days, giving a snapshot of wartime petty crime and looting.

> "Theft of two 7lb tins of Palm slab toffee.
> Two 10-year-old boys interviewed.
> Larceny of clothing coupons, money and gold Albert which she had pawned.
> Theft of sheets, clothes etc while owner was away – pawned by tenant to pay debts."

His notes refer largely to teenagers stealing food, including immense tins of molasses. Youth clubs, which had kept many teenagers entertained before the war, were closed and parents were preoccupied with war work. There was crime peculiar to a nation in a state of wartime emergency: looting and the black market. Contemporary references to the black market in diaries and letters are veiled – hints that silk stockings might be obtained from a certain market stall, or extra meat slipped into a favoured shopper's bag by the butcher. Some took to petty crime to pay off their debts, breaking into factories, robbing tills in pubs, breaking into empty homes whose occupants were on war work elsewhere. Deserted streets without street lighting were ideal cover for such criminal activity. This was not behaviour fitting the picture of the great British nation pulling together to win the war, but the population was starved of luxuries and in debt. For a minority this led to disaffection, and industrial unrest as the Government pushed workers to increase productivity for the 'war effort'. But financial worries were not purely the province of the working class. Joan Strange wrote in her diary in January 1940:

"Mother heard that her money, which used to bring in 5% then 3½% is now 2%! Everyone is grumbling about their drop in income, and no wonder and for what? Other direct effects of war are the rationing of food and petrol; increase of cost of living (it's gone up 12½% at least); unemployment among certain trades, especially among building and flower growing concerns in Worthing. Then we hear of the Russians dying of cold by the hundreds; sailors being mined, torpedoed; airmen suffering big casualties. Many people are yearning for a just and lasting peace and are endeavouring to keep bitterness out of their minds at all cost."

Income tax reached 50 per cent during the war years. Frank Forster lived in a depressed area of Chester, and although he had a job in an engineering works he still found it hard to make ends meet. In 1943 he wrote in his diary:

"Life for us has become a terrific battle for existence. We struggle to pay our way on the few pounds which we receive, aiming all the time at keeping some semblance of decency – we try our best to feed ourselves and those dependent on us with food which is good for them – though this latter is becoming more and more difficult."

The scarcity of certain commodities was exacerbated by high prices.

"We get more and more hard up. Our wages stay the same, yet the price of food, clothes and other things takes up an increasing amount of them. The few entertainments, such as cinemas, are having prices increased."

As workers struggled to make ends meet, there was industrial unrest. Frank Forster records strikes in March 1943.

WITH SO MANY ITEMS *in short supply, there was plenty of opportunity for the unscrupulous to make money. Stockings, cigarettes and luxury foods were all available on the black market if you knew who to ask. Government policy was to make things as fair as possible for everyone and this propaganda campaign aimed to discourage civilians from 'chiselling' each other.*

THE BLITZ BROUGHT OUT *the worst in some people. Many took to looting bombed premises either to keep things for themselves or to sell them on. If a shop window was broken during a bombing raid, wardens or police might be posted outside to prevent opportunists running off with the merchandise.*

"In various parts of the north of England there are [a] number of strikes occurring over the recent wage increase awards to the Engineering trade – in some instances only a few have been given the increase – a delay has been manoeuvred by the employers who say that the necessary alterations in the pay sheets will take some time – chaos has been created in the clerical part of the work because of shortness of clerical staff."

Strikes are becoming more frequent – the employers won't change their way of living and of making money.

Munitions workers often relied on buses to get to work, and many factories laid on special buses during these strikes. A month later Frank wrote:

"Strikes are becoming more frequent – the employers won't change their way of living and of making money – they are of the opinion that we workers should suffer and this won't do in wartime, especially when we are fighting for our lives. Since the beginning of this present war our work in the factories is telling on us more than it used to. There is evidence that the excessive time worked leads to tiredness, fatigue and the consequent train of minor things, which if left to develop make life a bugbear – yet we are supposed to carry on in the same way, we are expected to pull our weight, to obey all Government instructions, in short we have to put up with the added inconveniences without anyone giving us a helping hand."

Cities darkened by blackout, and streets empty of people as they sheltered from raids, brought out opportunist looters. When Mea Allan was bombed out in October 1940, she returned to her flat to check on her belongings.

THE AIR RAID WARDENS' *real job was to help the police to protect the public – and that meant the often gruesome task of searching bomb-damaged premises for casualties or trapped survivors.*

"Did I lose any cash? Nope. Had handbag with me in the shelter. Oh yes, I lost 2s 6d outstanding to Gas, Light and Coke Company! But probably it's buying a pint for some thirsty looter – they're a beastly lot: they actually wait about at night for houses to be bombed and then dash in and muckrake round for what they can find. I hope his beer chokes him."

The protection of an ARP warden's badge and identity card gave 'villains' licence to be on the streets when others where running for shelter.

"I remember refusing to enrol one man, who, early on in the raids, wanted to join our [ARP] post. He said 'I am always first on the scene of any incident. I have a small van and can be on the spot without delay.' I made a few discreet inquiries, and found that he was burglar, that his van was full of tools and that he made a point of driving all over the borough, particularly to business premises when they were hit – and diving straight into the ruins to find the safe."

This South London priest made a point of rescuing people's personal belongings from bombed buildings, as quickly as possible. Even then he was sometimes too late.

"It may seem that I was exaggerating the risk. But a family from one of the blasted flats came to collect their furniture, and found that a piano had been taken from the upstairs flat. Two other relatives came to ask me if they could enter their old mother's flat in Merrow Street, which had been blasted and made unsafe, and when I took them there, they found that all her trinkets, including her son's First World War medals, were gone. In fact, the very morning of the raid, the Borough Treasurers men came down just six hours after the bomb had exploded to empty the gas and electric meters in the blasted flats, only to find that every one had been broken open and rifled."

WITH PRICES RISING *but wages staying the same, industrial discontent grew into widespread strikes. Here in the shipbuilding yard at Barrow-in-Furness, then in Lancashire, workers walk out on a strike.*

Rescue workers showed immense compassion in risking their lives to salvage precious keepsakes from ruined homes.

"I always felt that these little salvage efforts were worthwhile. It is hard to realise that it was these small things that made such a difference to the morale of so many people. I suppose the secret of it lies in the fact that we showed that someone cared about the loss of their homes. It was important that there should be some visible link with that home as they took refuge in the bare, amorphous surroundings of the schools, which acted as Rest Centres for the bombed-out. Nothing helped their recovery more than the knowledge that their personal treasures were safe."

But nothing was sacred.

"When we recovered dead bodies, as soon as we found them I had to put them in an empty room under the guard of two wardens, until the stretcher party could remove them to the mortuary. Otherwise their clothing would be rifled, there in the midst of the darkness and dust and falling bombs. I often said that it was a good thing that I was not armed with a pistol or gun: I would probably have shot those whom I suspected of this kind of activity."

Bill Regan, the Heavy Rescue worker on the Isle of Dogs in London's East End, also salvaged people's belongings from bombed houses. At Christmas 1940, with an unexploded bomb on the other side of the street and his home in ruins, he was accosted by Lew Smith, a neighbour who lived a few doors away.

"Lew Smith is the agent of our landlord and he said, 'You haven't paid any rent for some time now Bill, what are you going to do about it?' I said, ' I've got one room with a boarded up window, two doors that have to be propped up and the rest of the house uninhabitable, so out of 15s6d [77 pence] for the whole house, what would a fair rent be for the one room?' He could think of nothing suitable to say, except that I couldn't stay without paying something. I said I would look for another place to live, and in the meantime, I would act as unpaid caretaker of our one room. He didn't see it that way, but reluctantly

WE ARE LIVING HERE 54 LETTERS IN 52 PLEASE THANK YOU KIND SIR

THOSE MADE HOMELESS *by the bombing had to rely on the kindness of neighbours, friends or relatives. Requests such as this one above were not unusual for postmen.*

LIFE HAD TO GO ON *for everyone. Many families would have to continue living amongst the ruins of their homes and being resourceful about finding shelter. Daily tasks, such as making or repairing clothes, were often carried out against the backdrop of bombed-out houses.*

agreed. Anyway he has a book full of empty, or wrecked houses, so he has problems and I have problems more worrying than he."

With wind and snow whistling through gaps in boarded-up windows, and with record low temperatures in many of those wartime winters, it is not surprising that Bill Regan was diagnosed with pleurisy.

In her job as a reporter for the *Daily Herald*, Mea Allan wrote an account of an interview with someone in the same rent predicament as Bill.

PREPARING MEALS
for the family still needed doing, even if the kitchen no longer had glass in its windows.

"Some London landlords are demanding rent for houses rendered uninhabitable by bombing. One business girl received a rent notice two days after blast from a High Explosive bomb had shattered the block of flats where she lives. It was a very heavy calibre bomb and fell less than 9 yards away. She told me yesterday: 'My flat is quite unliveable-in. The windows have been wrenched out, frames and all and there are holes in the walls. There isn't a door in the place. My front door, opening off the stair landing has been splintered into pieces as if it had been a piece of brittle toffee. There is no gas, no electricity and no water. The gas company have collected the meter-box, so evidently they don't expect the place to be lived in any more. The outside of the building has big cracks in it, and there's a crack running up one of my walls inside. When I leased the flat my side of the bargain was to pay rent, the landlord's to provide a flat to live in. I paid a month in advance and I reckon I owe two days rent from the expiry of the last month's up till the time I was bombed. But he has asked me for the whole of the next month's rent. A neighbour who had paid three months in advance up till Christmas went to the landlords and asked them for a rebate. They laughed at her and told her the place was not uninhabitable – she could still go on living there. Her place is even worse knocked about than mine. I think this is one of the most unpatriotic things I've heard of. I've heard it's happened to people all over London, even to poor people in the East End. I bet if I asked my landlords to dinner, they wouldn't even cross the threshold – they'd be so scared the building would topple down any minute."

When there was a lull in bombing Bill Regan went back to ad hoc labouring jobs, as money troubles continued to bite. But in January 1942 it was again bitterly cold.

"Layer of snow outside. Work tomorrow – unlikely. That means no pay. What an existence."

The next morning the weather was worse.

"Up at 6.30am. Thick snow. No work. Signed on at Labour Exchange, given a grey card, to go to Glaucas St, was given a broom to do snow sweeping."

CIVIL DEFENCE VOLUNTEERS, *the police, firemen, soldiers and civilians work frantically to rescue the children who are imprisoned under the rubble of a bombed school in London, 1943.*

At the end of the month the postman called with three letters.

"Received letter saying I owe £44.6.0 cost of the children's evacuation [to an Oxfordshire village]. Letter from Miller's Hospital, they want 10s 6d X ray charge for my left foot, done last August, when I smashed my cycle in a crash with a car. Letter from income tax people. What a day."

Phyllis Warner, after a visit to a London school, recorded the effects of bombing on the education of the new generation.

"The all clear of the previous night had not sounded until 3am, so that many of the children were looking heavy eyed. Education is suffering badly from the raids. On this particular day with a school working from nine till four, lessons were only possible for two hours – the rest of the day passed wearyingly in the shelters, for whatever other people do children must take shelter."

Evacuated children missed their homes, and despite conditions in London, the family ties in close-knit communities were a stronger pull than safety.

"I have pleaded with many parents, who replied, 'Well, if I'm killed, I want to take my Tommy and Alice with me – I don't want them to be left homeless in the world.' So strong is this feeling that parents will take their children to spend night after night on draughty subway platforms or in the foul air of vast overcrowded shelters rather than send them to the pure air and safety of the countryside. This evening I went up to a big London County Council housing estate, made up of vast blocks of flats for ex-slum dwellers, who were shifted here just before the war started. The flats themselves are super, but placed in a remote district, badly served with buses, and excepting the pubs, without a single entertainment facility. The children were mostly evacuated when war started, but soon came back and have been running wild ever since. In spite of two years with no schooling, the older ones have been able to pick up war jobs, which put plenty of cash in their pockets. They're a tough crowd, whose parents virtually ignore them, and they're all running around in the blackout with nothing to do but mischief. During the summer Joan has started an evening club for them – a heroic one-man job. The London County Council has let her have a hall, but nothing else. She has about a hundred young toughs there each night the club's open.

Joan Strange, whose sister Kit lived in London, came up from Worthing and visited flats in Kentish Town in 1940.

"The caretaker seems worried over the fact that in the blackout each night hooligan boys come round breaking windows – stealing bricks being used for the air raid shelter in the process of construction..."

Fuel was also in short supply, as munitions factories were given priority. In 1942 the government urged people not to use their central heating, or light fires until November. Kindly Bill Regan volunteered to help to deliver the limited supplies.

"Myself, Herbert and Robinson, went to Quebec and Montreal buildings, to deliver coal to the people living there. There has been a grave shortage this winter, and when the coalman has some coal, he supplies the people living downstairs but is too lazy to carry it upstairs, so that they have been without for weeks at a time. We deliver it to them now. Had a jolly time, but I nearly had trouble with some of the people. One old lady crawled from the top floor to ask for some, and I sympathetically carried 1 hundred-weight to her flat, and I'm nearly beat when I get there. Entering I find a robust fellow, and bigger than I, sprawled on the sofa. Granny can crawl down, I can lug it up, he sits round the fire. Another person had a cupboard full of coal, and wants more, while neighbours are without. 'If you can't get it in mate put it on the floor.' I do, all over it. One woman with three kids, borrows the money from another for ½cwt. I bung a 1cwt in, and skip out."

VERY YOUNG CHILDREN *didn't know what was going on – they just knew that they were frightened. Here, an air-raid warden comforts a toddler she has rescued after a raid during the Blitz.*

DURING THE COLD *wartime winters, if there was coal to be had, neighbours would work together to bring home enough for several households.*

7. All Hands to the Pump

"We are both quite convinced that in spite of the dirt, the long tiring hours the noise, and the annoyance of working for rather unhuman employers – and the general austerity of our life we are much happier than we should have been if we had remained at Benacre where we were continually wondering whether we were doing essential work. Now at any rate we are doing what the Government has asked women to do – and find the war doesn't get on our minds nearly as much as it did." Kathleen Church-Bliss, July 1942

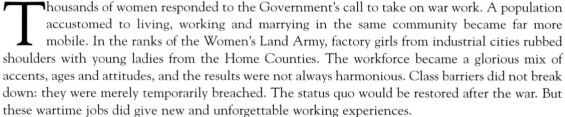

WOMEN WERE RECRUITED
into factory and war work,
particularly munitions.

A RECRUITMENT DRIVE
by the government was
designed to appeal to
women's patriotism.

WOMEN OF BRITAIN
**COME INTO
THE FACTORIES**
ASK AT ANY EMPLOYMENT EXCHANGE FOR ADVICE AND FULL DETAILS

Thousands of women responded to the Government's call to take on war work. A population accustomed to living, working and marrying in the same community became far more mobile. In the ranks of the Women's Land Army, factory girls from industrial cities rubbed shoulders with young ladies from the Home Counties. The workforce became a glorious mix of accents, ages and attitudes, and the results were not always harmonious. Class barriers did not break down: they were merely temporarily breached. The status quo would be restored after the war. But these wartime jobs did give new and unforgettable working experiences.

War created work peculiar to the needs of the war machine, such as the job of billeting officer. Those who remained in their peacetime jobs had to work under wartime conditions, with the added pressure that this entailed.

Kathleen Church-Bliss and Elsie Whiteman lived in the village of Benacre, where they ran a teashop. Both in their forties, they were two of the thousands of women who responded to government calls for more women to take up full-time war work. Family and friends tried to interest them in joining the WRNS or running hostels for the Land Army or Timber Corps, but these did not appeal. Visiting an Engineering Training Centre in Croydon changed their lives.

"The machine shop was fascinating. We saw centre lathes, capstan lathes, shapers, planers, mills and automatics all roaring away amidst a deafening clatter from the overhead shafting. Everyone appeared to be very expert and we watched with great interest. The centre lathes especially took our fancy, as the work needed constant care and attention, and we were told that this machine needed the most skill to work successfully."

Fired by this challenge, the two women enrolled on an engineering course. On a snowy February day they arrived in Croydon and, after training, started at Morrison's aircraft factory. It was a culture shock.

> "The factory building is really a disgrace. Broken windows let in the howling draught, the roof leaks and great puddles collect on the floor, the walls are splashed with oil and grease and the whole place is incredibly dirty and littered with filthy bits of equipment not at the moment in use. It is a frightful sight. These dirty conditions are made worse by the complete absence of hot water in the eight washbasins and lavatories provided for 300 girls."

Both these middle-class women joined the union, and Kathleen whiled away the 11-hour days brooding on the wrongs of the workers and dreaming up reforms to working conditions.

> "We are now members of a Trades Union. We are not quite certain of its name – but it's the Municipal and Something Workers. We joined in a most hole and corner way – and pushed our subscription over to the assistant shop steward – who looked furtive and said she had to be careful! She evidently lives in fear of the firm's Gestapo!"

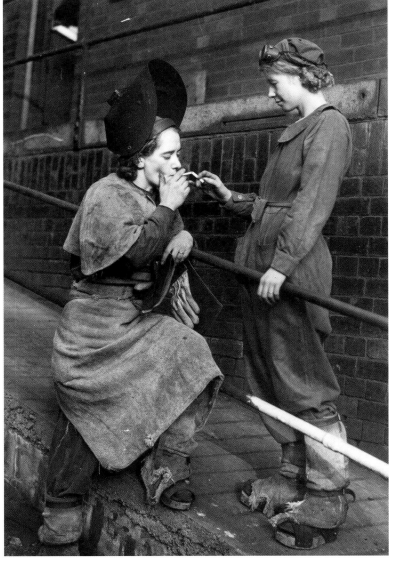

ESSENTIAL FACTORIES *such as steel mills could not have remained open without women to do the work. Here, they take a cigarette break without bothering to remove their safety gear.*

After five months they felt like old hands.

> "We no longer suffer from the acute nervous dread we did when we first came to Morrisons. Els, during our first fortnight here felt as though she were fielding bent double in the slips in a very important cricket match – poised on her toes ready for a movement in any direction and her hands darting from handle to handle. It was a very long cricket match and exhausting. Now she has long been able to straighten her back and relax and turn the handle with calm and detachment. In fact she is much put to it, in the mechanical jobs that crop up, to know how to while away the time – *A Midsummer Night's Dream* which she learnt by heart at the age of 16 has been a tremendous help to her. 'Now fair Hippolyta,' she declaims in a loud shout – as she retracts the drill – and so on scene after scene to the end. This talking aloud is evidently sound engineering practice as it seems to be pretty general – for looking round the shop one sees everyone's mouth is moving – though no sound can be heard."

The work was fiddly and exacting and great care was taken not to waste precious raw materials by making mistakes. It was worthy – but tedious.

> "We nearly die of boredom. The hours drag interminably, the clock never advances and Sunday seems a long way off. We think that

we might petition for a radio to relieve the tedium – which must be worse for those who are always doing the mechanical jobs – but doubt whether a radio would make itself heard above the awful noise. Looking round the huge workshop it seems to us that the hundreds of workers, though only separated from each other by a few feet are each shut away in an impenetrable box of noise – and live their separate lives for 11 hours a day hardly able to communicate with each other."

In May 1942 there was a heatwave. Combined with the pressures of air raids and poor working conditions, tempers were frayed at Morrison's.

ARMOURY WORKERS *were given an extra allocation of milk to counteract the effects of exposure to lead in their factory.*

"May 31: today Hilda was so hot – & so enraged with the Management for not trying to improve the ventilation that she threw a spanner through one of the windows in a temper! The resulting hole was a great improvement."

Kathleen and Elsie cycled to their wartime jobs. The bicycle was a much-prized form of transport in cities, enabling riders to swerve easily round craters, though the rubber shortage meant that tyres were scarce. Phyllis Warner summed up the worth of a bicycle.

"Even duchesses are riding bicycles nowadays; their value is more than a Rolls Royce"

Despite the disruption of routine daily life by air raids, Phyllis was impressed by the conscientiousness of people she encountered in her voluntary job at a feeding centre at the height of the 1940 Blitz.

"At the Feeding Centre today one of the things I notice most about the people who have just been bombed, is their anxiety about getting to work on time. You don't expect people who have just seen their home crash in rubble and have lost nearly all their possessions to be worrying about whether they'll be late for work, but in fact they do. Perhaps, because their jobs represent the one normal thing that is left, the only sober reality in a world turned to nightmare, and they just have to keep hold on what is sane and familiar. The whole tempo of London life has adjusted itself to this change. The rush hour has moved forward to half past four, and everybody leaving work makes an immediate and purposeful dash for the homeward bus or train – by six the streets are almost deserted. Home is no longer a place to live, it's somewhere to dump one's things and wash and change en route for the shelter, whether that is the cellar, the Anderson or the subway station. To many Londoners the chief irritation is having to transfer their dinner hour from eight pm to five thirty."

We are quite content to live one day at a time, for we all realise a long and hard road lies ahead."

Dr JP McHutchison, Director of Education in Dumbartonshire, noticed the same phenomenon in Glasgow in 1939.

"One quite noticeable feature of life in these early war days, is the smartness folks display to get their buses at night; from 5 to 6 o'clock, business people are more businesslike in getting to the bus stations and making sure of getting out of Glasgow before a possible alert holds them up. Even in this part of the country where real air raiding has not begun, there is a sort of 'rounded off' feeling at the close of the day – 'Well that's one more day over in peace and comfort'. We are quite content to live one day at a time, for we all realise a long and hard road lies ahead."

After Ernie Britton and his wife May had been bombed out in October 1940, May had gone to Dorset to live with her mother. Ernie found digs in Harpenden, Hertfordshire.

"I'm in the office now having swapped my London job with a colleague whose home was and still is in London. He used to travel out and back each day, occupying three hours daily."

BRISTOL WAS ONE OF MANY *British cities that suffered heavily because of the strategic importance of its docks. However, people still managed to make their way to work after a raid.*

A three-hour commute was just as much a consideration in wartime as it is today. Buses had to deviate from established routes because of bomb craters or piles of rubble. Trains travelled at 15 miles an hour as a precaution, since railway lines were an easy target for bombers and there were sometimes craters on the line. Phyllis Warner noted:

"One of the oddest things about our present life is its mixture of ruthless horror and everyday routine. I pick my way to work past the bomb craters and the shattered glass, and sit at my desk in a room with a hole in the roof – a block of paving stone came through."

As in other areas of the workforce, women stepped into office jobs to release men for the Armed Forces. Office talk inevitably dwelt on husbands, fathers, brothers and fiancés who were away. Phyllis Warner had a loved one in the Far East.

OLD FACTORY MACHINERY *could still do its job to perfection. Workers in Rolls-Royce's factories in Derby, Crewe and Manchester, producing parts for the Merlin engine to equip the RAF's Spitfires and Hurricanes, were trained to make parts to within an accuracy of one quarter of a thousandth of an inch.*

"Women do indeed get the rough end of war – whatever hell men may endure in the fight, they at least have the consolation of action and responsibility. They don't sit at home drinking tea and wearing their hearts out. What would we give for absorbing action and a conviction that we were playing a vital responsible part in the struggle – not sitting in dead alive offices."

As well as dealing with the uncertainties of war, people had to do their jobs under heavy blackout, as Ernie Britton described.

"In the factories it's not possible to have such a big scale shuttering so its always blackout and artificial light – not so good and not so healthy, never to see a bit of daylight except perhaps a snatch at midday break. During the last few weeks we've had fluorescent lighting (daylight) in our office and it makes a world of difference. As I had to be there Saturday and Sunday the first two weeks of its installation I thought it grand!"

Seventeen-year-old Monica McMurray was not enjoying her working conditions at Laycock Engineering in Sheffield in 1941.

"This eternal smell of oil combined with next-to-no ventilation and artificial light at work is suffocating, I think I shall have to try to get on the land."

As the engines of the British war machine, factories were especially at risk in air raids. Louie White was a milling inspector at the Blackburn Aircraft Factory, Roundhay, Leeds, during a heatwave in August 1942.

BOMB SITES NEVER FAILED *to attract attention, particularly if they were in famous places such as Trafalgar Square. The patriotic advertisement pasted around Nelson's Column is encouraging people to invest in War Bonds and thus help the government continue to pay for the war.*

"Very hot. About 12.40 the guns and sirens went. It was awful we all put on our tin hats and coats and went on working in them. We heard that it was Kirkstall Forge that had been hit."

In Croydon, Kathleen Church-Bliss and Elsie Whiteman recorded how air raids disrupted work.

"When we got to work we found the night shift had been in the shelters most of the night – and 48 bombs had fallen. Lily arrived rather late and very much shaken as all the windows of the train had been broken by blast and some of the passengers had been cut. We hadn't been in the place more than a few minutes before the alert went – & we started rushing to the shelters. Luckily it was some distance off. During the day various people were fetched away because their homes had been demolished – and Costello went off to enquire about his brother who had had a bomb in his road."

People could lose their jobs overnight thanks to the raids. Martha Cotton lost her job at the Welbeck Clinic in London. Her mother Peg Cotton wrote in her diary:

"The Clinic 'went' the other night! The Jerries are using land mines in the air raids. Like prize packages, these monstrous High Explosives are dropped now and then. And, when they fall, it is like a miniature end-of-the-world! These land mines explode above the ground, and blast buildings and people over wide areas.

Because of one of these land mines, Martha had to walk most of the way to the Clinic the other morning – the streets being impassable to traffic, with litter and rubble scattered about. Martha's soles were cut to ribbons with shattered glass – and her soul torn to bits with the sight of the people being excavated. When she arrived at the Clinic, the Out Patient Department was quite gutted by an oil bomb. Rescue work had ended, but drugs and instruments were being salvaged...Of course, Martha cannot get her degree now. There'll be no more lectures. She is deeply disappointed. One can not plan a thing these days! You just live, strictly in the present."

SALVAGE WORK INCLUDED *businesses, who needed to retrieve as much of their paperwork as possible, as well as valuables and personal possessions.*

ENTERPRISE AND INITIATIVE *were vital in war work, as they were in other aspects of 'soldiering on'. This 'factory', producing breech blocks for Sten guns, had previously been used as a hen house.*

In London's East End, Lylie Eldergill was on short-time after the garment factory where she worked was blitzed. As she wrote to her cousin, the newspaper and printing industries were hit particularly badly.

"As you know already the Air Raids have been simply terrifying, and the damage whichever way you go is appalling. Uncle Will's firm has been raised to the ground, two large buildings. Uncle went round Finsbury way the other day and the sight that met his eye was so shocking he was afraid to go further on or even turn back. So of course he is now out of work. There are now 37 printer and Newspaper firms done in."

Chronic paper shortages had also affected newspapers and printing firms. Doreen Manwaring's husband Len had been working a four-day week since the beginning of the war.

"Len's job at the *Evening News* is a bit rocky. They are having trouble to get the paper...our troubles are by no means exceptional. Everybody seems to be hit in some way. Men are losing jobs they have held for years, little businesses break down, the youth of the country is merged into the machinery of war, and our children have been out of homes for nearly a year now."

AIR-RAID PRECAUTIONS
INDIA HOUSE.

EMERGENCY INSTRUCTIONS
Room No. 403

Indication of an impending Air Raid will be given by the sounding of a Typhon Horn.

On receipt of the warning proceed at once by way of the MONTREAL PLACE staircase to Refuge Room "A" in the Sub-basement.

TAKE YOUR RESPIRATOR AND OUTDOOR CLOTHING WITH YOU

NOTE.—Before this room is vacated, all windows should be closed and the electric light switched off. All taps should be turned off in rooms containing gas connections.

The Senior Officer in the room is responsible for seeing that these instructions are carried out.

On arrival in the Refuge Rooms members of the Staff must initial their name on the Roll Call List displayed inside the Refuge Rooms.

Members of the Staff will remain in the Refuge Rooms until the "All Clear" signal is given.

("All Clear" is sounded by a handbell.)

THE GOVERNMENT ISSUED RULES *and guidelines for every contingency, like these instructions for evacuating the Indian High Commission in London in case of emergency.*

Melville Troy, an American, ran a small business importing cigars. He was 62 when war broke out and kept in constant touch with his family in the USA. On December 28, 1939 he described the effects of war on his business.

"At the office we have been discussing the business situation. We can get no cigars from Havana, as it is not permitted to send any money out of the country to pay for them. The cigar business will soon dry up unless this is changed, and the same will apply in time to cigarette tobacco, except that it may be easier to find a substitute for cigarette tobacco.

CIGARETTES WERE ONE *of the few pleasures most people could afford, though even they became harder to come by as the war dragged on.*

By June 1940, as cigar stocks disappeared from the market, Melville trudged round London selling cigarettes to customers.

"My own income from B & H is gradually disappearing with Havana cigars, and I am devoting myself to general cigarette sales. The commission is very small and the increase slow, but after sufficient time a little progress can be detected. I have just reached 50 accounts which in fact average nearly £20 a month on account of a few of them being large ones, but they are not found very often. The work is among small restaurants, clubs and ARP canteens."

To ensure some future income, Melville went to work for a tobacconist

". . . who distributes the popular lines of cigarettes and tobacco, which are not considered luxuries but one of the prime necessities of the working man and soldier."

SMOKERS WERE ASKED *to donate one cigarette from a packet, to be sent to a hospital for wounded soldiers.*

Just as Melville Troy found a new outlet for his wares, many people retrained or discovered new skills to fulfil the needs of troops or war workers. Ethel Mattison's sister Jenny joined a factory canteen.

"Jenny started work today, training for canteen management. She's awfully excited about it but tired out of course and has blistered hands from cutting up pounds of stewing beef!"

Britain's need for food had never been greater. The convoys were bringing in vital supplies but the country needed to produce more of its own food. Fit young agricultural workers were needed for the Forces, so the Women's Land Army provided land girls. Ernie Britton had married a farmer's daughter from Dorset and in 1940 his in-laws were struggling.

"Their one and only remaining man, has been called up and they have only got a young girl of the women's Land Army. She's a town lass, but I expect she pulls her weight although perhaps not like the old time country girl. This week they have a boy of 16½ starting. Theirs is a pretty hard life. Like most civil occupations, it's done by the old and the young."

While many had volunteered for war work, single women and married women without children had been conscripted in March 1941. For some this offered an ideal opportunity to get away from an office job. Monica McMurray could not wait to join the Women's Land Army and loved her new job, as she wrote in her diary.

"Oh! How strange everything in Stoughton seems, I wish I'd been here a few weeks. Home Farm is a lovely place, swimming pool, and tennis court. We seem to have a nice family of girls.
    Gosh! But are milk pails heavy!!! My poor muscles. We have spent a hard first day emptying three railway carts full of salt, one potash of salt and two white salt. I seem to be getting an appetite. I think I shall sleep tonight."

Monica was not a country girl, but she threw herself into the daily routine of agricultural life, getting up early, milking, hedging and ditching, planting and weeding.

"I have for the first time seen a birth! One of the cows in Hayle's Yard very graciously allowed me to see her son born. Unfortunately nearly all bull calves are killed on the following Wednesday. The work seems to be getting too heavy for me, I hate to say it, but I'm always short of that bit of extra energy needed, it's not that I'm lazy, I just get fagged and I did think I was getting tough."

Monica transferred to the Women's Timber Corps, an offshoot of the Women's Land Army. She was issued with the regulation breeches, pullover, two shirts, three pairs of army socks, two pairs of dungarees, hat and arm badge. What she did not know was that she would have to share a bed with another girl at her billet in Cumbria.

"September 30, 1941: find to my horror that we are without any water system or electric light. We have to wash in about a pint of water at which two have to join apparently. My first day of tree peeling – didn't last long, it poured."

Tree peeling was a particularly messy job as sap got on her clothes. Women in the Timber Corps were plagued by insects in summer, and snow and bitter winds in winter. Forestry work was extremely dangerous in high winds, and involved heavy machinery. Monica was eventually forced to leave after an injury to her foot.

CROPS NEEDED HARVESTING *quickly once they were ready, so the 'land girls' went out to work in force.*

"The last two years have been on the whole the happiest and brightest of any I have ever spent, yes even remembering the long walk to heavy work at Kirkhampton, cold and thick snow of the Ratlingate winter and the dreadful wood bugs. It's a sad, sad business this packing up and uprooting again, especially as my future now lies in the hands of The National Service Officer who can direct me into whatever he chooses."

The last two years have been on the whole the happiest and brightest of any I have ever spent

The country was in the grip of war, and the civilian workforce was subject to state control.

"July 28: kept my ordered appointment at the Labour Exchange. The only jobs I can choose from are, bus conductress (which I couldn't do because of my foot), hospital nurse which is ruled out for the same reason, factory trainee or unskilled factory hand – and I asked for a vacancy in AID, the officer said I could have a try, so along I went to the AID office in the big bank buildings. What questions I had to answer, triganometry, decimals, fractions, also all about my inspection and testing work."

WOMEN ALSO FORMED THE *wartime Timber Corps. As with everything else, no part of a tree was wasted, with the top branches going to make pulp for paper and the trunks into pit props for the mines.*

Two months later she entered the ranks of the AID based at Armstrong Whitworth's aircraft factory. Louie White, at Blackburn's Aircraft Factory, was working alternate weeks of days and nights. An ardent reader and socialist, she recorded regularly in her diary the shortage of work.

"Had so little to do all night, that I actually read one book before I went home next morning. I can't understand why we are doing nothing at work, an aircraft factory – while the Russians are fighting like mad. What can one expect with our government?"

Engineering was a reserved occupation, and men working in the industry were not immediately liable to call up for the armed forces. The part of Chester in which Frank Forster lived and worked was a depressed area. Like Louie White, he could not understand how there could be slack times when an all-out war effort had been called for. In January 1943 he wrote:

"For the past week or so in the 5" shop at Brookhurst [Engineering], we have been doing almost nothing but sit around and stand around – now a large number of us have had to report to the Labour Exchange this evening – transferred to other factories."

In contrast to these periods of short time and inactivity, in April 1943 Frank was employed on an urgent job – thanks to someone's bungling inefficiency.

> "So far this week I have worked on two occasions until 20:00 hours and now tonight until 21:00 hours. Our holidays have been cancelled until later – orders have been received from the War Ministry that a particular job is to be completed by Sunday night – we have been told that there are no definite hours to work to (that is, one can work as long as one likes, providing sufficient people are in work). The job in question is one of re-packing vehicles which were packed at the Ford factory and have been standing in their boxes for over 12 months – many of them are covered with rust."

Some factories had to relocate, thanks to the accuracy of German bombers. American Dick Cotton, husband of Peg, ran a factory making essential de-icing equipment for the RAF. During the Blitz in 1940, the whole family had to move, as Peg recorded.

> "The factory nearly went up in smoke the other night so it is being rushed out of town piecemeal on lorries. Dick had to go along of course. So we all grabbed what we could take in the car – and drove clear across England."

The entire factory moved to Bideford, in North Devon, uprooting hundreds of factory workers and their families from London and billeting them on the local population. The workforce, and their pets, travelled by train.

> "The train was so crowded, like most wartime trains, that the people were standing jam-packed in the corridors and in solid wedges of humanity in the luggage vans. Poor Mrs Maynard was completely exhausted. She had not only stood the entire six hours of the trip,

but had held the large and restless black family cat all the way. And think of the mothers with babies! And the poor youngsters being evacuated down here from bombed areas! ... When Dick returned to the Inn at about three o'clock in the morning he was quite worn out but enthusiastic about the welcome that his workers and their families had received. 'The town has been darned nice,' he said. 'The women simply marvellous. No one went hungry. Those WVS workers – I take my hat off to them! We've come to the right place.'"

The Women's Voluntary Service played a vital role on these occasions, acting as volunteer drivers to get families to their billets. Many factories had their own billeting officer – another job created by the war. Maureen Bolster was a billeting officer for an engineering factory. She regarded it as an essential but thankless job, as she wrote to her fiancé Eric Wells early in 1942.

"Lord what a job this is. Extreme tact and patience is necessity. A. Bright cheerfulness (even if you're feeling as cold as ice) is necessity. B. Lastly but not leastly by any means, comes sense of humour! That is vital. If I hadn't that I wouldn't have lasted a week at Vokes. Also one must be physically fit. One musn't mind getting soaked through, frost bitten, blown about, or over tired. Yesterday was quite a typical day in the Life of a Billeting Lady – alarm goes off at 6:45, get up, dress, come down to cereal, coffee and toast by the kitchen fire. Put on the old leather coat, sling Gertie gas mask round me, grab my torch and out into the darkness. Wait about in the cold for the bus and wish on my star if it's out. Clamber into the luxury coach hired by the firm, and endure nasty pipes, coughing noise and screeching factory girls."

ST DUNSTAN'S COLLEGE *for the Blind in Regent's Park, London, is forced to move its typists outside to work after their office has been badly damaged.*

This mixing of classes and accents was regarded as an opportunity by some. Former teashop owners Elsie Whiteman and Kathleen Church-Bliss were now clad in scarves and overalls as factory girls.

> "We have very much enjoyed the opportunity we have had of mixing with working class people on absolutely equal terms."

Women of all classes, mobilised into war work, found themselves living in close proximity with others. It was not always a happy experience. Pamela Moore received her call-up papers in the summer of 1943 and joined the Women's Land Army. She found that many Land Girls, freed from the restrictions of home life, threw themselves into a wild social life. She wrote to her fiancé after her first night at a Land Army camp at Yate, near Bristol.

We have very much enjoyed the opportunity we have had of mixing with working class people on absolutely equal terms.

> "To start with had an awful night's sleep, two girls sneaked in very late 'slightly merry', another one was up and down all through the night sick, and not being used to sleeping on the floor on a palliass my shoulders ached. There are seven of us in this great big hut, besides Beryl, Irene and myself who have all cuddled together for warmth, there are two other girls, very nice, and you can guess what the other two are like. The greater part of the girls are pretty awful, quite a number coming from Birmingham, but we three keep together as much as possible. One very di-da-di-da girl hasn't been seen since Sunday afternoon, when she said she was going to the station to collect her luggage. Altogether there are 66 girls in charge of the Lieutenant Colonel (can't remember his name for the minute) but of course affectionately known as – the Colonel. He really is a nice old stick, and tries to keep the girls who are friends with each other together. He calls us with his whistle at 6.15 each morning, breakfast is from 7–7.45, and the lorries depart after that. The lorry never came

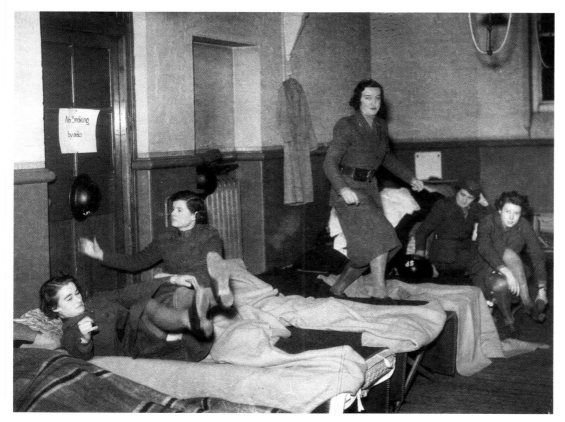

MECHANISED TRANSPORT CORPS *members slept with their clothes on while on duty. They had to be on call to drive ambulances or relief workers such as stretcher bearers to the scene of an emergency at a moment's notice.*

until 11 o'clock having been ditched, and we started work, picking spuds. The farmer was a very decent chap and works with us, probably to keep us on the job. We had a rotten lunch of rotten sandwiches, and when it started to rain at 4.30pm we packed up work. This wasn't too bad for the day, sort of broke my back in. But we walked most of the way back, and then it started to *rain*. I got soaked to the skin. I've had a hot bath in a filthy bath, some half cold grub, can't find anywhere to hang my wet clothes, they're here in the hut at the moment and it's not exactly a healthy state of air to sleep in. What a life!

The girls are all going to the shed that boasts a piano, but very few chairs, and they're all wooden, so picture Beryl and I lying on our stomachs on our divan-like beds with the smoke of the oil lamp our only light, getting up our noses, and the rain falling heavens hard on the tin roof, and I've already killed two spiders, once again. What a life!"

Veronica Owen, who had reluctantly been evacuated to Canada as a schoolgirl, returned home in 1942 keen to play her part in her country's war and became a Wren. She wrote to her mother in May 1944 about a new addition to her watch in the Coding Room at Fort Southwick, Portsmouth.

"Monica Newburn, a Canadian of 24, who is rather overbearing and always holds the floor with a penetrating voice, either talking about the numerous men who are in love with her and whom she is inclined to 'play' with – most of them Lt RNs, poor devils, or sex! She's staunch Roman Catholic, and lives with her sister married to a Lt RN. Well I've been very unkind and she sounds grim and really isn't nearly as bad as that – it's just that her talk is a bit much at times, but she is kind underneath and in some ways very amusing."

Veronica had been at boarding school, and was used to community life, but she still found living with some of her fellow Wrens a culture shock – particularly petty jealousies.

LOTS OF YOUNG WOMEN *later reminisced about having a great time during their war work. Released from the shackles of home, they could really enjoy themselves when they were off duty.*

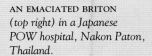

MESS PARADE FOR PRISONERS
of war at a camp on the
Burma–Thailand railway
(top left). Food supplies to the
camps were erratic, vegetables
were usually rotten by the
time they arrived and the
men often had to survive on
a measly ration of rice. As a
result they were chronically
underfed for the hard physical
work they were forced to do.

AN EMACIATED BRITON
(top right) in a Japanese
POW hospital, Nakon Paton,
Thailand.

THE FUNERAL OF A PRISONER
who died during the
construction of the railway
at Ronzi, Burma (middle
left). After the war, bodies
that had been buried in tiny
camp burial grounds like this
were transferred to one of
three war cemeteries that still
commemorate the victims of
the Japanese forced labour.

A PARTIALLY CONSTRUCTED
railway between Rangoon and
Bangkok (bottom left) had
been abandoned before the
war with 155 miles (250km)
left to build. Under the
Japanese, a labour force made
up of POWs started from
either end and worked towards
the middle, over mountainous
and jungle-clad terrain.

FORCED LABOUR IN BURMA

In Britain, a spirit of camaraderie mobilised the population into factory work, farm labour and voluntary service from fire-watching to ambulance driving. In the Far East, husbands and sons who were unlucky enough to be captured by the Japanese were treated as slaves and forced to work on the construction of the Burma–Thailand (or Rangoon–Bangkok) railway. This was intended to enable the Japanese to move troops and supplies between the two cities after they occupied Burma in 1942; the alternative sea route, via Singapore and the Straits of Malacca, was open to attack by Allied submarines. The horrific project later earned the name the Death Railway: it is estimated that 16,000 Allied prisoners of war and perhaps as many as 100,000 Asian 'pressed' labourers died of overwork, malnutrition or diseases such as cholera and dysentery as a result of working on the railway.

The construction required the prisoners to build two bridges over the River Kwai, subject of the famous film. Because of their strategic importance, the bridges were the target of frequent Allied bomb attacks, as was the nearby Japanese anti-aircraft battery. One night in 1944 three bombs overshot the battery and damaged the camp where the prisoners were housed, killing 19 PoWs and injuring 68 more. The wooden bridge was eventually destroyed in 1945.

ALLIED PRISONERS OF WAR ENGAGED IN BUILDING *the bridge over the Mae Klong river (renamed Kwai in the 1960s) as part of the Burma–Thailand railway, February 1943. The 11-span steel bridge, which was completed two months later, was supported by bamboo scaffolding. This and a wooden bridge nearby were the only means of crossing the river.*

THE CRAMPED QUARTERS *with little privacy were uncomfortable for many land girls. Others revelled in the camaraderie of living with colleagues.*

Some munitions workers lived in hostels. Miss Nora O'Connor ran the Burghfield Residential Club, which housed 1,000 female munitions workers. Eight hundred of the girls were Irish, and ages ranged between 18 and 60. They were employed at a factory near Reading.

"The making of munitions was hazardous in the extreme, involving the use of TNT and, in spite of rigorously enforced safety precautions, 'blows' did occur. Having refused one girl permission to go to a dance, I was immensely saddened by my next news of her – she had been killed by an explosion at work. The fact that a worker had been killed on duty didn't deter her companions; they showed neither fear nor hesitation in carrying on. Lack of clothing coupons was a source of frustration, but it nourished the initiative of a small group who organised a flourishing Exchange and Mart in second-hand garments."

Kathleen Crawley toured village halls, military hospitals and army and air force bases as an actress with ENSA (Entertainments National Service Association). On tour near Lincoln she stayed in a munitions hostel.

"We didn't know quite what to expect yesterday, but it turned out to be the hostel of a Clax factory here and nearly all the girls are Irish. I suppose all munitions hostels are like this. The corridor of bedrooms looks like a prison. All the rooms are tiny and two of everything. The food seems alright though it's rather muckily served, but I think we'll enjoy the week – it's a change anyhow. It has masses of bathrooms and the water is always boiling. What appealed to us were the laundry sinks, wringer and ironing room. The entire company has washed everything, and dried and ironed everything with one speck of dirt on it. It was such a novelty to have it all there when you wanted it. There's a games' room here with darts and ping pong which Betty Fuller and I intend to be proficient at by the end of the week. The only trouble is that it's such a noisy place and none of the factory girls even try to be quiet after 7 in the morning."

Dirty sheets in boarding houses, leaky roofs in the dressing rooms and an uncertain power supply are all described in her letters home to her mother. This was theatre under 'wartime conditions'.

"Last night's venue was terrible. It was so unbelievably awful that we thought we were having an actor's nightmare – the not knowing your lines or having half a mile to run and being late for your cue. Well, it was a village hall we found ourselves in – we've been playing many of these lately. There were no tabs [front curtains], the lighting was no better than 6 candle power – really it wasn't. The doors in the hall had to be opened to let light onto the stage! The stage was surrounded by camouflage netting – filthy dirty and smelly – which we had to remove. Anyway we could have borne with all this – they'd never had a play before. The Entertainments Officer didn't even know it was a play, and the whole audience sat the whole way through without a sound and without any applause till Eric told them the play had finished. Even the cat must have found it tiresome – she had four beautiful black kittens during the show."

On tour in Scotland in 1944 she wrote:

"Tonight's show is too funny for words. Four times the lights have gone out and we've continued playing by torch light from the wings!"

THE ENTERTAINMENT NATIONAL SERVICES ASSOCIATION *(ENSA) sent shows to entertain the troops on active service but also put together concert parties to boost the morale of civilians in underground shelters.*

NOT ALL OF THE ENTERTAINMENT *was of a high standard and ENSA was nicknamed 'Every Night Something Atrocious' (or Awful). But in their headquarters in Drury Lane, the heart of London's theatreland, they had access to professional-quality props and costumes.*

WITH MOST ABLE-BODIED MEN *away on active service, some jobs had to be taken by the very young. This pit worker from the Rhondda Valley in South Wales is 14.*

Kathleen was horrified by some of the conditions in which those on war work had to live. Her brother had joined the Forces and she thought him lucky compared to the Bevin Boys, after the company had performed at one of their camps. A chronic shortage of miners, coupled with severe wartime winters and the increasing needs of industry, led to drastic measures from Ernest Bevin, Minister of Labour. Many skilled miners had entered the forces, and in December 1943 the Bevin Boys were called up to replace them in the mines. They were chosen by a random ballot to ensure that this form of conscription applied to all classes and backgrounds. John Whisson was working as a clerk at the Ministry of Supply in London, and had just qualified as an emergency motorcycle despatch rider. He had hoped to join the army when he was called up in February 1944. Instead he was sent to Moor Green Colliery, in Eastwood.

During the winter months it was not unusual to find, on waking up that the walls above our beds were covered with hoar frost.

"Unfortunately the Nissen huts which served as dormitories for groups of twelve were not heated. During the winter months it was not unusual to find on waking up that the walls above our beds were covered with hoar frost."

The new young miners spent a month training before going down the pits. Michael Banister wrote up his experiences for his school magazine three months later.

"The lecturers were all mining men, and though they no doubt knew their jobs, some clearly had difficulty in imparting their knowledge to the trainees, who were in any case, for the most part truculent and in no mood to receive any information on the now abhorred subject of mining. During the whole of my period of training I never saw the coal face. Any knowledge I gained was derived almost entirely from the lecture room and hence was purely theoretical."

Writing his first letter home, Noel Humphrey described the training equipment.

JUST A FEW WEEKS *of training was given before the new recruits were exposed to the harsh realities of pit life. In total, nearly 48,000 young men joined regular miners from 1943 to 1948. Scrapes, bruises and accidents were commonplace, but fatalities were comparitively low.*

"We were given a helmet, boots, overalls and a pair of white gym shoes. The helmets are made of cardboard but it looks like black bakelite. The boots are studded and they have a metal toe-cap. I am billeted with a boy from London. It is very nice here with this miner and his wife. There is plenty of good food here."

In another letter home to his mother in Pulborough, Sussex, Noel described his first trip underground.

"There is a funny feeling in one's stomach first, but it soon passes off. About half way down it feels as if you are going up again. On the way up it feels as if you are going down again before you reach the top. We all have electric lamps which weigh about six pounds. In some of the tunnels there are electric lights and you can walk with ease while in others you have to bend your head."

Among his fellow Bevin Boys was the future leader of the Liberal Party, David Steele. Another future MP, Geoffrey Finsberg, was a Bevin Boy, as were the entertainers Eric Morecambe and Jimmy Saville. David Jedwab was an idealistic 17-year-old in 1944, when he described a day at a pit in Lancashire.

"When I am not in a particular hurry, I like to walk across those fifty yards of surface slowly, and sometimes – on nice fresh mornings – rather hesitatingly. This is all that separates me from the choking depths into which I shall descend shortly. I feel sorry to leave the fresh air and hear the wind rustling among the grass and hedges. My gaze turns up at the great tall chimney in front of me. Together with the pitshafts, with their clumsy looks, it makes a gruesome site in the dark. I take one last look at the sky that is gradually beginning to be filled with a pale light and, make my way to the lift cage."

The cage took David and his fellow miners down 1,000 feet (305m).

"Down here it is strangely quiet; only the dull thudding sound of our steps breaks the silence and the former garrulous chatter of the men has become a strained and tense silence. Soon we are walking, supporting ourselves on our knees, along four foot high passages and tunnels, now crawling on all fours, now on our stomachs by drawing ourselves forward with the elbows, and now climbing up brows as steep as Welsh mountains."

Michael Banister trained at Doncaster and was posted to Bedlington Colliery in Northumberland in February 1944. He was assigned to help a 17-year-old who had been down the pit for three years, and the two teenagers managed a junction on the haulage roads.

"It is not pleasant work, but it is far short of 'hard labour'. In fact I have one of the best jobs in the pit. In comparison with that of a member of the Forces, it has its merits and demerits. It holds no glamour of uniform, no regular three monthly leaves, and very slight chances of promotion. But we have a home life with its undeniable advantages. We have regular and definite hours of work, and weekends entirely free; and we have a longer expectation of life!"

THE BEVIN BOYS WERE *conscripts, selected at random from all those who were due to be called up in any given week. From December 1943 till the end of the war, 10 per cent of all conscripts aged 18–25 were assigned to mining work.*

Despite their increased life expectancy, many Bevin Boys resented losing the chance to serve their country *above* ground. While military conscripts were awarded campaign medals for serving their country abroad, the young miners who had served their country at home did not have their contribution officially recognised until 60 years later.

8. News and Propaganda

"Well, it certainly is a comical war! At least on the wireless: our own short-wave transmitter broadcasting in a dozen or two foreign languages, and every country frantically doing the same. Everybody it seems is trying to lecture everybody else into doing what the first everybody wants done – And then German broadcasts in English! Can anything be more Gilbertian for example, than the German announcer on 49.2m wave length wishing his listeners a good night's rest after he has done his best to make sound sleep for many people difficult to come by, with his harrowing accounts of the result of Britain's continuance of the war: or his colleague from Hamburg tonight concluding his 9–10pm 'news' – but really militant propaganda – by saying: 'Since this is Sunday we will conclude our broadcast with the hymn The Day Thou Gavest Lord Is Ended'. Verily a mad world my masters." Dr JP McHutchison, October 1939

As the light shone through the wireless dial into dimly lit and blacked out homes, many could not resist twiddling the knob from the BBC Home Service across myriad tiny European stations to Berlin. The wireless was a new weapon in modern warfare. War news in 1914–18 had been carried by the only means available: the newspapers. Great war correspondents like Frank Gillard pre-recorded reports from the frontline, heard hours later in British homes. Limited filming had taken place in the trenches of the Great War but in this new war the camera lens transferred images of battle straight to the retinas of cinemagoers. It was all subject to censorship but the population was able to follow the progress of the allied armies as they had never been able to before.

Dr JP McHutchison found he could not resist tuning in to German radio stations.

"What a depressing 'nightcap' the German news broadcast in English is – one must really cease listening, but curiosity as to what new lies they are spreading is always strong."

Listening to these German broadcasts in English must have made the population recognise the reality of spies and a 'fifth column' (a phrase borrowed from the recent Spanish Civil War to describe enemy sympathisers), and the necessity for slogans like 'Careless Talk Costs Lives' and 'Be Like Dad, Keep Mum'. Examples of disturbingly accurate information, broadcast to shake the morale of the civilian population, were scattered throughout contemporary diaries. Dr McHutchison lived on the outskirts of Glasgow, which rated a mention in the German 'news' in English in late 1939.

'CARELESS TALK COSTS LIVES' *was a campaign based on the fear that spies might be listening in on any casual conversation. Any remark that might diminish public morale was also seen as playing into Hitler's hands.*

"Last week local interest was created in a mention of Clydebank (Queen Elizabeth), Dumbarton (Blackburn Aircraft Works) and Alexandria (Torpedo Factory). The green painting of the Blackburn Works was noted."

The Germans were not averse to attempted interference with BBC programmes. In October 1942 Joan Strange cut out a story from her daily paper and stuck it in her diary. She added her own ear-witness account of this bizarre attempt at German propaganda.

CARELESS TALK COSTS LIVES

"Nazi radio voice butts in on BBC news. The voice has butted in for the last 3 days now. It's absolutely childish. He is not nearly quick enough and is devoid of all wit.

CIVILIANS WERE ANXIOUS *for word from the front line. Radio was the source of any 'breaking news', while newspapers were anxiously scanned for reports of battles and lists of those killed or missing.*

EVENING PRAYERS
*and hymn singing
were a feature of life
in shelters run by the
Church Army and
were often broadcast
as part of the BBC's*
Sunday Service.

Tonight all he could think to say was 'That's a lie' or 'Of course' then 'That's a lie' again, a most feeble effort!!"

The mystery voice interrupted the BBC Forces programme with a running barrage of abuse of Winston Churchill and Foreign Secretary Anthony Eden. But the Germans were not alone in their use of the radio as a weapon of war. The BBC World Service, funded by the Foreign Office, started broadcasting in German after the Munich crisis in 1938. By the end of the war it was broadcasting in 45 languages. Messages were even sent to the Far East, where prisoners of war listened secretly in the camps. The BBC Home Service broadcast uplifting messages from evacuated children to their parents; the young Princess Elizabeth encouraged the children of the Empire; and Queen Elizabeth broadcast to the Women of America in 1941. Dr McHutchison and his mother were regular listeners to the Sunday service, which was broadcast by the BBC and was one instance of how simple propaganda could raise morale.

"Tonight's broadcast service was relayed from a shelter in London and was almost too poignantly pathetic in its setting. The hymns sung for the most part by folks now homeless and sheltering every night in the crypt of the church had a significance they never had before, and that their authors could never have imagined possible. It moved me, and it must have moved all the angels in heaven, to hear the voices of the grown ups and children singing, O God, our Help in Ages Past; the King of Love My Shepherd is; Holy Father in Thy Mercy, Guide Me Oh Thou Great Jehovah and Abide With Me. One felt surer of our victory somehow after listening to such a service from such a place."

FOLLOWING THE DEFEAT
*of Field Marshall Rommel
by General Montgomery
at the second battle of
El Alamein, Churchill
broadcast to an eager world
audience on November
29, 1942. He discussed
and celebrated the Allied
victories in North Africa,
describing the events as a
"bright gleam of victory".*

In rural areas many people were not connected to electricity, and went to great lengths to listen into the wireless. Crystal sets were not uncommon, and a conventional wireless set could be powered by an accumulator – a cumbersome type of battery taken to a central depot for recharging.

Switching on the wireless in the evenings was how the British population got their war news, concerts and light entertainment in their own homes. Great literary names like George Orwell and JB Priestley attracted large audiences. Prime Minister Winston Churchill used the radio to great effect, cajoling and encouraging unity on the Home Front. The wireless brought the news vividly to life for people far from the action – sometimes perhaps too vividly. Leonard Marsland Gander (who later became a war reporter) was the wireless correspondent for *The Daily Telegraph* during the early years of the war:

POPULAR AUTHOR
*JB Priestley drew huge
audiences for his radio
'chats' – only Churchill
himself was more popular.
Some people criticised
Priestley for painting too
rosy a picture of 'Little
England', though in
fact he was a committed
socialist and his talks were
eventually cancelled because
of complaints that they were
too left wing.*

"July 15, 1940: there is great interest in the sensational running commentary (recorded) given by Charles Gardner on Sunday on an air fight he watched over the English Channel. He included such phrases as 'Oh boy, oh boy, this is the best thing I've seen', as young men were crashing to their death – it was strong meat for some listeners."

The wireless was a source of comfort too. In Somerset, Ann Lee Mitchell found herself exhausted and often depressed about wartime events. But she would turn that button and, as the set warmed up, listen to the magic words 'It's That Man Again'.

"Very tired, had some supper on a tray by the fire and giggled weakly at the absurdities of ITMA on the wireless."

Mrs E Innes-Kerr had worked for the BBC in Malaya, and after escaping to England she rejoined the Corporation in London.

"Sometime in the middle of 1943 the BBC's Engineering Division organised voluntary spare time munitions work in the evenings. When this was started most people in our department said they would willingly give up one evening a week to munitions, but when it came to choosing an evening, everyone was adamant they could not do Thursday evening, because that was the evening for ITMA with Tommy Handley. Maw and I were regular listeners to this, but it quite surprised me how certain everyone was, even the intellectuals in the department, [that] they were not going to miss Tommy Handley's programme. Honor and I elected to do our munitions work on Monday evenings, and we used to go straight from the office. We worked from 7–10pm making lamp sockets for aircraft. Probably about 30–40 of us in a big room. The radio was tuned to 'Music While You Work'."

RADIO COMEDY CONTRIBUTED more than anything else to raising morale and It's That Man Again, starring Tommy Handley (right), was the most popular show. It was said that if Hitler had chosen to invade at 8.30 on a Thursday evening, there would have been little resistance. The title parodied a newspaper headline cliché, used whenever Hitler made some new territorial claim, and its abbreviation to ITMA mimicked the wartime habit of abbreviating the names of everything from the RAF to ENSA.

There has been a lot of discussions in the papers lately about the ban on 'slushy music' on the BBC

Daphne Pearson was a guest on one of the hit wartime shows, as she wrote to her mother, swelling with pride, in February 1941.

"Do you remember you saying I wonder whether you'll ever do 'In Town Tonight', well I was on the air last night and this morning. Only one had to say exactly what was written and not much choice. Odd words I was allowed to correct – we had five rehearsals and I got colder and colder and at 6:15 I could not stand it any more and said I must have a drink – this was hailed with great cheer. So into the nearest pub and I drank three brandies and ginger ales before I could warm up. During rehearsal they said we were very cold and lifeless. Most of the BBC having moved into a cinema without any heating, I'm not surprised."

In their sitting rooms, couples swayed to music played on the gramophone and dance music played live, by the likes of Henry Hall and his Orchestra, and broadcast via the wireless. In a letter to her sister in America in 1942, Ethel Mattison recorded censorship of the type of music broadcast by the BBC.

"There has been a lot of discussions in the papers lately about the ban on 'slushy music' on the BBC. No doubt you have heard about it. According to The Sunday Times, Tinpan Alley are very upset about it and fear that their voice will not be heard this side of the Atlantic. Personally I think the loss will be all theirs."

BRITISH TROOPS ADVANCE *through the dust and smoke of the battle at El Alamein, 1942 (top left).*

A GERMAN PANZER CREWMAN *lifts his hands in surrender to a British soldier (top right). Hitler had ordered Rommel to battle on to the last, but Rommel disobeyed, preferring to save the lives of some of his men and retreat to fight another day.*

GERMAN AND ITALIAN SOLDIERS *are taken prisoner after the battle (above left). About a third of the Axis troops – some 35,000 men – were killed or wounded at El Alamein, with another 13,000 taken prisoner.*

A 4.5-INCH FIELD GUN IN ACTION *at El Alamein (above right). Monty had 1200 tanks to Rommel's 500, and he also outnumbered the Germans in terms of artillery and infantrymen.*

FIELD MARSHAL ERWIN ROMMEL *(right) earned the nickname 'the Desert Fox' because of his wily generalship. After leaving Africa he played a strategic role in the defences of the Normandy beaches, but was later suspected of involvement in the July (1944) plot to assassinate Hitler and forced to commit suicide.*

VICTORY AT EL ALAMEIN

For the first three years of the war there was little good news to tell the British people and the government struggled to keep people's spirits up. Finally, though, in November 1942 General Montgomery's decisive victory over the German Field Marshal Rommel at El Alamein gave the propagandists a genuine triumph to shout about.

The conflict in North Africa had got under way when Italy entered the war on the German side in June 1940. The Italian forces soon surrendered after the onslaught led by General Wavell, but in 1941 Rommel was put in charge of the elite tank force known as the Afrika Korps. In June 1942 the Allies underwent a humiliating surrender at Tobruk in Libya, which gave huge quantities of stores into German and Italian hands.

The tide turned, however, after General Montgomery took command of the 8th Army. The two forces met at El Alamein, a bottleneck on the coast 250km west of Cairo, whose position hampered Rommel's battle plan and supply lines (which had been leaked to 'Monty' courtesy of the code-breakers of Bletchley Park). The Germans suffered heavy losses and eventually retreated back into Libya. It was very much 'the beginning of the end' of the North Africa campaign: Winston Churchill observed, 'It may almost be said, "Before Alamein we never had a victory. After Alamein we never had a defeat."'

LIEUTENANT GENERAL Bernard Montgomery (above), wearing his trademark beret, watched the Axis forces retreat from El Alamein. Like Rommel, but unlike his predecessor Auchinleck, 'Monty' was greatly respected by his troops, who said that he was 'as quick as a ferret and about as likeable'.

ROMMEL'S FIRST ATTACK was knocked back by the land mines that the Allies had laid, because Monty refused to follow the retreating Germans. He was awaiting the arrival of 300 Sherman tanks (left). These tanks – new, powerful and vastly superior to anything Rommel had at his command – ensured an Allied victory.

Newspapers published tales of the courage and dedication of men in the forces, particularly the RAF. But listening to the voices of those airmen on the wireless was far more effective. In August 1941 Dr McHutchison was glued to his set.

"Some recent broadcast talks by airmen, pilots and gunners, have impressed and moved one by their quietly-spoken, calm and almost matter of fact tones, no bravado, no consciousness of bravery, but only a sort of quizzical modesty about their exploits, a kind of very boyish interest in deeds of superb skill and daring – the typical English sporting spirit."

Phyllis Warner went to see a similar production in her local London cinema in August 1941.

"Went to see *Target for Tonight*, the new film of a bombing raid in which all the actors are active members of the Bomber Command. It was slightly eerie to sit in that cinema after black out time, and watch on the screen all the sinister routine preparations for a raid and the planes humming nearer and nearer their goal, knowing that any minute the warning might shriek that German bombers were upon us here. My experiences of raids being exclusively that of the target, my sympathies drifted to the German AA gunners down below rather than to our side up in the plane – until they were on their lonely and perilous journey back, when something about their simple cheerfulness took hold of the imagination, and made those minutes painfully tense. It is above all a memorable film, one presented in undertones, but which keeps recurring to the mind days later."

Not everyone agreed with these sentiments. Lucy Kemp spent much of the war waiting for her husband Teddie to return from his voyages to North America with the transatlantic convoys. While he was away from home in February 1942 she went to the cinema.

"The war news is so — , and I have been getting so keyed up waiting for Teddie that on Saturday I thought I should explode, so went to our village cinema for relaxation. We led off with Donald Duck, which was very funny, then a propaganda thing about 'more ships'. This consisted of a man reciting some poem with fade-ins and fade-outs of convoys, mostly being bombed! I thought 'Good Heavens', and then settled down to Wuthering Heights."

'WAR WORK NEWS'
was a special newsreel sponsored by the Ministry of Supply, enabling working people to keep up with the news during their lunch break. This film is being shown in the canteen of the London Passenger Transport Board.

Propaganda films were used to boost the morale and productivity of factory workers. Elsie Whiteman and Kathleen Church-Bliss were among the workforce at Morrison's Aircraft Factory in Croydon.

"At dinner time today the Ministry of Information film 'Let's finish the job' was shown in the Canteen. The place was crowded to suffocation as all the windows had to be shut in order to put up the blackout – and every worker in the place was there – including all the office. It was really a very wonderful film – designed to show by illustration how every excrescence however minute on the body of the plane sets up resistance to its passage through the air – and in consequence slows up the speed. It was very cleverly devised and must have been planned by a skilled engineer. The right and wrong ways of doing jobs was also shown in an amusing and narrative form. The moral was, that how we finish the job is all important. Old Els who has so often wondered whether her slow careful work was justified, came away inwardly uplifted as obviously you can't be too careful. They told us that rough finish can make a difference of 25 mph to a plane's speed."

MOBILE OUTDOOR SCREENS *were an enterprising way of raising money for the war effort during the Battle of Britain. Here crowds gather in the street to watch a film about the RAF on a screen mounted on a truck, which will move on to the next 'venue' when the performance is over.*

Factories, schools and villages adopted ships, planes and even whole squadrons, and were treated to visits and flypasts by the men whose work they were supporting. Salvage campaigns exhorted the population to 'keep a rag bag' (four old collars would make a new map for the RAF); food leftovers were collected in huge bins by the WVS to feed pigs; and paper was collected to make munitions (one propaganda photograph showed Queen Mary's secretary donating a huge pile of her old letters to this campaign). Joan Strange recorded some of the efforts in Worthing in November 1941.

> "We've ransacked the house and collected all sorts of old bills etc. there is a big national competition for paper with a £20,000 prize for the winning county. There were stacks of old forms all ready to be collected at the town hall."

Dustcarts pulled a separate salvage cart behind them for recyclable materials. In 1944 there was a book recovery and salvage drive for the Services, blitzed libraries and munitions.

> "School children are collecting the books and we turned out 130 today which were removed triumphantly in two sacks – up to today about 50,000 have been received."

RECYCLING PEAKED *during 'Salvage Weeks', like this one in St Pancras, London. Waste paper could be used in munitions factories.*

SUITABLE BOOKS *would be forwarded to servicemen or used to rebuild the stocks of bombed libraries; others were added to the recycling heap.*

MORALE BOOSTING *was never far from the government's mind. These children wear 'V for Victory' caps donated by the British War Relief Society of America.*

MINISTRY OF HEALTH *says:*—

Coughs and sneezes spread diseases

Trap the germs by using your handkerchief

Help to keep the Nation Fighting Fit

POSTERS REMINDED *people of the need to keep the nation healthy so that the war effort could be maintained.*

Three thousand disused slot machines from Britain's railway stations were recycled as part of a campaign for iron and steel scrap, as well as the infamous railings. Telephone boxes carried a poster declaring: 'I'm on war work, if you must use me be brief.' Some people gave up their home telephones as part of their war effort. On the underground, posters encouraged people with colds to keep their germs to themselves so as not to take sick leave and harm the war effort. The 'V for Victory' campaign even spawned a V for Victory hat, worn by one enterprising woman in London. The most productive campaign was 'Dig for Victory', which used front gardens, bomb craters and public parks to produce vegetables; the People's Park in Grimsby produced 15 tons of onions one year. In his school essay in September 1940, D Madge recorded the success of the allotments at the Kneller Boys School in Twickenham.

"Ever since war began the school's field has been dug up into allotments 16 by six yards. All of them bear vegetables of some kind such as turnips, carrots, beetroot, cabbage, marrows, potatoes, brussels sprouts etc. They are all worked by the boys themselves. The ground is very dry and the things aren't growing so well but the weather is breaking now and looking more like rain. Boys could come up to their allotments during the holidays, which owing to the war were only a fortnight. Just before the holidays a boy in the school stole most of the fruit from the orchard, but it was not long before he was found out. A lot of the vegetables are now being sold to the school and the money which we get is given to the Red Cross. Boys are still doing their bit 'Digging for Victory'!"

'DIGGING FOR VICTORY' *meant making use of all available space: these women are picking tomatoes that have been grown in the 'garden' of a petrol station.*

Joan Strange held an allotment in Worthing, and picked up tips on vegetable growing from her fellow allotment holders.

"March: help! I've not written this old diary for nearly a week. It's the allotment's fault! The weather has been so good that I've gone up most evenings and got too tired digging to write the diary. The two oldish men on the next plot have helped me a bit as they are taking over a bit of Ken's plot, which is already dug. There is a very friendly spirit up there."

'Make do and mend' was a watchword for housewives. Sheets were turned 'sides to middle', and people were encouraged to save and reuse scraps of string and paper. Joan Strange and her mother used their needlework skills to raise hundreds of pounds for wartime causes.

Only when a severe Blitz has temporarily stopped printing or circulation has this voice of the people failed to present its messages

"January 24, 1944: mother is very busy making trolley cloths from a linen sheet given her by Miss Bridges marked 1882! It's an enormous sheet and will make dozens of such-like things for sales. In this case it's for a Prisoner of War sale 'something new from something old'."

Despite the proximity of Fleet Street to the City of London and wartime paper shortages, the papers were still published and were a vital source of news, propaganda campaigns, recipes and handy hints for 'making do'. Peg Cotton, as an American, was impressed when she described wartime newspapers in early 1945.

> "For years these have been but two scant sheets of paper. Paper makes munitions. Yet these rationed newspapers have carried on throughout the war. Only when a severe Blitz has temporarily stopped printing or circulation has this voice of the people failed to present its messages, heartening, or heart rending, every day, so surely as that day would dawn."

Talking to 'the press' in wartime had its risks. In January 1941 May Chalmers, whose husband Archie was the Sheriff of Oban on the west coast of Scotland, innocently recounted her local news in a *private* letter to a close friend, Mea Allan, who happened to be Assistant News Editor on a national newspaper, the *Daily Herald*. There were to be embarrassing consequences after May recounted the dramatic results of enemy bombing in Argyll.

> "I'm still slightly sick when I think of the last visitation when they got the boat full of the Aga Khan's stable and only one poor horse got ashore and none of the greyhounds. Somehow the animals cause me more sorrow than the men who passed out, even more upset than the Sunderland which thought the sea was twenty feet lower opposite Kilbowie and crashed scuppering the whole crew of twelve."

EVERY OPPORTUNITY to encourage people to save, repair, reuse or recycle was taken by the government. This leaflet contains instructions for making slippers out of an old hat.

MAKE DO AND MEND: war workers in a London factory relieve the monotony of rationing and utility clothing by refurbishing hats.

The two women kept up a chatty and frequent exchange of news in the early years of the war. Mea Allan wrote back a week later on 8 January:

"Today, on the desk, in comes a Press Association slip about the Aga Khan's bloodstock in France having been purloined by the Germans – and I am in charge. So being a conscientious Scot, I pen little notes to some of the items, and one of them is, 'It may interest you to know that one ship of a convoy bombed off Oban Argyll Scotland, had on board the Aga Khans' horses and hounds. Only one horse swam ashore. The rest were killed or drowned.'"

Mea Allan was the first woman to be appointed to a Fleet Street news desk and was always delighted to beat her male colleagues to a story.

"Now how was I to know, when nobody told the innocent sweetheart of 50 rampin' stampin' newsmen – how could I know that for the past week every other journalist on every other paper in the kingdom had been trying to find out who that horse belonged to?? 'Where did you get this story and *how* did *you* get it?' they bellowed. If the Edinburgh office did ring you up I hope you weren't annoyed; they are very nice people. If we get an exclusive, tops!"

CARELESS WRITING *also cost lives and letters from the front frequently included the line 'I'm not allowed to say where we are'. Postal censorship was a labour-intensive business and the censors knew scores of languages between them.*

But May Chalmers could not share her enthusiasm after a brush with the police, which revealed that all calls from journalists were monitored.

"You have got me properly in the soup – Oban Inspector of Police rang up yesterday and then the County Police from Lochgilphead. The only saving thing about it all is that they have been

decent enough not to tell the Sheriff. If they had done so he would have certainly shot me or put me in the sea, so if our friendship is to continue, will you promise, honour bright, *never* to pass on anything I tell you? It is rather a revelation to learn that the County Police listen in to any conversation on the telephone which *comes* from a reporter, and I was congratulated on the way I ticked off the Edinburgh man although being told off as well. Gosh to goodness if Archie knew! It's just too awful to contemplate and I'm completely sunk. You probably think it's a storm in a tea cup but it means a lot to me and apparently the AK episode was *terribly* secret."

Censorship of news, and of letters going abroad, was all part of the war machine, designed to prevent fifth columnists from discovering scraps of information useful to enemy agents. Blue pencil was used to erase words and place names deemed to give away vital information to the enemy. Newspapers had to submit stories to the Ministry of Information to be 'passed by censor'. Mea Allan described the procedure.

"One rings for A Boy. When A Boy comes, one says rapidly over one's shoulder: 'Ministry – at once!' If there's a raid on The Boy puts forward Union rules and won't go out. He will if the office car is at the door to take him. Later one of our men at the Ministry phones over corrections – copies have to be corrected and sent to subs [sub editors]."

THE FALL OF SINGAPORE *island at the southern end of the Malay Peninsula and a vital part of the British Empire, is considered to be one of the biggest defeats in the history of the British army. Moreover it was an indication of Japan's fighting prowess.*

Contemporary diaries and letters summarised the war news every day. When the island of Pontillaria was finally taken in the Italian campaign, one British woman even named her daughter Pontillaria. The population was kept relatively well informed, despite the censor. Phyllis Warner had a shock when she opened her newspaper in February 1942.

"Started the day feeling cheerful, but was horrified at the lunch time headlines. Japs land in force at Singapore. The papers are cruel – they put the worst news in the biggest headlines, with no thought of those of us who suffer. I can't believe that this is true, that with all the defences of Singapore Island the Japs can land in thousands. But the radio holds out no promise of better news."

If the headlines appalled, pictures could be far worse.

"What is going to happen to all our men? There won't be a chance of evacuation. Are they all to be killed or taken prisoner? I do wish I hadn't seen those horrible *Picture Post* photographs of what the Japs do to their prisoners."

News of Russia's continued stand against invading German troops was recorded day by day in many diaries. The population was inspired and heartened by their Russian allies. Phyllis Warner went to a festival of Russian films in London, and she could not help comparing Stalin's inspirational speeches with the propaganda issued by the British Government.

"Where are our War Office nabobs and political boneheads who were convinced the Russians wouldn't last ten days? Sitting up and taking notes on how to fight a war tooth and nail and not by a series of gentlemanly retreats, I should hope. Stalin's call to the Russian people 'Rise to defend your land' . . . 'be ruthless' . . . 'create guerrilla bands' . . . 'make conditions unbearable for the enemy' . . . 'rise in your millions', is a pretty shaming contrast to our War Office instructions to the Home Guard that weapons and explosives must on no account be improvised, and the official invasion leaflet which told us to hide in shelters till the fighting was over. I wonder if I would have the courage to sling a milk bottle at a parachutist: I hope to God I would."

The women must be prepared to kill to protect their children.

Scrapbooks of newspaper cuttings show that by 1941 the British public was aware of the extent of Jewish persecution. One article even predicted that the number of Jewish victims of the 'final solution' would be six million. Mea Allan mixed with other journalists and with government officials all day, and was privy to classified information. Her vivid description of a German air raid, in a letter to a friend, included this in October 1940.

"If it's not High Explosives its landmines – our own if you please, wot the Germans pinched at Dunkirk!! If that's news to you swallow it and forget it!!"

DAPHNE PEARSON *became the first woman to be awarded the George Cross, after rescuing a pilot from the burning wreckage of his bomber aircraft. She is seen here following her investiture by King George VI at Buckingham Palace, November 1941.*

It was the job of the newspapers to provide morale-boosting stories too. Daphne Pearson was splashed all over the newspapers in 1940. Daphne had been only a few hours short of gaining her pilot's licence at the outbreak of war, but she was turned down by the Women's Air Transport Service (whose ranks included Amy Johnson). Instead she joined the WAAF (Women's Auxiliary Air Force). At two o'clock on the morning of May 31, Daphne was asleep in her bunk at an RAF Coastal Command Station in Kent. A noise stirred her from sleep and she was alarmed to hear the rattle of a plane's labouring engine and a terrible crash. Leaping out of bed, she rushed out and found a plane in flames. She pulled the injured pilot free and then, as an enormous bomb exploded in the fuselage, threw herself over him to protect him from the blast and shrapnel. Daphne was awarded the George Cross – the first member of the WAAF to be honoured for bravery. Three months later she wrote to her mother from Malvern:

THE MOST DISTINGUISHED *female artist of her time, Laura Knight (above) painted a number of works under the auspices of the War Artists Advisory Committee, including a portrait of Daphne Pearson.*

> "I am staying here until Wednesday – Dame Laura Knight is painting me – am full of conflictions because we are so busy on our station."

Dame Laura Knight, one of the official war artists, painted many extraordinary scenes of life on the Home Front, from women handling enormous barrage balloons to heroines like Daphne.

THE INSPIRING STORY *of Daphne Pearson's heroism led many other women to volunteer for dangerous war work, such as ambulance driving.*

> "I am being painted in a tin helmet and holding a rifle – Air Ministry will be furious but Dame Laura says my helmet is rather like a bonnet effect on the back of my head and the rifle makes a good line – WAAFs are not to carry arms controversy is still waging and this will upset the apple cart. Dame Laura is adamant and firm."

Daphne was itching to carry a gun *officially*, particularly with the Germans poised for invasion on the other side of the English Channel. In a modern war Daphne might well be put into more frontline duties. Instead she found herself being used as a feisty role model for the women of Britain, to garner new recruits. She travelled all over the country, often at very short notice.

> "Apparently everyone hates recruiting, very few officers remain. It is very thankless and the department certainly gets more curses than thanks."

Poor Daphne was soon disillusioned with her new role, as she wrote to a friend:

> "Am longing to smell fresh air and see clear skies. My eyes are glued to papers and innumerable forms, and all electric light. I long for a jersey and slacks and water and unspoilt grass."

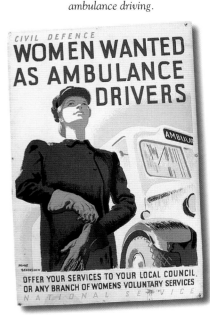

CIVIL DEFENCE
WOMEN WANTED AS AMBULANCE DRIVERS
OFFER YOUR SERVICES TO YOUR LOCAL COUNCIL, OR ANY BRANCH OF WOMENS VOLUNTARY SERVICES
NATIONAL SERVICE

'WAR WEAPONS WEEKS',
*held in towns and cities
throughout the country,
were extraordinarily
successful fundraising
events. Making Hitler look
ridiculous was part of the
propaganda.*

In addition to her public relations and recruitment work, Daphne was sworn into the RAF CID (Criminal Investigation Department) to vet civilian workers for connections with fifth columnists but her skills acquired in her pre-war career as a photographer were ignored.

Risking her life for that of an injured airman had brought her glory, but not job satisfaction. Her role in the propaganda machine did give her a chance to visit her mother and home on the Cornish coast at St Ives, a town filled with refugees and artists.

> "Am to do Cornish recruiting for 8 or 9 days as it is St Ives and Penzance War Weapons Week. I come down by train on the Thursday 24th and look round and confirm arrangements of Friday. On Saturday be present at the opening of the War Weapons [Week] St Ives. In the evening attend a dinner and meeting and Boxing Match at St Ives."

Her public relations itinerary continued at St Just and Helston. This was a prestigious role, and Daphne had a corporal to drive her and another officer to accompany her. Her appearance at War Weapons Week parades was intended to act as a fund-raising boost. In one week Liverpool raised £11,500,000 in voluntary contributions, and even small towns raised enormous sums of money in these regular events.

War Weapons Week at Twickenham on the outskirts of London had a different flavour. It was opened by Miss Chili Boucher on May 17, 1941, featured a parade of bulldogs, a wild west show, fan dancers and white mice, and was kicked off by a football match between Teddington Wanderers and the Free French Forces. Seven days of free entertainment followed, to encourage people to 'Lend Like Helen Be Merry And to Hell With the Jerry'. The *Twickenham and Richmond Times* carried an exhortation from Jimmy Knode:

> "Lend all you can to your country. Remember it is not a bit of good hanging on to your 'cash', it will never win the war in your pocket, or hidden under the bed, or in the cupboard,

MARK IV TANKS PARADE
*the streets of Alton,
Hampshire, during
War Weapons Week.
A Spitfire was the first
Alton and District purchase
and by the end of the war,
the area had funded five
Lancaster bombers.*

the old iron pot, under the floor boards, behind the old man's picture on the wall. Some people are even crazy enough to string the money round their necks so that when 'Mr Hitler' calls to collect, he gets the lot. Now be sensible folks, take a bookmaker's tip and be on a sure winner. Lend all you can during the *War Weapons Week* for the sake of dear old Twickenham. Make up your mind today and get ready to part with your hidden treasure before old Nasty knocks the lid off the tin."

It obviously worked, as Twickenham raised £593,344 that year. The activities of one Twickenham secondary school gives a snapshot of wartime fundraising. Living on the outskirts of the capital, boys from the Kneller Senior Boys School spent many happy hours picking up 'souvenirs from Jerry'. These pieces of shrapnel and bomb debris were sent to other towns to be put on display, raising money for Spitfire Funds. In his notes for assembly in October 1940, the headmaster recorded other fundraising efforts made by the boys that month.

"Air Raid Exhibition in Hall in aid of Red Cross. Wallis the organiser is worried at lack of support. Please announce the exhibition and the charge ½d.
L Smith of Form 2PB has organised a show in his garden and has given me 4/6½ in aid of the Red Cross. Give him a public word and praise for his initiative.
Ronald Whiting Form 2PA has collected by various means £1.4.6 for Red Cross and £2 for London Air Raid Distress Fund. He has received a personal letter from the Lord Mayor of London, thanking him."

Even family pets were drawn into fund raising for the war effort. Tinker, a Birmingham cat, sold her kittens in exchange for donations to the Red Cross Penny-A-Week Fund.

SHRAPNEL LITTERED
London's streets during the Blitz and children made a game of seeing who could collect the most. The salvaged metal was then recycled at the local scrap depot.

9. Making the Best of It

"Farewell to theatres, movies, dances, dinner parties and such pleasures; we pass our evenings in dug-outs, trying to read write or talk or play bridge, so far as the rattle of guns, the roar of planes and the crash of bombs will allow."
Phyllis Warner, September 1940

WESTMINSTER COUNCIL *offered a prize for the best dressed London shelter at Christmas 1940. The centrepiece here is a patriotic portrait of the King, Queen and Prime Minister surrounded by the Union Flag.*

In the midst of war, and the inevitable separation of family and friends, there was an added poignancy to parties and celebrations. Families toasted the photographs of dead sons and husbands. At Christmas, Wrens hung out socks for Father Christmas and then took turns to creep round in the dark and fill them. Women wrote to faraway husbands, describing tiny, precious objects gathered to poke into socks for their children. Women on the YMCA tea-car run filled stockings for men spending Christmas Day at anti-aircraft batteries and barrage balloon sites. Couples married in the midst of air raids, babies were christened, and dance halls thronged with swaying couples (this might be their last evening of happiness). Going out could be dangerous: several dance halls and cinemas were bombed. Many civilians felt guilty at the contrast between life on the home front and the life of men in the front line.

Phyllis Warner's gloomy prediction that the war signalled the end of social pleasures had a ring of truth. Cinemas and theatres had closed at the outset of war, though they soon reopened. But she soon found that shelterers, as they scuttled underground at night, made the most of this new opportunity to socialise. Two weeks later she wrote:

"We really have quite good fun in our basement shelter. Last night somebody brought a guitar, and we sang negro spirituals, sea shanties and part-songs until lights out."

By December these shelter singsongs had developed into large social occasions.

"Ten of us went to a singing party tonight to our nearest public shelter. It houses about 250. We sang John Brown's Body, Genevieve, Under the Lilacs, Upidee, Juanita, Drink to me Only,

EVENINGS IN THE SHELTERS *could be long and tedious, so people enlivened them with whatever entertainment they could think of. Here the citizens of Bermondsey, south London, take part in an 'educational debate'.*

Shenandoah, Sweet and Low and the Swanee River with the whole company joining in the easy ones. This shelter has a programme committee and I was interested to see this week's schedule. Monday – Keep Fit Class, Darts. Tuesday – Concert followed by a religious service. Wednesday – Musical Evening – contributions welcomed by members of the shelter. Thursday – religious service. Concert by Father Adams and Father Knight of the Parish Church. Friday – Whist Drive. Saturday – Keep Fit class. Religious Service followed by dancing. The shelter is lucky in having an excellent piano lent 'for the duration' but people think it is safer down there than in their own homes. The shelterers seem to be enjoying their social activities so much that I wondered if they would ever want to go back to their own family life again."

A PARTY COULD DEVELOP out of an otherwise routine evening if someone had a musical instrument. Here, the residents of Ramsgate, Kent, enjoy themselves in an underground tunnel.

Phyllis lived in the Mary Ward Settlement in London, where young intellectuals and idealists, often university students, lived in the slums and did voluntary work there.

"In our settlement shelter, we have devised a programme which provides a different fixture for every night of the week. Chief limitation is the necessity for sleeping in the shelter nearly all the club members who come to the classes. We have physical training on Mondays, choir on Tuesday, play reading and dramatics on Wednesday, organised games on Thursday, debates on Friday and dancing on Saturday – shelter dancing is strenuous because it has to be done on a concrete floor. Play reading and the debates are outstandingly successful, much livelier than they were in pre-Blitz days."

A war-weary population grabbed every opportunity for fun. There were trips to the pantomime, theatre and ballet; and above all there was the cinema, visited several times a week by many diarists. Many of the films were morale-boosting tales of courage and 'derring-do'. Dr JP McHutchison, a veteran of World War I, was not a frequent cinemagoer but in 1940 he was at an evening show at The Picture House in Glasgow when the red 'Air Raid Warning' sign flashed up on the screen.

> "The manager was clapped heartily after he made the announcement, and only two persons left (and they may have been ARP workers.) In my desire to get back to Airdrie, I left in ¼ hour and was only the fourth person to leave. Such courage on the part of the large audience in such a vulnerable building, made one proud and confident of our ability to stand up to Nazi terrorism. Folks too on the street were quite nonchalant as I made my way (the warning still on) to the bus stand, and the all-clear went after 20 minutes, just as my bus was leaving the station."

Going out held its own dangers, particularly in the blackout, as pedestrians picked their way past bomb craters and sandbags. Ernie and May Britton lived in the London suburbs.

> "We used to go to the pictures on Saturdays but now May is working and gets so tired we don't go as she very much needs tea and generally we prefer not to be out o' nights. Getting home in the blackout is a bit of a burden and it takes the gilt off."

Double summer time had been introduced to benefit farmers, but it also benefited theatre-goers like Phyllis Warner.

THE SHOW MUST GO ON:
Peter Glenville and Patricia Tucker in the 1940 production of Shakespeare's All's Well That Ends Well.

NOEL COWARD'S NEW PLAY Blithe Spirit, *a frothy comedy on the improbable subject of a man haunted by the ghost of his first wife, starred Margaret Rutherford as the eccentric medium Madame Arcati: it was just the sort of escapism wartime audiences wanted.*

"The theatres are all packed out because everybody is having an orgy of play-going whilst the black out still permits. There aren't many shows to choose from, but just because there are so few, the casts are all-star and the acting super. This is particularly true of *Blithe Spirit*, Noel Coward's airy trifle of wild improbability which Margaret Rutherford, Cecil Parker, Fay Compton and Kay Hammond make appear positively credible. How like Noel Coward to concoct even now a comedy that is completely original and adroitly fitted to the times. I went to a matinee on a stuffy Turkish-Bath day of pouring rain, with an incipient headache and a sullen temper, and in no time was laughing delightedly at its utter nonsense."

Going for an evening out in the provinces was an even better experience, a rare indulgence for Phyllis in January 1942.

"Came down to Oxford to spend a weekend with Maisie. GR took me to dinner at the Mitre, and to the theatre to see *Hedda Gabler*. I hadn't been to an evening theatre for six months so it was quite an occasion. Strangest sensation was walking home afterwards through streets thronged with people. In London after dark you only see wardens and policemen, and an occasional belated pedestrian tearing home. Sitting indoors you only hear footsteps at long intervals – the slow tread of the police or the hurried patter of an occasional passer-by – in Oxford you hear footsteps all the time, leisurely, carefree ones at that."

Mollie Dineen went to a New Year's Eve Dance to see in the year 1942, while she was looking after evacuees in a tiny Welsh village. The number of male partners was boosted by men from the nearby RAF camp.

THE WINDMILL THEATRE, *with its notorious nude tableaux, defied many of the Lord Chamberlain's decrees and after the war was able to boast, 'We never closed.'*

"The floor was frightfully crowded, but who cares anyway. It was my first dance for over two years, and I was very nervous at first, but the boys were good and I danced with John, Bill, Harold and Ted and enjoyed every moment. Soon it is 12pm as the clock strikes, the band played the National Anthem and not a sound is heard; hundreds of men and women, many in uniform stand stiffly to attention, ready to stand and defend their land as the New Year dawns. Then cheers and kisses all round."

Pamela Higgins, a widow living in Cheshire, had cut down on her entertaining because of the war. But she wrote to her son Stephen:

ENTERTAINING THE TROOPS

While those at home made the best of their leisure with singsongs in the underground shelters and evenings out in the local dance hall, professional entertainers toured the world in an effort to boost the morale of troops on active service. They also performed for those engaged in war work at home, such as munitions workers and hospital staff.

ENSA (Entertainments National Service Association) was the brainchild of theatrical impresario Basil Dean and was operated by the NAAFI, which also operated canteens for servicepeople. It had to cover a vast area of the globe and work in difficult conditions, so not all the shows were of a very high standard. The association was quickly nicknamed 'Every Night Something Atrocious' (or 'Awful'). But for up and coming performers such as Tommy Cooper and Frankie Howerd, ENSA provided steady work and a respectable salary of ten pounds a week.

Some of the top names of the day, including singers Vera Lynn and Gracie Fields, top comedians Tommy Trinder and Arthur Askey, and a theatre company from the Old Vic that included Sybil Thorndike and Laurence Olivier, travelled in uncomfortable and sometimes dangerous circumstances in order to do their bit for the war effort.

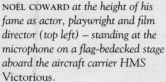

NOËL COWARD *at the height of his fame as actor, playwright and film director (top left) – standing at the microphone on a flag-bedecked stage aboard the aircraft carrier HMS Victorious.*

ENSA CONCERT IN NORMANDY, *1944 (top right). ENSA gave two shows at each location, sometimes in a barn, sometimes out in the open. The set and props would be packed up and moved on to the next site.*

A TYPICAL ENSA 'THEATRE': *singer Ruth Howard entertains RAF personnel from the back of a lorry (middle right) in an olive grove in Italy, during a visit from the popular bandleader Geraldo. The first ENSA concert was given at a camp in Surrey just a week after war broke out; the last in India, in August 1946. In the intervening seven years, ENSA gave an estimated two and a half million performances to an audience of 500 million.*

GEORGE FORMBY PLAYS HIS UKULELE *for troops in the ruins of a Normandy village (bottom right), only a few hours after the D-Day landings in June 1944.*

FILM ACTRESS PHYLLIS STANLEY *performs for navy personnel on the packed deck of HMS Nelson (left). Several of the sailors have perched on the barrel of a 16-inch gun to give themselves a better view of the stage.*

"Next Sunday I am having about 12 to 15 people to tea and the following Friday the 12th I am having a dinner party. Last week I felt so depressed I thought 'come, this will not do at all', so I telephoned to various friends that live near to ask them to come and to put on their prettiest frocks. I don't think the men will change. Everyone was delighted and thought it a marvellous idea. The meal will have to be very simple, soup, cold tongue and chicken and sweets."

In 1941 an anonymous diarist went to the President's Dinner, United Kingdom Commercial Travellers Association (Grimsby branch). His fare was luxurious.

"For dinner we had hors d'oeuvres, oxtail soup, roast chicken, brussels sprouts, roast and mashed potatoes, trifle, fruit tart, cheese and biscuits, celery and coffee. There was also a bar. Not so bad after two years and four months of war!"

At times the contrast between life on the Home Front and life on the front line gave civilians a guilty conscience. But places of entertainment were not immune from the trappings of war. Phyllis Warner had a memorable night out at the Savoy Hotel in London

"Tonight I had a delirious return to peacetime living – I put on formal clothes and went to the Savoy, where gaiety survives even in an air-raid. At 9pm we were driving in pitchy darkness through completely empty streets – with the guns thudding overhead and shrapnel pattering down on the sidewalks. I wasn't too happy about it, having seen a few cars with large shrapnel holes in their roofs, and was glad to find myself in the hotel Air Raid Shelter, where guests dine dance and sleep. The Savoy doesn't pretend that there isn't a war on. It

A BIT OF LUXURY, *1944 style: a buffet in the dance hall at the Royal Opera House, Covent Garden.*

YOUNG LONDONERS, *and servicemen and women on leave, flocked to dance halls for an evening out. Forces clubs, such as the Merchant Navy Club (above left) were a popular way to enjoy leave or time off duty. The Lyceum Ballroom (above right) had been closed as a theatre in 1939 because of a plan to demolish it to improve traffic access to Waterloo Bridge. This plan never materialised and it remained one of London's most popular dance and jazz venues for many years after the war.*

makes no attempt to disguise the forest of girders which support the ceiling, nor the piles of sandbags that prop up the walls – beyond painting them red, white and blue that is. The Air Raid shelter used to be the Lincoln Room, and although Lincoln's statue has disappeared behind the boarding of the windows, the Stars and Stripes still decorate the walls. There were about three hundred people dining and dancing including Lord Beaverbrook, Minister of Aircraft Production, and Mr Herbert Morrison celebrating his new appointment as Home Secretary. An elaborate six-course meal was good testimony to the adequacy of our food supply, and evidently the bombs on each side of the hotel had had no effect on its cellars. As we danced to Carroll Gibbons Band the guns added unrehearsed effects, so that we had 'a nightingale – *bang* – sang in – *thud* – Berkeley Square – *crash*' and 'Franklin D – *woof* – Roosevelt Jones – *smash*.' Nobody appeared to mind...As the perils of the streets and the absence of taxis make it impossible to go home till daylight, the hotel provides its dinner guests with mattresses and pillows in the safety of the basement. It is an experience to sleep in evening dress on the floor of the Savoy! Hundreds of guests slumber side by side in this de luxe shelter. Its spacious first-aid room contained only three casualties, victims of the rain of shrapnel...As we drove through the streets in the drizzly dawn, people were emerging from shelters to be greeted by the coffee-stalls and mobile canteens that are now so quickly on the streets at the All Clear."

While nightlife in the capital may have been dim but undaunted, things were somewhat different up in Shapinsay in the Orkney Islands. Teenager Bessie Skea was disgusted that the adults had seen fit to stop all forms of entertainment when war broke out.

"There won't be any more fine times until this war is over. Shapinsay is too bad; they've stopped everything; dances, concerts, ploughing match, shows; practically everything that can be stopped. Of course we have a great many Terriers [Territorial Army] away, thirty five I think, and the older people believe it isn't right to have anything enjoyable – but what on earth is to hinder us having Red Cross concerts in aid of the troops? All the youngsters are complaining and longing for a dance – myself included – and I do think it's too bad. They won't even have a Farmer's Union Social! There is the SWRI, Women's Guild and Bible Class of course, but nothing else except knitting socks! The rest of Orkney is not cutting out anything – but it's no good grumbling."

Munitions worker Louie White recorded few parties in her diary. Her main forms of entertainment were trips to the cinema, but in January 1944 she went to a dance thrown by her firm, the Blackburn Aircraft Company, where she was currently working the night shift.

> "Got up at 4pm and ironed my burgundy dress. After tea I got changed and went to Blackburns dance. Met Vivien who had brought a Polish soldier called Casmere. She introduced us and we all kept together. We went to work but I was too tired to do anything at all."

Social occasions were enlivened by the presence of glamorous foreigners. Dance halls were crowded with young men and women, often in uniform, far from home, clutching at an evening of escapism. Christmas rarely offered such escapism, bringing as it did thoughts of those far from home. Three months after the start of the London Blitz, the nation celebrated Christmas – rather quietly in the case of Phyllis Warner's family.

> "There was little present-giving except to the children, and little card-sending on account of the paper shortage. Everyone so faithfully obeyed the instruction to post early that in thousands of households the postman didn't call at all on Christmas Day.
>   We entertained ourselves by showing the films we made in the days of peace, and a nostalgic display it was. Gendarmes in the Champs Elysées, the roofs of Moscow, Ascot Races, Henley Regatta, New York Harbour and the shining decks of the Empress of Britain – sights that seem to speak of some far off idyll. But no doubt when peace returns we shall look back half nostalgic for the excitements and endurances of the war."

A year later Christmas celebrations had become even more frugal. Like many others she spent Christmas day in the office.

> "This is a most un-Christmassy Christmas, Christmas cards are pretty well in abeyance because of scarcity of paper, and presents are very nearly out too because of the necessity to cut consumption. I've sent no cards at all and only three useful gift tokens. It will be a Christmas without chocolates, or fruit or nuts, and short of drinks and cigarettes; there are

no Christmas decorations, the stores look much as usual, and I haven't heard a single carol. Most un-Christmassy of all are the fantastic prices being charged for ordinary goods, holly at 6d a twig is typical of this racket...I'm going to stay in London and work at the office as usual on Christmas day, a dreary prospect. But I'm in no spirit for Christmas cheer while P is in danger in Malaya."

Newspaper and radio warnings urged the population not to travel at holiday time, as trains were already crowded with troops coming home on leave and parents of evacuees visiting their children. Long queues formed for tickets. Christmas trees, when they could be found, were decorated with coloured buttons and earrings. Ethel Mattison, with no children of her own, managed to find a tree for her sister's children.

"Today I brought home a Christmas Tree and potted it and have put it in the scullery for a surprise...We are collecting things piecemeal, such as quarters of sweets and odd bars of chocolate. Other things seem plentiful enough, I mean decorations, books and toys, but of course there is no fruit at all."

EVEN AT CHRISTMAS *essential war work had to go on. These women have taken a short break to decorate their London factory before returning to their sewing machines.*

Toys were sold at inflated prices and rescue worker Bill Regan scavenged the bombsites of the Isle of Dogs to find presents for his daughters. Old toys and dolls prams were refurbished, and as toys became scarce people made wooden toys and toy animals.

On a visit to see her sister Kit in London in July 1941, physiotherapist Joan Strange from Worthing was astonished to see Londoners still enjoying some of the peacetime pleasures in Hyde Park.

NURSES IN WESTMINSTER
Hospital sing carols to the patients on Christmas Eve.

"In Hyde Park there is a central dump for rubble etc – it's a young mountain with a road over it. I wonder how many houses have helped make it – thousands? Next to the mountain were the bowlers, playing hard! Hundreds were bathing in the Serpentine and allotments abound everywhere! The orators very amusing. Hyde Park is also an anti-aircraft gun centre and ARP shelter centre, horrid. But the grown ups still sail their boats on the round pond."

After the retreat from Dunkirk in 1940, many people gave up their holidays to continue in war work. A year later Ethel Mattison, who worked at the Food Office, dealing with ration books, wrote to her sister in America:

accommodated a massive rubble dump, an ARP shelter and an anti-aircraft gun centre, but there was still plenty of space to stroll around on a fine spring day.

"It has become official that we are to have only one week's holiday this year. I think this is plum crazy and very short sighted, especially for people working in conditions that prevail in our office – no natural light and a very inadequate 'conditioned air' system. I think it likely that most people will find it necessary to take a week off sick. However to make the most of the summer Eileen and I have decided to have weekends on the river such as we had last year. It won't be the same without the men of course, but it should do us good physically. It's a cheap way of spending a weekend and very restful and peaceful."

Holidaymakers found accommodation difficult to get, as boarding houses and hotels were full of troops and evacuees. Phyllis Warner stayed with friends when she spent a week in Devon.

THE SERPENTINE,
in London's Hyde Park was a popular place to swim in the summer – but gasmasks still had to be near at hand.

"The holiday has been heaven. Nothing much to it, a few bathes, some dancing, some tennis, some walking, a lot of lazy sitting in adorable little country pubs, bending the elbow and chatting idly, and occasionally laughing uproariously. I wonder if I ought to have enjoyed it so much in a world in which thousands are dying in man-made agony, millions losing their most cherished hopes and treasures, a world in which it is the best and most splendid who are falling in combat daily. This is the same guilty feeling I used to have in the year before the raids when the agony was elsewhere. A winter of London blitz removed that trouble – I snatched at such pleasures as came my way without a pang. But now that life is placid here, I'm beginning to worry again."

SPECIAL AGRICULTURAL CAMPS *were set up to enable young city workers to help out on farms during their summer holidays – and yet another government recruitment campaign encouraged people to join in.*

Men in the Forces were sometimes given leave at short notice. Munitions worker Louie White spent a romantic week at the Yorkshire seaside resort of Scarborough in June 1943, when her husband Jack was given a week's leave from the RAF. They had been married a little over two years.

"In the morning went in a canoe on the lake. It was grand better than rowing. Saw a bomber on the North Beach, one of ours that had come down during the night. It broke up later in the day. Saw another convoy complete with barrage balloons. Heard gunfire out at sea. Went in the pool after dinner, then in a canoe again after tea. Spent our last night on Castle Hill. The two bays were beautiful, and the sea was like silver."

Heard gunfire out at sea. Went in the pool after dinner, then in a canoe again after tea.

A few days after that week of sparkling sea and sand, Jack was shot down and listed as missing, presumed dead.

Apart from the restrictions of travel and accommodation, holiday preparations in themselves were far from simple, as Joan Strange recorded in August 1942.

"It was a great effort getting ready for a wartime holiday – in addition to the usual arrangements to be made about patients etc I had to fix up a deputy at the Report Centre, two canteens and fire watchers. Then we had to tell the Warden we should be away and tell him our key was at Mr Tyrers. We turned off water, gas and electricity and only half drew the curtains to enable ARP wardens to look inside in case of incendiary bomb trouble. I got 'emergency' food cards for two weeks and arranged for our paper (*Daily Telegraph*) to be delivered at the Shepherds. If you cancel its delivery altogether it's impossible to get it again on our return."

Joan and her sister Kit were among the thousands who responded to a government campaign to take a working holiday on a farm. They cycled 60 miles to an agricultural camp.

"We arrived soon after 7 o'clock and discovered it is a real camp of tents. I'd hoped it might be in a building. We'd been told to bring plates, cutlery and a tea cloth, and we had an evening meal straight away. We were given a ground sheet and blankets and a straw mattress! The camp is in a lovely situation there are between 250–300 people. To bed early and slept fairly well.

Aug 24: Up at 6am and queued for breakfast at 7am. Then queued again for work. There seems some difficulty about work. The farmers send in lorries for so many people but usually there are more people than the farmers need. We were not lucky so took our bicycles and rode to Harpenden. It was a lovely day.

Aug 25: Eleven of us went by lorry (with about 30 others – terrific pack) to Stranghams farm where we were met by a very nice foreman. We were shown how to stook wheat and we worked well all day. We had a meal at midday provided by the camp – bread and margarine, meat (dehydrated) pies and tea made at a neighbouring cottage. We all earned 5s10d and arrived back in the lorry at about 7:30. Most of the people are from London or the north and there are a few foreigners. Something is organised in the camp most evenings but Kit and I go to our hard and boney beds early."

The holiday was not an unmitigated success for these two middle-class ladies. Pouring rain turned the camp into a quagmire and so, as there seemed little work to do, they cycled up to London to stay with friends.

FERNANDO THE BULL
greets a land girl making her rounds at the County Farm Institute in Sparsholt, Winchester.

NO-ONE WAS TOO YOUNG *to do their bit — schoolchildren were also recruited to holiday work on the farms.*

For newly widowed munitions worker Louie White, working on a farm far from her factory job in Leeds was an adventure and a delight. Her diary entries, which had become brief and monotonous after her husband had been shot down, suddenly sparked to life. He had been missing 54 weeks by July 1944, when she and a friend, Peg, travelled by train to Crayke Castle in north Yorkshire.

"A lorry came to meet us, and what a laugh we had bundled together. The castle where we are spending a farming holiday at Crayke is lovely. Built on top of a hill with the village just below, it looks like a grim fortress, but looks much bigger and milder when you ride up the drive to the door. The window is a real castle one with bars and a very wide window sill."

Although she was staying in a fairytale castle, Louie shared a room with eight others. They worked hard and played hard.

> Went to a dance and rode back in the lorries under a lovely harvest moon. The sky was full of planes lit up.

"Went to Sparrows Field and weeded carrots, not bad at all. Finished at 5 came home in a lorry. At night went to a dance in Easingwold. Had a marvellous time.
    July 6: Weeding again.
    July 7: Last day at weeding. Went to a dance and rode back in the lorries under a lovely harvest moon. The sky was full of planes lit up."

School children were also asked to go and work on farms in their holidays, all as part of the nation's drive for more food. The basic raw materials for celebrations were scarce, as Phyllis Warner described in her diary in April 1941.

"Went to Aunt Jennie's Golden wedding. There were many apologies for a meagre feast, but probably it compared favourably with 1891, when tomatoes and grapefruit and canned goods and other things we now lament were still unknown. But 1891 had its advantages, at least they had a chance to get married in peace, and not the way their youngest daughter did last autumn, having to keep dashing into the church crypt during the ceremony, and into the coal cellar during the reception."

The romance of a couple's wedding day was heightened by the uncertainties of war. Peg Cotton's daughter Alix had a fairytale wedding when she was married to a naval flyer, Peter Dean, in October 1939.

"The service was to be at four-thirty. Firstly, because English law prohibited such after six pm and secondly, because the blackout must be considered. In spite of the war, the 100-odd gas masks accompanying the guests, and Pete's orders to report back to his Naval Air Base on the very next day, nothing could detract from Alix's loveliness as she came down the aisle of that old English church on her father's arm in her pale blue costume, her Grandmother Cotton's tiny ermine hat and muff, and a corsage of pale pink roses and lilies-of-the-valley. Awaiting her stood Pete and his Best man, Rob D'Almaine, Lieutenant on a submarine, resplendent in their Naval uniforms. They seemed young heroes of a new Crusade."

A PACK OF BOY SCOUTS *set up the drinking water for their fruit-picking camp on a farm near Cambridge. The boys worked to a rota, taking it in turns to pick the fruit or to stay in camp and do the chores.*

The new Mrs Dean soon discovered she was pregnant but Pete Dean was never to meet his daughter: he was killed test-flying a new plane. On doctor's orders Peg Cotton had to keep the news from her daughter until the baby was born a few weeks later. Penelope Marianne Dean was christened on September 11, 1940. The Blitz had just begun its nightly tune as Peg Cotton wrote her diary that evening:

"I am writing, with the tea trolley as desk, in the lower hall. The rest of the gang are asleep – apparently. There has been, and still is, an almost continuous roar of guns. The flat shivers and trembles with the impact of solid sound upon its walls. The top of the trolley vibrates beneath my arms. Well, it seems that, indeed, one can get used to anything! Besides, what else can one do save carry-on? Penny was to be christened this afternoon at 4:20, but at that hour the Jerrys and the RAF staged a dog-fight right over Regency Lodge. Shrapnel fell in the courtyard. Endeavouring to do as everyone else does – carry on as normally as possible – I continued to arrange the flowers, and chatted with the family and Dorothy and Tony, who had joined us about four o'clock, just before the Siren went. Well, the 'All Clear' finally went, shortly before 5 o'clock. So Dick drove us around to the church – St Paul's Church, Avenue Road, a block from our flat, the same little church in which Alix and dear Pete were married almost a year ago, on October 7, 1939.

"We were all grouped about the baptismal font, and Mr Malet, the Vicar, had just given baby her name, 'Penelope Marianne' and had baptised her for the third time, 'And of the Holy Ghost,' when the Sirens went, and the Devil was upon us again. 'Shall I proceed?' asked Mr Malet, 'Or do you care to go down to the shelter?' We elected to finish the ceremony. Then rushed Penny home in the car – the men following on foot, keeping under the trees as the AA guns were in action. Alas, none of the Godparents could attend the Christening, and only one friend, Hartley Davies, appeared – because of the darned raids. However, we (the family) and Dorothy, Tony, Hartley and Mr Malet assembled here afterwards in the flat, and drank dear little Penny's health in sherry and had a piece of Martha's fine fruit cake, iced, and decorated with pink and white ribbons. Elsie and Frank almost got to the Christening. But the 4 o'clock raid drove them into a roadside shelter, and the AA fire kept them under cover until too late. A shame!"

A 1940 WEDDING *goes ahead as planned, despite the fact that the church has been destroyed during the Blitz.*

DESPITE THE DEVASTATION *the well-to-do could still get married in St George's, Hanover Square (right).*

Phyllis Warner went to a wedding in Cambridge in November 1940 and expressed the pleasure of leaving the Blitz behind and going to

". . . simple functions at which one has friends rarely seen in wartime. This was a cheerful informal gathering and most of us seized the chance to stay overnight and sleep in a real bed. On a clear autumn morning the lovely pinnacles and towers of Cambridge looked more gracious and heart-lifting than ever. I got a lift back to London by automobile – a rare treat nowadays – we enjoyed the ride like ten year olds."

BECAUSE OF RATIONING, *wedding cakes had to be less decadent. There were ingenious ways of solving the problem however – the shop assistant (far left) explains to a bride-to-be that the icing effect is achieved with painted cardboard and rice paper and lifts off to reveal the real cake below.*

10. Friends and Enemies

"We were allowed one large case and one piece of hand luggage. It was all so exciting, I was going to England, though I had not the foggiest notion what to expect, or even where exactly in England I was going, and didn't care. Mother cried. She was not a crying sort of person, I just couldn't understand it." Klaus Ulrich, June 1939

Refugees from the Nazi regime had been arriving in Britain long before war was declared on September 3, 1939. Those with friends in Germany and Austria were well aware of Hitler's hostility to the Jews, but appeasement of Herr Hitler was the watchword of the 1930s and the British government was not keen to offer asylum to persecuted men and women. With hindsight, the facts of the final solution are now known and the persecution that preceded it. But concentration camps existed even before the outbreak of war – a fact that was also known by some Britons. Isabelle Granger, a schoolmistress, spent her holidays travelling on the Continent. She was passionate about the alpine meadows scattered with wild flowers, and equally passionately concerned about her many friends scattered through the countries that Hitler was eyeing greedily.

"The young Scheus, thank God, have got a job. Their baby is alas, with Herta's mother in Vienna, under police supervision, so all my good plans for fetching her are useless – her disappearance would coincide with Mrs Puegger's loss of pension, and her son's going to a concentration camp. The rest of my friends are trickling out or shooting themselves. Three months of ceaseless correspondence have resulted in three Jewish friends of mine getting jobs – one here, one in France, one in the United States and that's been my sole contribution to 'civilisation'. One of my best friends, a pacifist from the Wachau, disappeared, I got news last week from a servant of his to say he was proud to say he'd denounced the 'infamous traitor'."

By the summer of 1939 her letters to a friend in British Columbia had become angry and bitter at the bureaucracy she was dealing with in her attempts to help refugees.

JEWISH REFUGEE CHILDREN *arriving in England from Vienna, c.1938. Well before war broke out, Jews across Europe realised that living under Hitler's regime was becoming dangerous.*

"We are conditioned by bolts from the blue, sudden phone calls, appeals that must be answered at once, an important feeling that if I don't act at once by ringing up a committee in London, or wiring a committee in Vienna, or standing in a queue in order personally to hand in some poor wretch's papers, then something will go badly wrong for someone, and that it will be my fault. It's like existing in a lunatic asylum, my head is crammed with shibboleths and rules."

Many with close friends and contacts in continental Europe had recognised the dangers of Hitler and his National Socialists long before war was declared. On September 3 millions of Britons listened to Chamberlain's historic announcement that 'this country is at war'. Isabelle Granger felt a sense of relief.

"That day for me has no war significance, quite on the contrary it signified a personal cessation of hostilities and a relegation of the struggle to other people – a calm and comforting conception."

Isabelle had already given a home to a German friend, Elisabeth Gruber, known as Lillibet, who with the advent of war was classified as an enemy alien. In May 1940, as Britain's continental neighbours were falling under Nazi rule, Isabelle wrote to British Columbia again.

MARTHA ULRICH *and her son Klaus had this portrait taken at the beginning of 1939, hoping it would appeal to an American sponsor and allow them to escape from Germany. Klaus brought the photograph with him to Britain. Martha was to die in a concentration camp.*

"If you get this, and if you hear we're blown to atoms here, would you please do something for me: get in touch and make sure my executors give my remnants of fortune and life insurance to Lillibet. I feel as her nationality is still enemy she'll need a good deal of bolstering up, and she knows all my interests and what to do with all the people I've guaranteed lately."

Miss Granger was one of those sympathisers in England prepared to act as guarantor to refugees, by giving their names and bank account details to the government. In Germany, Martha Ulrich had a portrait taken of her and her son Klaus, which she hoped would appeal to an American sponsor. An aunt and her family had escaped to America in 1938, but in June 1939 Klaus was found a place on the kindertransport. In later years he told his story.

"We were allowed one large case and one piece of hand luggage. It was all so exciting, I was going to England, though I had not the foggiest notion what to expect, or even where exactly in England I was going, and didn't care. Mother cried. She was not a crying sort of person, I just couldn't understand it."

This was not a trainload of excited modern children rushing from carriage to carriage making new friends.

"We were cowed, you have to remember what we had been used to."

On the journey through Holland, Dutch friends met the train with a bag of food for the hungry 12-year-old. But when he arrived at Liverpool Street station the reception was very different.

"We were taken to a nearby gymnasium and sat on benches round the wall. Strange people came, looking not at us, but at the labels round our necks."

OVER 500 YOUNG REFUGEES *arrived at Harwich on the steamer* The Prague *on December 12, 1938, and were taken by special train to a holiday camp in the nearby seaside town of Lowestoft. Most were Jewish; the rest were 'non-Aryans' of one sort or another, or the children of anti-Nazis. For many it was a baffling and distressing time.*

Despite his limited English, on arrival in Britain Klaus Ulrich began to write his diary in his new adopted language. The scruffy pencil entries were very different from the neat Gothic script he had employed in Germany. He had been taken in by an Oxford don, Mr Moore, and his wife.

"Two or three years earlier I had been given a notebook, a rather elegant affair with a cloth binding and plain blank pages. There are entries for two 1938 periods in, for a ten-year-old pretty good German writing. Then there is a gap until that Autumn of 1939, when I noted that I asked Mrs Moore to teach me to darn my socks, because I needed to be able to look after myself. The handwriting had changed from that of a neat well-ordered German ten-year-old's to that of a rather disturbed English child – tangible evidence of an inner turmoil."

Like Klaus Ulrich, many refugees were taken in by complete strangers. On April 21, 1939, in the genteel seaside resort of Worthing, Joan Strange welcomed a family of Jewish refugees from Vienna: Mr and Mrs Beermann and their children Henry and two-year-old Elizabeth.

"The Beermanns are impressed with English ways, for instance that we do not lock our front doors in the daytime – that our police are friendly – that they are allowed free entry to cinema etc. For months fear has reigned in their hearts, now – safety and self-confidence."

Easing them into their new life, Joan got Henry a library card, found him a bicycle and within two days he was celebrating St George's Day at St Paul's with hundreds of other scouts. She and her elderly mother put up the Beermanns in their own home, but Joan was preparing for their successors. Although she was an active member of the town's refugee committee, Joan had used her own money to buy a house in Canterbury Road. In December she wrote in her diary:

"There are over 1,000 aliens in West Sussex and as Worthing is the only place with a committee, about 500 in Worthing."

Joan acted as a taxi service, taking her protégés to register at the police station, giving the children days out at the seaside and taking families for drives into the surrounding countryside. After Poland's collapse, she recorded the impact on her new friends.

"September 18: Our refugees are depressed about it but they were cheered up on Saturday morning when Mr Ritter heard a most interesting broadcast from a German woman belonging to a secret anti-Nazi society, urging women to prevent more bloodshed. She hopes to broadcast again next Saturday. The end of her speech was jammed."

MANY OF THE REFUGEES *were educated at 'International Schools', such as this one at Pauntley in Gloucestershire. As well as coping with the stresses of being evacuated from home the children, some of whom were often very young, also had to learn to speak English and adjust to the way of life in another country.*

That anonymous broadcaster was not mentioned again. Mr Ritter, the avid listener, was one of many Jews who escaped and anglicised their names – in his case from Rittesheim. Just as many of these refugees took a decision to speak only English after their escape, this anglicisation of names was common practise. Klaus Ulrich did the same, changing his forename and surname. He spent the summer of 1939 at Eastbourne, taken in by a young couple, until war was declared.

> "That made me into an 'enemy alien'. Though it was some time before that reality took hold, it was significant to me none-the-less. I had been an outcast so long, and during this lovely summer I had started to belong. Now it was back to being an outcast. All the people with whom I came into contact were as pleasant as ever they had been. But it is certain that, just as I felt outcast for being a beastly Jew, now I felt outcast again for being a beastly German."

Foreigners were classified as either friendly aliens or enemy aliens, with accompanying restrictions. The Cotton family in London, being Americans, were friendly aliens and had to conform to a midnight curfew. Joan Strange had both groups among her circle of Worthing refugees.

> "Friendly aliens can go outside the five mile limit from Worthing – not so the Beermans who are 'enemy aliens'! They may leave only with police permission."

In May 1940 Joan began to record the internment of the men and its impact on those living in her 'refugee house' at Canterbury Road.

FOREIGNERS LIVING *in Britain had to register with the authorities. The queues in Golders Green, north London, shown here, were so long that a subsidiary office had to be set up in a local church.*

"May 23, 1940: We had all Canterbury Road to tea and Mrs Schleichter and Peter too – nine of us! The women who've lost husbands are so sad and upset, almost as if they were dead. It's because the men are not allowed to write and Mrs Thorneycroft telephones to me to say the men are being moved to —?"

This secrecy and internment was an understandable precaution in time of war. Isabelle Granger felt the tension as her numerous refugee friends in London were sent to internment camps.

"Every ring at the bell seemed to herald Lillibet's departure. It cluttered up our lives too, as well as making us nervous and apprehensive. I always came home to find babies screaming who had been left to spend the day while their young mothers trudged from the Home Office to Scotland Yard, trying to find out where their husbands had gone to; and old ladies who couldn't afford a phone and whose English was too shaky to warrant their using one so they sought information about sons and husbands – Lillibet has these to cope with all day and to feed and generally prop up. Now, thank God, enough dust has been raised against this disgraceful persecution of our allies, to put at least a temporary stop to the wholesale internment – though I shan't stop interfering till they let out Friedl Scheu, one of the best brains and most honest and lovable of all democratic Austrians."

INTERNMENT OF ENEMY 'aliens' and known Nazi sympathisers began shortly after the outbreak of war, when fears of invasion were at their highest. The original intention was to deport the internees to the British Dominions. However, in July 1940 a German U-boat sank the SS Arandora Star *off the coast of Ireland, killing 800 internees and prisoners of war bound for Canada, which lead to the policy being abandoned. Many 'enemy aliens' spent the rest of the war in internment camps on the Isle of Man.

I had been an outcast so long, and during this lovely summer I had started to belong. Now it was back to being an outcast.

Dr Enoch, a Jewish research chemist, had escaped from Germany in 1939. He had managed to establish himself in business, but as an alien had to appear at the tribunals set up to root out Nazi sympathisers.

"We were interrogated very thoroughly. We were questioned not only about ourselves but about our families, our ancestors, our friends. Those who came out worst were interned immediately. For the others it was only a question of time, as the fear of spies, of 'Fifth columnists' became really grotesque. So I was visited one day, by two officers of Scotland Yard, who demanded to see the attic of our house. I had recently installed a small room into it, and for light a small roof window was put into the roof. Some people had intimated that this roof window had been made with the purpose of giving light signals to the enemy. One of the officers took a chair and looked out of the window. I don't know what he expected to see."

His job at a pharmaceutical laboratory gave the police added 'grounds' for suspicion.

"Three officers came and asked me, what would happen if I would bring some of my typhus bacilli in to the water supply system. Apparently they thought I could do this by pouring them into the sink or flushing them down the toilet."

On June 6, 1940 his turn arrived for internment. Two officers from Scotland Yard came to get him.

"I was allowed to take with me only the most necessary things. I declared that I could not leave the laboratory, which contained dangerous bacteria, without control."

His escort allowed him to contact an assistant to put the laboratory in order, then he was whisked away. Two days later he was taken to the racecourse at Kempton Park, which had been surrounded with barbed wire for its new role as a holding point for internees. None of the men was allowed newspapers or any form of war news. Friends did manage to track him down and send a basket of strawberries and chocolate, but on June 13 the internees were on the move again.

"We were led through an espalier of soldiers with fixed bayonets to a train, which brought us through the night to Liverpool. In the train to Liverpool I experienced the only sign of friendliness from our guards: A young soldier said: 'I am sorry for you boys.'"

Under heavy guard the men arrived at Onchan on the Isle of Man, where enemy aliens aged 16 and over were interned.

A NEW HOUSING ESTATE *in Huyton, Liverpool, was converted into an internment camp. Here, the internees are collecting straw for their own beds.*

"We were accommodated in a big block of boarding houses, which was surrounded by a double fence of wire netting. There were rooms for two to six people who had to sleep mostly in double beds."

Earlier arrivals had purloined furniture, cooking utensils and blankets, leaving the rooms ill equipped for newcomers. Dr Enoch found the food 'very bad and entirely insufficient'.

"Most tormenting was [that] we did not receive news from our families nor of the war. At irregular intervals the camp commander issued some communications, which were hung at two places in the camp, but these were mostly entirely vague. As just at this time the big catastrophes happened in Holland, Belgium and France, a great nervousness developed, which was stirred up intentionally by the Nazi elements in the camp.
Twice a week we were allowed to write letters of 24 lines each. In urgent cases we could also send telegrams. After more time we were also allowed to receive letters, these and those from us took about 12 days. After the postal connection had been established the mood improved considerably."

LONDON POLICE ESCORT *a group of 'alien' women and children to the railway station, from where a special train will take them to an internment camp.*

A GROUP OF HUNGARIAN JEWS *arrive by train at the Auschwitz-Birkenau camp, Poland, June 1944 (top right). On arrival at the camps, male and female prisoners were segregated, so that husbands were separated from wives and mothers from sons.*

VICTIMS OF THE BUCHENWALD *concentration camp, liberated by the Americans in April 1945 (top left). On the middle bunk next to the vertical post is Elie Wiesel, who went on to achieve international fame as a writer and academic, and won the Nobel Prize for Peace.*

PRISONERS WERE FORCED *to abandon everything in their possession before entering the camp. Here (middle left), personal effects litter the snow-covered railway tracks leading to Auschwitz.*

AT THE START OF THE WAR, *Poland had a Jewish population of three million; by the end it had been reduced to 500,000. Here (bottom left), four prisoners look despairingly out of the cramped and crowded railway carriage that is taking them to a concentration camp.*

'THE BADGE OF DISHONOUR': *a Jewish couple in Budapest, Hungary, wear the yellow stars that they have been ordered to display prominently so that they can be easily distinguished from non-Semites (inset right). Many Jews who had lived in mixed communities were deported to Jews-only ghettos and they were forbidden such basic privileges as travelling on public transport or attending public places of entertainment such as cinemas.*

NAZI ANTI-SEMITISM AND THE FINAL SOLUTION

Within two months of Hitler's rise to power in January 1933, the first concentration camps – including the notorious Dachau – opened their gates to those deemed to be enemies of the Nazi regime. This was followed in April 1933 by laws to purge Jews from the civil service, legal profession and theatre. Jewish newspapers were outlawed, and beaches and swimming pools became out of bounds.

Capitalising on middle-class resentment and insecurity in the years of post-war recession, the *Judenboykott* of April 1, 1933 targeted Jewish businesses throughout Germany. An active policy of Aryanisation forced Jewish managers and workers out of their jobs, and Jewish companies were sold cheaply to new Aryan owners.

In 1935 mixed marriages were banned and Jews deprived of the vote. In 1938 passports were stamped with the letter J, while those with non-Jewish names were forced to adopt the name Israel or Sara to single them out.

Jewish organisations and clubs were forced to hand over membership records, and meticulous lists of wealthy Jews were compiled by the police and the Ministry of Finance. In October 1938, 15,000 Polish Jews were deported to concentration camps and on November 10, the day after Kristallnacht, orders were given to arrest as many German Jews as could be given cell-space; the prime targets were the wealthy. The camps of Dachau, Buchenwald, and Sachsenhausen were each ready to receive 10,000 inmates.

A GROUP OF JEWS FROM WARSAW *are herded towards the transport trains. Young and old alike were forced to walk arduous distances in harsh conditions, before being crammed into cattle cars for long and uncomfortable journeys to the camps.*

AN ARMED GUARD LEADS
*a group of Germans to a
commandeered hotel on the
Isle of Man where they will
be interned for the duration
of the war.*

Another internee being sent to Liverpool offered to swap with him, so the two men went to the camp commander.

"He asked me how old I was, I said 36 years (in effect I was nearly 44 years old). Moved by our entreaties he intimated that I should take the place of the other man when his name would be called. We thanked him and I ran back to my house, packed my things in the greatest hurry and arrived at the gate. The roll call was already in full swing. Apparently the name, Rosenthal, had been called up already, but it was repeated once more at the end of the list. I called 'here' and passed the gate as the last one."

They were packed on to a ship at the Isle of Man port of Douglas and arrived in Liverpool four hours later. This chance to escape from internment in Britain had given Dr Enoch a sense of relief and optimism – a mood that changed when they were loaded on to the SS *Ettrick*.

"We were led from the upper deck, deeper and deeper, until we had to pass a passage through barbed wire, which was so narrow we could pass it only in single file. This separated the under the water-line holds of the ship from the other parts, which were sealed off hermetically by the barbed wire well. We descended into this airless and lightless inferno. About 1,600 men were pressed into our dungeon. On top of us, but separated by the barbed wire, were 1,000 German prisoners of war. In addition there were very many guards on board the ship. Long rows of tables and benches were in our quarter, furthermore many hammocks, but although these covered the whole available space, they were hardly sufficient for a third of the internees. The others had to sleep on or under the tables. It was impossible to get at night time from one place to another without crawling over rows of sleeping people. We had to eat, smoke and sleep in the same place, and in the same place were the toilet buckets.

In day time we had to queue for hours to reach the wash room, the toilets, the kitchen, the hospital, or a little space of fresh air in the outside board of the ship. Even the air here was contaminated by the many sea-sick persons who could relieve themselves only here outside the common quarters, and that only in day time."

Miss Nora O'Connor was Deputy Commandant of an internment camp for women who had originally been interned on the Isle of Man before moving to the mainland.

"The internees were sent to us for screening by M15, before being released to the United States or other neutral countries, where sponsors awaited them with open arms and open purses. They were mainly German and Austrian Jewesses. They came from all walks of life, intellectual, business, professional, and domestic service. The internee with the really dramatic background was Friedelinde Wagner, who bore a startling resemblance to her illustrious grandfather. Hitler's unbounded admiration for Grandpa's works and for all the ideology which the name Wagner implied, accounted for the presence of Friedelinde amongst us. After some months, and several interviews with MI5 she was released 'without a stain upon her character', to study music with Toscanini in South America, but not before she had caused me agonies of frustration trying to teach her to dance."

Nora had been a bridge hostess for troops on the south coast before she took up the post of Deputy Commandant. She organised fancy dress dances, indoor gymkhanas and bridge drives to entertain the women while they waited to be released. The next intake was 70 internees who were being repatriated to Germany as part of a prisoner exchange.

"I was warned 'They could be dangerous.' It appeared to the Establishment that anyone wishing to be return to 'the Vaterland' was a potential danger. This struck me as rather pessimistic. Many of the women in question had been interned because they happened to be within reach of Regulation 18b [allowing the internment of people suspected of being Nazi sympathisers] at the outbreak of war, possibly travelling in Allied ships or on holiday in Allied countries and naturally wished to return to their homes and families."

THE INTERNMENT CAMP *on the Isle of Man consisted of seaside hotels and houses fenced off behind a barbed wire barricade.*

However. as the 'ragged RAF' was shooting down German planes in the south of England, it is not surprising that there was widespread and palpable unease about 'aliens'. Maureen Bolster was a billeting officer for an engineering works, finding accommodation for workers who were attached to the factory.

"The day before yesterday I billeted a man called Fingerhut. He was a foreigner of sorts taken on in the drawing office. Then yesterday I had a phone call from an irate landlord! Did I know I had landed them with a *German* born in Berlin, only just released from internment on the Isle of Man, and who had to report to the police every few days? Dear oh dear! I had to spend half yesterday afternoon trying to pacify the poor wife – apparently the man went there and said 'My name is Fingerhut – I am a *German*,' and demanded this that and the other – a fire in his room and special food etc. I think the poor little woman thought the invasion had begun!"

Even Joan Strange, who had many friends among the refugee population, was nervous occasionally. Drivers were encouraged to pick up hitchhikers as one way of saving fuel.

"We picked up an Austrian refugee near Godalming – at least we hope he was! Jack said he might have been an escaped prisoner! Anyhow we only took him a couple of miles."

Isabelle Granger, who dedicated so many years to helping refugees from the Nazis, got the sack from the Foreign Office in 1940 because of these humanitarian activities.

"We were visited by a very pleasant CID man who said certain allegations had been made against us, and he named them – I was a Government official living with a German [her refugee friend Elisabeth Gruber]. We had been heard to criticise the Government, though

as he explained, we had every right to do that, but the Alligators [those who had made the allegations] hadn't liked that. We had met casually in a foreign hotel and finally we were passing on information to Germany through America. The detective was kind and stayed to supper where he met Margery and two other English women, and the tough fiancé of one of them and Friedl Scheu – who was horribly overawed at the presence of the police, it recalled raids in Larochegasse. He assured Lillibet and me that he was convinced the allegations had been made by spiteful people, and that there was no word of truth in them – he inferred that as such specific lies had been told, the Alligators were well known to us, and led us to believe that they might have been found on the staff [of her former school]. This doesn't altogether surprise us, as we knew one or two had strongly resented our being right about Hitler – you cannot imagine how big a crime it is to have known all along that he was a menace. He said we ought to hear no more about it. He came to tea a week later, and played with two Viennese children who were with us, and swopped stories of thief catching, for the children's Hitler atrocities, which they related freely."

You cannot imagine how big a crime it is to have known all along that Hitler was a menace.

The kindly sergeant's report led to no further action from Scotland Yard.

The French were regarded as 'friendly aliens'. But just how friendly were they? Nora O'Connor, promoted to Commandant of an Internment Camp, helped to answer this question.

"The Friendly Aliens were men and women, many in underground movements, who had escaped from their occupied countries, enduring much hardship en route, and sought refuge in Britain. A number of them tried to impress us with, 'I am a personal friend of General de Gaulle.' The Croix de Guerre was prominently displayed on their bosoms, but MI5 required credentials more convincing than this pectoral show of patriotism before letting them loose."

THE INTERNMENT VICTIMS
were not only German: this group includes Japanese, Finnish and Romanian 'aliens'.

Many aliens were 'adopted' by Britain. The chemist Dr Enoch returned from enforced exile in Canada in February 1941. His research led to the production of a tetanus anti-toxin and a vivicillin for swine fever which he tested on himself, his success hitting the headlines in April 1944. Klaus Ulrich became an engineering apprentice and a British citizen and went into the British aircraft industry. He never saw his mother again: she died in a concentration camp.

Prisoners of war were also pressed into war service in Britain. In the Orkney Islands, Italian POWs built a tiny chapel, complete with Italianate frescos and a concrete statue of St George. All over the country prisoners of war were building sea defences and working on farms and in forestry.

Mariele Kuhn, whose husband was half-Jewish, was asked to act as an interpreter at the Head Injury Hospital at St Hugh's College, Oxford. Many of the German conscripts she met had been wounded in the Allied advance after D-Day in 1944. On September 28 she met Johann Mosig from Silesia. He had been captured in France and flown to England after a few days in a field hospital. The 18-year-old had been wounded in the back and his spine was broken in two places. She recorded her visits to the damaged man in her diary.

"I was rung by the hospital to come over and do some interpreting while the neurologist examined Mosig more closely. I was to find out exactly how he was hurt – it seems he was running, when he felt a big blow in the back, tumbled forward and could not get up again. He has no pains in his legs now, is just completely 'dead' from his chest downwards.

October 3: Found Mosig, called Fritzly by the nurses, on his tummy, his face buried in his arms, his back had become so very sore from lying on it. The nurses are really sweet to him, anxious to see him happy and make him comfortable. Why wasn't he happy they asked me? Well, I thought being a physical wreck at the age of 18, a prisoner of war, in a foreign country, were quite good enough reasons for not being radiantly happy!"

After a few days 'little Mosig', as Mariele called him, started to chat.

"Showing me stacks of photos from home, father, step-mother, brothers, sisters, half-sisters, goats, kids, and chickens! He read the two books I took to him as well as the magazines.

Told him that some of the books we'd collected for German POWs, were given by Jewish emigrants. When I tell him anything like that he just shuts his eyes and can't look at me. It does not fit in with all the things he has been told all his life."

Mariele Kuhn's humanity towards these German POWs is extraordinary, bearing in mind that she and her half-Jewish husband had been forced to flee Germany. She took sweets and souvenir postcards of English cities; she knitted scarves, and wrote letters home for those who were paralysed or blind. When patients died, she wrote letters of condolence to their families and even took photographs of their graves to send as a memento. Mariele had volunteered to interpret for the wounded POWs, but was soon employed by the British Red Cross as an official visitor. This official status, and the Red Cross armband, made her feel more at ease, particularly when she was abused by Allied prisoners who were in the same hospital.

Extraordinary friendships were forged across the divide of war. Evidence of this is provided by a small collection of letters in broken English addressed to Percy Patten in Brighton. Evidence of his kindness comes from a former POW writing from his home town of Hanover in December 1946.

THE ITALIAN CHAPEL *on Lamb Holm, Orkney, was built by imprisoned Italian soldiers under the guidance of the craftsman Domenico Chiocchetti, who also painted the ornate interior and the altarpiece. The chapel is constructed from two Nissen huts joined end to end and from other materials found near at hand.*

"I am really glad to be a free man again. On this place I will have to thank you for all the kindness you have done to us. What this means for a prisoner of war I can't tell, and you have taught us that we are human beings. Through you I have got such a good impression from the English people I thought I will never get. You will never be forgotten by me and always remain an example for me."

11. Our American Cousins

"These youngsters heard something of the plight of their less fortunate British cousins and wanted to do something to help. They pledged themselves to save a cent a meal a day toward that end. The idea was quickly adopted in the city's schools and Sunday schools and funds sufficient to endow a Sunshine bed in perpetuity was the result."
Constance Logan Wright, November 1942

Five months before the USA entered World War II, a prominent American couple attended Independence Day celebrations in a small Cornish town. America had fought with the Allies for the last few months of World War I. The transatlantic relationship was long and complex, tangled in the web of history. Britain's wartime Prime Minister, Winston Churchill, was born to an American mother; Lady Astor, the first woman to take her seat as an MP in the House of Commons, was an American; and many American heiresses had married into the British aristocracy in the late 19th and early 20th centuries. But to the bulk of the British population, America meant one thing: the movies. By the end of World War II, American GIs were the stars of their own movie, carrying off the hearts of 70,000 British GI brides.

Before GIs crossed the Atlantic to join the war, the 'Bundles for Britain' scheme brought clothes, blankets and hospital supplies from well-wishers in America. Britain's first year of the war was fought mainly at sea, and it was the plight of men serving in North Atlantic waters that stirred US sympathies, as Mrs Bingham, wife of the former American Ambassador to London, recorded.

"Newspapers carried vivid and stirring descriptions of the hardships and constant peril endured by these men [on trawlers and minesweepers in the North Sea and Atlantic], and survivors of torpedoed vessels began to straggle into our ports after harrowing experiences and miraculous rescues at sea, in pitiful condition and in increasing numbers. So Bundles for Britain was started. By February 1, 1940 the first shipment of 1,000 sweaters, 1,000 helmets, 300 pairs of mittens and 1,000 scarves was on its way to Britain. The first of 234 shipments."

Torpedo victims even found bundles waiting for them in such out-of-the-way places as Ponta Delgada in the Azores. An American-built British minesweeper was christened *Miss Bundles* in recognition of this American help. When the Blitz started, Bundles for Britain were sent to help victims of the raids. Constance Logan Wright

TO HELP EKE OUT *the ration allowance, the Women's Voluntary Service (WVS) set up a clothes exchange where families could swap clothes that their children had outgrown.*

'BUNDLES FOR BRITAIN' *contained gifts of clothes, blankets and other necessities from charitable Americans. Less dependent on imported goods, the USA never suffered the shortages that Britain did.*

reported back to the American well-wishers after a trip round recipients in Britain.

"The Lady Mayoress of Portsmouth said that she had been continually handing out 'Bundles' of garments, for after the raids it had been her job to tend to the people who had been bombed out and find clothing for them. She said it was remarkable the difference these gifts had made in the people. When they arrived to see her without any proper clothes, they were dirty and depressed, but when they left clean, and with new things to wear from Bundles their depression vanished. They were bright and cheerful once more and had gained courage to face their troubles. Bombed families had been without any clothes at all, except for what they stood up in, and very often those had been torn to pieces by the blast. With the clothes that Bundles had sent they had been able to clothe 4,000 women."

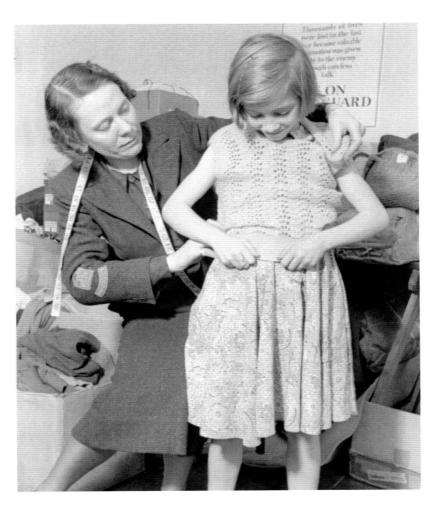

The naval base at Devonport made the city of Plymouth a constant target for German bombers. At the height of the Plymouth blitz, special trains were organised to take civilians from the city into the relative safety of the countryside. Passengers snatched what sleep they could in fields and under hedgerows. Mrs Bingham visited the city in 1942 to see what American aid had achieved and what more was needed.

THE BRITISH WAR RELIEF Society of America organised fund-raising events throughout the war and sent 40 per cent of the proceeds to Britain in the form of charitable donations. This little girl has lost her home – and most of her possessions – in a bombing raid, so the American gift of clothing is greatly appreciated.

"After 57 consecutive nights of bombing during the enemy's savage attack on their city, the people of Plymouth emerged to find Bundles for Britain on hand to help – the first civil relief agency to reach them."

This aid was not just for the civilian population. Anti-aircraft gunners, and many other servicemen and women, were supplied with refreshments at their posts by 105 mobile canteens provided by the Americans. A young British airman wrote to them:

"If only the unseen, unknown, kind hearts who gave us this welcome Bundle for Britain could pay one visit to our aerodrome to see for themselves how much this daily spot of comfort and cheer means to us."

City hospitals had to cope with routine medical care as well as those injured in air raids. Among them was Cardiff Royal Infirmary, one of the hospitals that was sent a mobile surgical unit from America. Constance Logan Wright reported back.

"Cardiff Royal Infirmary's working capacity was reduced by two thirds. When the buildings became practically useless through enemy action, this hospital built up an efficient mobile division. American ambulances rushed to the scene wherever bombs had fallen."

This nation seems inexplicably proud of defects in its national character.

Ambulances, bedding and surgical instruments were sent to 57 London hospitals and 91 provincial ones. But it was the plight of British children, bombed out or orphaned, that prompted extraordinary kindness from their transatlantic cousins. According to a 'Bundles for Britain' leaflet, two very small children from Niagara Falls adopted the Sunshine Home for Blind Children.

> "These youngsters heard something of the plight of their less fortunate British cousins and wanted to do something to help. They pledged themselves to save a cent a meal a day toward that end. The idea was quickly adopted in the city's schools and Sunday schools and funds sufficient to endow a Sunshine bed in perpetuity was the result."

The American town of Barnstaple funded a wartime nursery for orphans in its Devon namesake. Once America had entered the war, some US servicemen 'adopted' war orphans, sponsoring them with gifts of money, and at Christmas in 1943 Santa Claus arrived at orphanages and children's hospitals in a 'four-engined sub-stratosphere bomber' courtesy of the US Air Force. Some Americans and Canadians had joined the British Forces long before America joined the war. Bob Raymond served in the RAF before joining his compatriots in the USAF. He was well placed to observe the tensions between allies.

> "Every Canadian I've met, dislikes the officers of the RAF. I believe it is due to the fact that the officers cannot conceive of anyone not talking in the breezy staccato manner that is their natural mode of expression, and their being equal to them – the officers – in intelligence and efficiency. That rule applies to the English, for all but the well-educated classes, speak with an accent and act in every way as inferior beings. But the rule certainly

THE FOOD FLYING SQUAD *was another charitable organisation supported by US aid. Here the service, manned by the WVS, provides food for those made homeless in the Coventry bombing raids of April 1941.*

FOOD FLYING SQUAD
U.S.A. TO BRITAIN. MINISTRY OF FOOD

does not apply to the Dominions' personnel over here. I'm wondering what's going to happen on some of the long flights. The Canadian aircrew get along fine with English sergeants and other colonials, but they are as flint and steel to RAF officers."

British society and its class distinctions were incomprehensible to many American and Canadian personnel. Bob Raymond wrote in his diary:

"I sometimes feel that England does not deserve to win the war. Never have I seen such class distinctions drawn and maintained, in the face of a deep effort to preserve a democracy. With powers of regulation and control centred in the hands of a few, the abuse and preservation of the Old School Tie is stronger than it ever was on every side. In that, I am not affected and can remain aloof, and claim an unprejudiced onlooker's viewpoint. It has been well and truly said that General Rommel of the German Army Afrika Korps would never have risen above the rank of NCO in the British Army. This nation seems inexplicably proud of defects in its national character."

Efforts were made to promote a harmonious understanding between the natural allies. Dick Cotton, whose Rola factory made aircraft parts and had relocated to North Devon, was drafted in to talk to the British while the USA was still neutral. As his wife Peg wrote in 1941:

"Help the English people to understand the how and why of our actions nowadays; that our sympathies are with England, but that we are a very large nation peopled by a very large and varied public and governed by a system that is truly impelled by the people. And the American people, as a whole, are not yet ready to enter this war. They have no desire to."

AMERICAN GENEROSITY also provided Christmas presents for British evacuee children. Here, Father Christmas – played by a woman – hands out toys to a group of evacuees in Henley-on-Thames, Oxfordshire, 1941.

Phyllis Warner, who had spent a year in the USA on a teacher exchange scheme, was also recruited as a lecturer to the British Forces, teaching troops about the Americans.

"I made my debut as an approved lecturer to his Majesty's Forces, by visiting an isolated AA Battery to deliver an oration on America. I felt very shy about it, but a powerful drink in the Officer's Mess as soon as I arrived gave me Dutch courage, which I needed when I entered the hall to the sound of a stentorian 'Eyes Front'. There are several hundred men on the site so I had a lively audience who asked good questions – for once they kept off Hollywood and gangsters. Afterward I was charmingly entertained to dinner by the officers, so it was quite a social function."

UNLIKE BRITISH SOLDIERS, *the GIs always seemed to have money to spend and soon earned a reputation for being extravagant and fun-loving.*

The silver screen was much to blame for the British view of Americans, as GI bride Avice Wilson recalled.

> "Due to weekly visits to the local cinema I vaguely thought of Americans as being movie versions of New Yorkers and the soldiers would be the same, but in uniform, highly mechanised and rushing around."

In her California home, Londoner Florrie Elkus had been avidly following the war news from Britain, concerned for her large circle of friends and family all over England. Her sister Ethel Mattison wrote to Florrie on December 13, 1941:

> "I think of you when I am coming home from work in the blackout, and wondering if you hate it as much as we all do. One gets used to it but it is always unpleasant except on moonlight nights. I hate to think of you personally suffering any discomfort from the war (you've had enough to put up with worrying about us) but all the same, the general feeling is one of satisfaction that America is now in with us."

Ethel, like many diarists and letter writers in this period of the war, overflowed with admiration for the Russian struggle to expel the invading German Army.

> "December 20, 1941: The Russian successes are staggering – it's no wonder that everyone is bounding with enthusiasm for our Eastern allies. At the moment it's a big contrast with our lukewarm attitude to America. The press is largely to blame. For months it has uttered paens to America – whilst for years previous to 1941 practically every newspaper had proclaimed that Russia was a corrupted and weakened tyranny."

ONE OF THE LUXURIES
*American soldiers never
seemed to run out of was
chewing gum.*

America's entry into the war in December 1941 brought with it an invasion of GIs (an acronym for General, or Government, Issue – referring to their kit). Even now the term GI conjures up images of dances, jazz, jitterbugging, and gifts of the unobtainable: nylon stockings, chocolate and chewing gum. The first Yanks arrived in the small Somerset town of Wellington in 1942, as Anne Lee Mitchell wrote in her diary,

> ". . . followed by trails of children who can't leave them alone. Three hundred have now arrived and there's a forest of tents in the field behind the Griffins – lovely for them as they're woken at 5am by terrific chatteration, laughter and blowing of whistles!"

The free and easy reputation of the GIs had already reached Somerset when Anne returned home one evening in October.

> "Electrified to find a huge Negro in the kitchen – Gertie much flustered, explained it was her 'coloured friend, cycled over from Cross Keyes' to see her. When she brought my supper she said he had brought a bottle of beer and would I like a glass!! She then asked if she might go out for a bit with him, from which I sternly dissuaded her, pointing out that Nasty Incidents happen in the Blackout. Gathered from Gertie's face that any such incidents happened weeks ago!"

Bottled beer was at a premium in wartime Britain, so this was a handsome gift. This was the era of segregation, when black and white Americans served in separate companies. In Anne Lee Mitchell's quiet corner of the West Country, a black face was unknown – unknown and possibly therefore to be feared. The rumour mill got to work.

> "Lurid tale going round of a respectable Mrs Burton, who, followed by a negro last night, lost her nerve, and broke into a run under some dark trees. In a flash he was on her stabbing and slashing her neck with a knife. She screamed, luckily was heard by a cyclist (her brother in

law) who came to her rescue, and took her, dripping gore, into Mrs Ball's for First Aid. Man since arrested, but another one is missing from the camp. I trust I don't encounter him in the hay shed when I go in there of a dark evening. Wish the camp were further from our goats."

Troops of any nationality have always acquired a reputation when billeted amongst civilians. Whether these and other incidents were apocryphal or not, they still reflect a certain unease about the proximity of GIs amongst the locals. Peg Cotton was aware of the faults of her countrymen.

"Almost always, alas, it is the small incidents brought about by small people that build up an adverse 'blanket' opinion. For instance, the reckless driving here of American jeeps and motorcycles along the narrow, twisting English roads. In Instow alone, we have four different smashed walls from accidents. The walls are private property. Their owners don't think much of Americans! Frank Heaver's car was run into by an American Jeep. Its driver – in a tearing hurry, and on the wrong side of the road at that – hops out and goes up to Frank, who was ruefully looking at his damaged hood. 'Can't you get out of the way? Don't you know there's a War?' I feel gratified and proud when I see and hear of all the nice things, the decent things, that most of our American boys do here in England. And they love children. They will go out of their way to speak to a youngster. I was standing in a bus queue at Barnstaple one day when an American Jeep drove into the adjacent parking place and stopped. He looked us over – a line of women with laden shopping baskets, and the usual lot of children, too young to be in school or left at home alone. The young man suddenly straightened up, reached over into the back of the jeep, and then climbed out. Both hands were full of candy and gum. He went down the long queue, giving every child (even those in their Mother's arms) a share of the sweets. 'Hi, Buddy!' or 'Here, young lady!' he'd say – and grin shyly when the women thanked him. 'Shucks! It's nothin', Ma'am.' He went back to the jeep, and was asleep before our bus appeared."

THE AMERICAN ARMY *was strictly segregated, with black and white men serving in separate companies. Here, members of the first African American troop ever sent to Britain discover the delights of a local pub.*

THE ATTACK ON PEARL HARBOR

Britain needed the help of the USA and Russia to win the war against Germany, but until the surprise attack on the US Naval Base at Pearl Harbor, Hawaii in December 1941, Britain had held the western front alone. Although the Americans provided crucial support in the form of money, goods and military hardware, President Roosevelt had avoided his country joining the conflict directly.

In a bid to discourage Japanese aggression in the Far East the US Pacific Fleet had been moved to Hawaii. The Japanese reasoned that their planned attacks on the British colonies of Malaya and Singapore would result in America joining the war against them, so their solution was a pre-emptive strike to neutralise the Americans in the Pacific before they could mobilise. Attacking with over 350 planes launched from six aircraft carriers, the assault decimated the Pacific Fleet while it lay at anchor. Following this 'date that will live in infamy' as Roosevelt called it, American involvement in the conflict was certain and the war entered a new phase that would lead to thousands of GIs and American airmen being welcomed to England to join the struggle.

PUBLIC AND MEDIA OPINION *in the USA had been against involvement in the war, but the unprovoked attack on the Pacific Fleet convinced ordinary people that it was not only inevitable, but justified.*

DIVE BOMBERS FORMED *part of the second strike wave, dropping three bombs on the forward portion of the destroyer USS Shaw which was in drydock under repair. While efforts were being made to flood the dock, a fourth hit her ammunition magazines, resulting in a spectacular explosion (right) that completely destroyed her bow.*

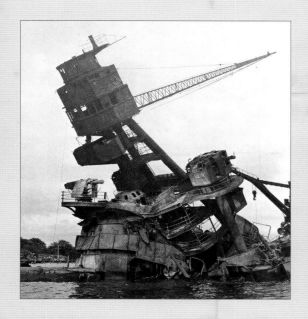

MANY OF THE CRIPPLED SHIPS
were salvaged and repaired
following the attack. However,
the USS Arizona (top left) was
too badly damaged, and the hull
remains at the bottom of the
harbour to this day. There were
2,350 fatalities during the whole
attack, including 68 civilians,
and 1,178 injured. Of the
military personnel lost, 1,177
were from the Arizona.

A JAPANESE PHOTOGRAPH
(top right) showing the attack on
Wheeler Army airfield. The air
base was one of the first places
to be targeted by the Japanese,
grounding the planes that were
stored there.

AERIAL BOMBARDMENT
caused the majority of the
damage in the attack, but five
Japanese Midget submarines also
entered the harbour. The USS
West Virginia (middle right),
seen here in the foreground sitting
low in the water following attack,
was reportedly the victim of the
first torpedo of the attack.

THE FLAGSHIP OF THE US FLEET,
the USS California (bottom
right) was one of the primary
targets of the attacks. A bomb
hitting below decks set off
her anti-aircraft magazine,
accounting for 50 of the 98 crew
members killed.

When 300 more Americans arrived in Wellington, Somerset, at the end of October 1943, Anne Lee Mitchell (like many other war-weary Brits) welcomed the diversion.

"The camp behind the Griffins is a clamour once more, while groups of greenish-grey figures lope about the streets. Curious how a slight change in uniforms gives a foreign air. I hear the officers are a nice lot. Let's hope they'll brighten our winter for us, like Leslie and Briggs and the rest did last year."

On the whole, British families took the GIs into their hearts and their homes. Through a hospitality scheme, British families offered their homes in a gesture of friendship to GIs on leave. The Americans had a reputation for abundance. Kathleen Crawley, who entertained troops and war workers with ENSA, wrote home from Colchester:

AN AMERICAN SOLDIER *billeted to your house meant that you could be assured of generous gifts of rationed luxuries such as tea.*

"On Friday we went to the famed American camp and found all that had been promised us – to begin with, at each of our places at table were 40 Chesterfield cigarettes, two Mars, two packets of fruit sweets and a packet of chewing gum. After that we had hamburgers and chips and beans and I had two large plates of delicious coffee ice cream. After that we were given sherry and koka kola, and after that there was a sort of dance. It was great fun – most of the officers were extremely nice."

Peg Cotton opened her Devon home to fellow American servicemen on leave. They provided an exciting diversion for the whole household, including her granddaughter Penny.

"They come over to Springfield – big, husky chaps with a real appreciation for a sing-song, a game of Bridge, a meal in a home, even though the meal is a distinctly wartime one. They come like the Greeks, bearing gifts – of tomato juice, candy, gum, cigarettes, and even a cake now and then. They remember Penny with special fruit drops and oranges. They talk of their homes – their parents – their wives – their children – their girl friends. They exhibit snapshots of all these human bits and pieces that make up the whole special 'Heart Experience' of each man – the thing he's eventually going to fight for, Home and Family and his Right to enjoy these things in Independence and Peace."

THE CONFIDENT MANNER and affluence of the American soldiers made them popular but also caused resentment, particularly with British servicemen who did not enjoy the same advantages.

Peg Cotton's husband Dick was one of the team in charge of procurements for the Allied invasion of Normandy. In the run-up to that campaign, Bill Virgil Evans the 1st breezed into the lives of Anne Lee Mitchell and her husband Mike one evening in March 1944.

"Our USA, one Bill Virgil Evans the 1st, arrived after lunch, a nice young lad with fair hair and blue eyes, feel I can deal with him fairly easily. Thrilled with home comforts and a big bed, his first for two years. We now await Bill, to whom Mike intends to give solemn warning of the perils of Wellington Women. Tonight he's told us all about the war, the colour question, sex ditto, and America's 'attitood'. He doesn't talk as much as *hold forth*, but is very delightful and I s'pose we too had everything taped at 22."

The tall handsome Texan loved to dance, play cards and share the details of his life 'back home'.

"Quite overcome by Bill's showing me a photo of fine twin baby boys – his own – and the smiling blonde he told me was 'one of his best girls' is his wife! His first baby, a girl, died at five months and he has only seen his sons once, they are nearly two now. And he seems such an infant himself! Amazing! He slept out on field manoeuvres last night, and says it was not so bad, he covered himself over with leaves. Enlivening tales of his tough upbringing in Texas – his Ma used to go out drinking and leave him alone, he found her liquor once (aged 7) and was comatose under the table when she returned. He thinks the world of 'Mom' I may add – 'A fine little woman, plenty tough, yes Ma'am'!"

It was their mores, money and easy manner that made the Yanks such a novelty. War-weary British civilians like Anne-Lee Mitchell enjoyed their encounters with their ebullient allies.

"While doing the farming a USA van drew up, full of officers, and Babs in her best attire enthroned among 'em, clutching three carnations. She'd been whisked off to be Matron of Honour at a USA wedding in Taunton! Bride and groom complete strangers but still. Great party at Sanford to celebrate this, we rushed back to cobble supper and take Bill into the Snells for a party, inebriated wedding guests and the band, they played and we danced in and out of chairs and drums. Bill consumed lots of neat whisky and whirled us round Texan-fashion, and when we got back at 12:30am, insisted on playing blackjack."

Peg Cotton recognised the cultural differences as her part of Devon swarmed with American troops.

Bride and groom complete strangers but still.

"The swaggering, boisterous antics of thousands of GIs bewilder the Devonians. In the pubs the American soldier treats the English beer and 'whiskey and soda' like soda-fountain or milk-bar drinks. That is, he drinks all he wants – without discrimination. He mixes drinks – and, in treating his English girl friend, he mixes her drinks! The result is not one to enhance the reputation of American young manhood. Windows are broken. Heads are broken. Hearts are broken. The English, because they do not understand, look askance at the Americans' free and easy ways."

Whatever British views of the Americans had been before they arrived, GIs were destined to have the romantic lead in this movie. Where once the Poles had held sway over the hearts of British women, the Yanks were about to take over. Avice Wilson was a teenager in Chippenham, Wiltshire.

"In January 1944 the second lot arrived, the 4th Armored Division. By the time they left many of the boys had been adopted by families, every girl in the town had an American boyfriend, sometimes two, and some had worked fast enough to get married. As a family I think we were impressed with the 'action' of the GIs. Something needed doing or getting? Right we had it as soon as possible. Admittedly the Americans had greater resources than we had at that time, but it was the combination of drive and confidence that never failed to dazzle us."

Peg Cotton was watching on the sidelines, with some misgivings.

"To the GI, no matter who the girl is, she becomes Millie, or Jane, or Babe, at once! There is no formality. The girl, to begin with, is uneasy when the American boy tightly links his arm in hers, as though they were very close friends. But in a very short time she accepts this as natural. She walks with nonchalance, hand-in-hand, with her American boyfriend. She chews gum. She boasts of the candy and sugar (both strictly rationed here) that he gives her. She is more leg-conscious than she ever was – wearing sheer American stockings – from the PX [American Forces supermarket]. She thinks all Americans are millionaires – and would like to marry one – and go to live in that country where everything is done by Modern Magic. I creep inwardly at the disillusion of some of these girls in the future."

SOME 70,000 WOMEN left England for the USA after the war as 'GI brides'. Here an American soldier and his wife have a farewell dinner with her family before setting sail for their new life.

Cliffs and beaches along the Devon coast were closed off as troops rehearsed for D-Day. Machine-gun fire, explosions and loud American voices disturbed the peaceful wartime countryside. Peg Cotton witnessed all this and sympathised with the locals who had to put up with it.

OUR AMERICAN COUSINS

DANCING AT THE RAINBOW
Corner, London was strictly
for white GIs only.

Aware of the needs of their troops far from home, the American Red Cross started clubs for GIs in major cities. Anne Chalmers volunteered as a hostess at the American Red Cross club in Bristol.

"There was no mistaking that we were on American territory, since it was their flag that was visible, their music that was being played on a radiogram, and the whole atmosphere was alien to any Brits, who, at least temporarily, left their native soil. Hand painted portraits of wolves heads with their bodies clad in American uniforms, graced the walls of the club. I talked to one of the Red Cross women and asked what hostesses were supposed to do. She replied that we had to dance with the men, talk to them and circulate. We were not supposed to stay with one particular one all the evening. There was a room with a piano, a lounge where soldiers could read quietly or write letters, a games room and a large ballroom with a stage, upon which well known bands would play for the Saturday night dances. There was also a canteen downstairs where food was provided, the kind that every resident in the United Kingdom currently dreamed about, since there was a plentiful supply of bacon and eggs and other 'goodies' which were severely rationed, and sometimes unobtainable as far as our own population was concerned. There were also bedrooms and bathrooms upstairs, so that soldiers who visited Bristol, but were not stationed there, could stay and enjoy the club's amenities. In the club there was often a sense of unreality, away from what was going on outside, with an exciting, stimulating feeling of not knowing what was going to happen from one day to the next. The American soldiers had brought with them a new dance called the Jive, and taught it to us, which was just as well as most of them were not very good ballroom dancers."

This club was only for white GIs. Black GIs had their own club elsewhere in Bristol, where they were allowed to bring their white girlfriends. Many of them were very homesick, and though the new environment could mean freedom and fun, some were miserable and lonely off duty. There were reports that troops from the southern states took violent action on one occasion when they heard of black troops going out with white girls: several were stabbed. The next morning black and white officers held a combined meeting to decide how best to separate the warring factions. Black soldiers were to be allowed out on alternate evenings, and this applied to the whites too. When dates were made, girls had to make sure whether it was a 'black' night or a 'white' night. Sally Peters was a 'donut girl', one of the hundreds of American girls who arrived in the wake of the GIs to bring them some home comforts. She wrote to her mother in Virginia:

"All day I handed out cigs, life savers and chewing gum – The 'boys' are wonderful – they are so glad to talk to an American girl. I have been running the Donut Dugout this week. That is the small building taken over by the Red Cross to give the boys some place to go other than pubs. It opens at 3pm and serves only coffee and donuts but has writing rooms, lots of fireplaces and big comfortable chairs. Tonight the Special Service Officer was supposed to have one of the bands appear for a concert at the Dugout, but they never showed up, so I gave some of the boys dancing lessons while one of the GIs played the piano. We also did a little singing of songs.

"I was out dancing with a naval flyer last night – I shall be extra nice to him – they are all such grand guys. It sort of makes you feel

SEGREGATED SOLDIERS
like these black Americans were often detailed to support roles rather than front line duties.

BLACK AMERICANS
with white girlfriends had to frequent the black servicemen's clubs, or British establishments such as the Bouillabaisse in Soho, shown here.

strange to think that they won't all come back . . . somehow I just can't blame them for getting drunk on their leave and staying that way for a couple of days – I think that the most good I've done so far is listening to the several I've been out to dinner with – one lad from California overstayed his leave a day and a night because he wanted to go out again with me – not that it was just me, but someone had to listen to him and be interested in what he had to say – I got a letter from him yesterday thanking me. Saturday night was very gay – evening dress dancing etc. Could have been any Saturday night at home. I had a wonderful time and even pinned a decoration on the Colonel – Danger hangover under construction."

She also visited the Grosvenor House Hotel in London, which had been requisitioned for US Army officers. It served 4,000 meals daily in the hotel's grand ballroom. The American Red Cross sent mobile canteens over with the troops. Although Sally wasn't able to tell her mother in her letter, she was serving GIs in special training for D-Day at Ilfracombe in Devon.

"5.4.44 Today I drove a 4 ton truck! Our clubmobile for the 1st time. It wasn't so hard, just had to remember to drive on the left hand side of the road, know when to double clutch and how to use the 4 gears! Edna drove out to the camp where we picked up a jeep to lead us out to the boys who were to be served. The terrain changed from lovely rolling downs to rolling sand dunes and that's where we got stuck! We put a couple of urns of coffee and five or six 100-doughnuts into a jeep and I went with the major and the jeep through the sand dunes to the place we were looking for. We placed the urns on top of the hood of the jeep, made the boys line up on both sides and served them coffee, letting them help themselves to the doughnuts. Incidentally, the major made me wear one of the GI steel helmets, but as I was wearing a bunch of narcissi in my hair I objected. Besides the helmet is most unbecoming – but he was firm. I got the best of him, sticking the flowers in the strap right in front. One of the GIs made some comment about my Easter bonnet, so I stuck it in the netting they wear on their helmets. I met the same boy three hours later and he was still wearing it! If only you could see me bouncing around in that jeep holding on to one sloshy coffee urn and that helmet bouncing around on my head."

Young women being 'shipped to the US' to join husbands whom they scarcely knew and families they had never seen.

As the war in Europe came to an end in May 1945, there were already many GI brides – and more to come. It was a trend frowned upon by many in Britain. Mrs Paroutaud's father was one of them.

"Our English relatives were appalled to see 100s of their young women being 'shipped to the USA' to join husbands whom they scarcely knew and families they had never seen. I never saw my father again. He was old and broken by the grief of the war. My brother who would have been 21, was missing in action at Tobruk."

Despite her father's opinion, she was married in June 1945, and joined the other GI brides being shipped out Stateside the following year. They were allowed a baggage allowance of 200 lbs and were housed in a camp staffed by German prisoners of war.

"Everything at that camp was an acute embarrassment – there was a physical inspection with all clothing removed."

Avice Wilson's husband-to-be, Johnnie, was one of the team organising the operation.

"Between the Army and the Red Cross everything the girls could possibly need was supplied, from baby bottle nipples to notepaper. Some girls neglected their children shamefully, others didn't know how to take care of them. Here the Red Cross girls did a valiant job, they took the children while their mothers were being processed, dried the tears of the homesick and bolstered the courage of girls who were having doubts about their journey."

To while away some of the time on board, Avice wrote letters home to her parents.

"There are 36 in a cabin, about 50ft by 13ft, so we are very crowded. Two tiered bunks, no proper place for hanging clothes so they are all around the sides. The bunks have a canvas bottom and mattress, and Hilda's is next to mine almost like a double bed. As this is a troopship there isn't much comfort, but it's worth any discomfort to join Johnnie. Three mothers and babies went off the ship, as the babies were ill. One girl received a cable 'Don't come, not wanted' and her passage was cancelled."

Just as they were ignorant of the American way of life, some of these women knew very little about the husbands and fiancés they were going to join.

12. The Final Assault

"More lovely weather, and sunbathing – these hot days, smell of lilac, and general air of well-being certainly helps one to bear the suspense. If it were not for the terrific air activity – fleets of giant bombers, transport planes and gliders – I'd think the second front only an evil dream."
Anne Lee Mitchell, May 1944

By 1944 an optimistic note was palpable in diaries and letters. The population was exhausted but felt victory was in sight. Hitler was on the run, and the country had survived the onslaught of thousands of bombs. But like any cornered and wounded animal, the Nazi beast would make a final vindictive and terrifying attack on the weary civilians on the Home Front. Unaware of this sting in the tail, the population talked of little else but the opening of the second front. It had been predicted and anticipated by some since 1942: soon the great day would arrive. With hindsight, it is known that the D-Day landings were the beginning of the final Allied victory over Hitler. But as he mused in the beauty of a spring morning, in May 1944, Mr C Jory could not predict certain victory.

"Are we in this coming invasion going to get one more set back, is the purely bad luck or the criminally unforeseen and mismanaged going to put us back from peace for another year or more? A lot of people must be wondering the same thing, and many thousands, millions maybe, with men and boys in it looking with dread to what the next few weeks will bring to them, whether in the whole it is victory or defeat."

BY THE SPRING OF 1944 southern England was full of American soldiers preparing – unbeknownst to the local civilians – for the Normandy landings. Here, a soldier takes a moment to help the children with their skipping on a street lined with equipment awaiting shipment to France.

In the West Country, Americans were massing for this invasion, troops blocked the roads and soldiers slept under hedgerows. Jory went down to the West Country for a few days and was impressed by the American hardware as the US Army readied itself for D-Day.

"By day and night their lorries and trains and all sorts of queer vehicles with mysterious loads are on their way to the west. There is more purely American traffic on the main road all the 24 hours than used to be there on the busiest summer day (holiday traffic) in peacetime. One marvels where all the petrol comes from! The high spot for me of this road traffic was to see one of the huge amphibious vehicles overturned across the main road. It is a six

VILLAGERS AND FARMERS *living near Slapton Sands in Devon discuss the news that they are to abandon their homes to allow American troops to practise their manoeuvres in secret. Some of the farmers, returning home the following year, found that their land was appreciably less productive than it had previously been.*

wheeled open truck on land but underneath is a propellor shaft and quite a useful looking propellor. This particular craft overturned by hitting a wall in swerving to avoid a lorry that cut in front. The job of righting it (or her) was done most expeditiously."

In Somerset, Anne Lee Mitchell recorded the unbearable tension of this waiting game.

"Such a perfect day again, this loveliness almost frightens me; it seems as if it's the end of everything – nothing so perfect can last. Yet each day brings new wonder. Today it is the lilac opening. I think we are all jumpy over the second front, we expect to hear it's begun every day, yet it's always the same old news: raids, raids, raids. Such a lot of heavy gunfire rumbling yesterday, I really thought it had started."

Anne and her friends had been entertained and charmed by many of the Americans camped on the town, including her lodger Bill Virgil Evans the 1st.

"Found Babs and Marion in the Sanford [a local pub] very gloomy because they think all the favourite US officers have gone. Long and tender goodbyes last night though no one said they were going. Bill came in late and had a sad little chat, asking us to look after his trunk 'in case anything happens' and giving me his folk's addresses. He seems to feel he may go off to battle any day now. How grim it is. We both lay awake last night, tossing and turning and thinking of all our friends waiting for the fateful zero hour."

That was at the end of April and, had she but known it, there was still more than a month to go. The gorgeous weather and the suspense continued.

"May 11: More lovely weather, and sunbathing – these hot days, smell of lilac, and general air of well-being certainly helps one to bear the suspense. If it were not for the terrific air activity – fleets of giant bombers, transport planes, and gliders – I'd think the second front only an evil dream. Alas! I fear it's bound to come."

When at last D-Day arrived, streams of hyperbole, patriotism and the possibility of peace poured into diaries and letters. The nation had held its breath and released it in one prolonged cheer. Unkindly, just when the future looked rosy, Hitler's new weapon (promised via Lord Haw Haw's broadcasts) burst from the skies. After nearly five years of war, this was devastating. Londoner Bill Regan, hardened to the sight and sound of bombs by his job as a rescue worker, was not alone in his feelings.

"Peculiarly, everyone is unanimous in their dislike of these things. They make a bigger mess than the bombs ever did. Some have a different note somewhat like an outsize bee, and they have a proportionate sting. Bill Brackin told me he dreaded nightfall; Wright and Pryor have said the same. There is not one man I know who is getting used to it; if anything it is getting everyone down. The sound of a motor far or near brings everyone to their feet with no exceptions. Not only is this so at the depot, but also in the streets. Kids playing happily, grown ups going about their affairs, next minute the streets clearing, as if by magic. You can see by their expressions, and the way they seem to go – 'let me get out of this'. You can feel the uneasiness. Unlike the old days when everyone waited to help everyone else."

It was the RAF who nicknamed these jet-powered V-1 flying bombs 'doodlebugs', but they were also known as buzz bombs. Miss Andrews was living in Tunbridge Wells where the local population had their eyes glued to the skies, watching the clouds of silver barrage balloons and listening for the buzz of the V-1s.

"People tend to be more jittery because of the inhuman aspect of the thing – once the engine stops, you know nothing can prevent disaster, and in London you don't see the fighters intercepting. We had guns all round us for a week or two, making it dangerous to move about outdoors, then they moved away and balloons have gradually crept closer. There are thousands of them (literally) stretching about 35 miles in width, and from here to London in depth, and at all heights. They are very successful in exploding doodles in the air; though sometimes a fast one will merely break the cable and sail on (one is going over as I write)."

RAF BALLOON DEFENCES *against the 'doodle-bugs', September 1944. Dispensing with the need for a pilot meant that the V-1 could be half the size of a conventional bomber plane, making it more difficult for anti-aircraft guns to hit.*

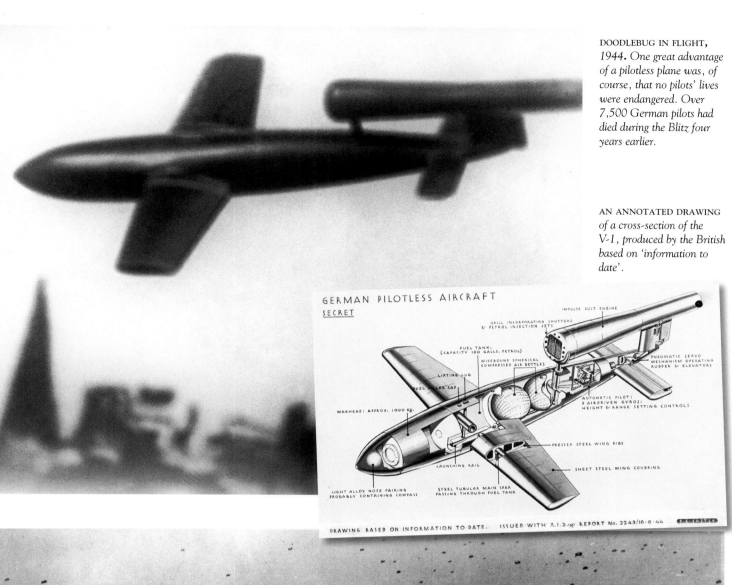

DOODLEBUG IN FLIGHT, 1944. *One great advantage of a pilotless plane was, of course, that no pilots' lives were endangered. Over 7,500 German pilots had died during the Blitz four years earlier.*

AN ANNOTATED DRAWING *of a cross-section of the V-1, produced by the British based on 'information to date'.*

GERMAN PILOTLESS AIRCRAFT
SECRET

IMPULSE DUCT ENGINE

GRILL INCORPORATING SHUTTERS
& PETROL INJECTION JETS

FUEL TANK,
(CAPACITY 130 GALLS. PETROL)

WIREBOUND SPHERICAL
COMPRESSED AIR BOTTLES

LIFTING LUG

FUEL FILLER CAP

PNEUMATIC SERVO
MECHANISM OPERATING
RUDDER & ELEVATORS

AUTOMATIC PILOT:
3 AIRDRIVEN GYROS:
HEIGHT & RANGE SETTING CONTROLS

WARHEAD: APPROX. 1000 KG.

PRESSED STEEL WING RIBS

LAUNCHING RAIL

SHEET STEEL WING COVERING

LIGHT ALLOY NOSE FAIRING
PROBABLY CONTAINING COMPASS

STEEL TUBULAR MAIN SPAR
PASSING THROUGH FUEL TANK

DRAWING BASED ON INFORMATION TO DATE.   ISSUED WITH A.I.2.(g) REPORT No. 2243/16.6.44

THE ALLIES LAND IN FRANCE

The tide had been gradually turning in the Allies' favour, but once a foothold had been gained in Hitler's 'fortress Europe' the weary British population could feel confident that it was only a matter of time before victory was theirs and they could steel themselves for one last push. If the battle of El Alamein had been, as Churchill put it, 'perhaps the end of the beginning', then the beginning of the end came on the Normandy beaches on June 6, 1944 – 'the D-Day landings'.

The purpose of D-Day was straightforward – to break through the German defences, advance on Paris and liberate France from German occupation. To achieve that aim, it was necessary to land a force of over 150,000 troops, mainly British, American and Canadian, backed up by 8,000 sailing craft and 13,000 aircraft. It was the largest and most complex operation of its kind in the history of war.

'Operation Overlord', as it was called, was under the command of General Eisenhower and the landings took place at five different points along the Normandy coast – beaches that were codenamed Utah, Omaha, Gold, Juno and Sword. Fierce German resistance on Omaha led to great loss of life on both sides, but eventually the Allied forces prevailed and began to take control of northern France.

THE BRITISH 2ND ARMY, *Royal Marine Commandos, make their way up Juno Beach at 8am on D-Day (above left). Behind the assault troops, old ships were being towed across the Channel and sunk to provide sheltered anchorages for the Allied craft.*

THE ROLE OF THE AMERICAN PARATROOPERS *– seen here flying over the English Channel – was to land along the 100 mile (160km) front on the Normandy beaches (above right). Bombers also attacked the bridges over the rivers Seine and Loire, preventing German reinforcements from reaching the scene of the fighting.*

AMERICAN SOLDIERS ABOARD *(middle right) an LCI (Landing Craft Infantry) on their way to Normandy.*

PACKED INTO AN ASSAULT CRAFT *on their way across the Channel (below right), these Canadian soldiers are equipped to start fighting the moment they land. About 14,000 Canadians stormed a 5 mile (8km) stretch of Juno Beach that morning, with the objective of capturing the seaside towns and advancing inland to cut off a key German supply line.*

D-DAY WAS A MASTERPIECE *of planning and organisation that both troops and back-up had been rehearsing for months. Here (left), barrage balloons keep watch overhead as vast quantities of US troops, supplies and equipment are unloaded onto Omaha Beach the day after the landings, to support the Normandy Campaign. This part of the conflict lasted nearly three months, but eventually Paris was liberated on August 26 and Brussels on September 3 – five years to the day since war had been declared.*

LONDON UNDER ATTACK *again: a V-1 flying bomb explodes close to Westminster. Big Ben and the Houses of Parliament can be seen on the right.*

Jory, who was a journalist, summed up the first week of living with the V-1s, which Hitler's propaganda chief Goebbels had proclaimed as the first of the new secret weapons designed to bring Britain to its knees.

"A week's intimate experience of this secret leaves us slightly bloody, but unbowed, and he will have to try something a lot better than that! First was on Sunday night or early Monday, just one that put a railway out of action, quite a lucky shot in the dark, as beyond setting the missile in a general direction and loading it with fuel for a certain (or more or less uncertain) distance that is all the control there can be over it. Two nights later there were more and it was announced that they *were* flying bombs or pilotless or robot planes. By Friday they were coming regularly and quite frequently, day and night and we fired at every one enough stuff to sink a battleship without doing them any harm, and upsetting the populace by the increasing row all night. By night they were easily seen in flight, level and straight about 1,000 feet up, because of the red glow from the petrol driven engine placed on top of the plane, itself not quite half the size of a Spitfire. Fuel exhausted, noise would stop, light go out and ten or 15 seconds later there would be a loud explosion as 1 ton of bomb in the nose struck ground. Blast was tremendous and mostly lateral and buildings for good quarter of a mile radius were wrecked. By Saturday night (when one fell 100 yards from flat and broke windows in it, killing six in houses in Downton Avenue opposite) they were coming over from 50 to 100 in night and alerts were more or less continuous. We seemed to have no answer, and it was obvious that if something effective were not done quickly there would be a considerable amount of panic; exodus on quite biggest scale since 1940 Blitz began. Goebbels and crew were telling the world London was in flames, that MPs had fled, that we all lived in shelters."

The following week, which he recorded as the "42nd week of the fourth year of war", Jory declared that he could not write about the wider war, because he had to write about the war as 'it affected me in particular'. He was in bed with a bad cold in his top floor London flat on the night of June 24.

"Listening to pilotless planes in large numbers passing over and bursting near and far when one did *not* pass over, but hit the roof of my flat over dining room with engine still running. The final noise before the burst was a fierce menacing roar like the snarl of a thousand tigers. Then came the explosion and everything seemed to be going down in a ruin about me. I was not more than 25 feet away from point of impact, with the concrete roof, the walls of the corridor between my bedroom and dining room all there was between us. I was at that moment half turning left towards bedroom window in opposite direction from where the plane came. I felt I had been hit in the face from direction of window, a sharp and hot blow. For a minute I could not see owing to cloud of black dust and I suppose smoke. Meanwhile the building rocked, debris rained down and I got to the centre of small room feeling blood already running from left side of face and head. Then for an appreciable but short time there was absolute silence, then shouting began in the street and lower down in building."

ALMOST 2,500 V-1S exploded over London between July 1944 and January 1945, killing over 6,000 people. Here, workers survey the wreckage of a railway goods yard in the East End.

On hands and knees he looked for his torch, searching through the head-high rubble in his bedroom. By its light he surveyed the random damage. The wardrobe doors had been ripped off but the clothes inside were unscathed. The dressing table mirrors were unbroken but the grandfather clock had been blown from one end of the room to the other. He went to what remained of the window and shouted for help.

"A fireman in the yard below heard me and shouted that he would get on fire escape. I said: 'Don't do that come up the stairs instead.' So he and another did, though in places the landings had been blown away, stepping from one top rail of stairs over a three foot span with a 60–70 foot drop he got to my room window-sill and came in. He agreed that the only way out was via the window, so I went first dropping in to the other fireman's arms at last."

CIVIL DEFENCE RESCUE *crews help to remove casualties from a London building damaged by a V-1, July 1944.*

FOLLOWING A V-1 HIT *that destroyed an entire street in south London, this man returned from walking his dog to find that his wife was one of the victims. A policeman offers tea and sympathy to the now homeless widower.*

THE GREATEST INTENSITY *of hits occurred in Croydon, South London. In total, 2,419 V-1s hit London (including this one in Ilford, Essex above), killing over 6,000 people.*

Jory's dog, Bill, had been lying under the bed when the flying bomb hit.

"The three of us passed out the Airedale, Bill, who was so amenable that he must have been dazed. Then I was helped to walk over piles of debris, every floor being wrecked but main stairs intact, to first floor, where in corridor my wife had been sheltering and was unhurt. In opposite corridor several people were buried under debris from ceiling and flats on either side."

One hundred pieces of debris were removed from his face and head when he arrived at the hospital. As he lay waiting to go down to theatre for an operation to remove a piece of glass from his left eye, the flying bombs still droned overhead.

"I had no idea then if my left eye had been saved. It was heavily bandaged and was a bit troublesome. So was my head, part of which had been stitched. A fractured skull had been feared I learned later."

THE FINAL ASSAULT

The next afternoon he was transferred to another hospital in Chertsey, Surrey, to recuperate. He travelled in a Green Line bus converted into an ambulance. The 30 mile journey took over five hours, as the ambulance had to pick up so many other casualties along the route. In September that year he returned to work – the surgeons had saved his eye.

Hospitals had to postpone their normal work to treat the casualties. Anne Lee Mitchell had an agonising wait to have a breast lump removed in the summer of 1944, and could hear the rockets overhead as she lay in her hospital bed.

In Tunbridge Wells, Miss Andrews watched the skies as Spitfire pilots shot down the V-1s over the Kent countryside.

"At school we had to quarter the children close to indoor shelter. We kept a spotter who blew a whistle on hearing a bomb approach and then all dived for shelter. The worst worry was the approaching public exams. A very sympathetic notice from the university empowered us to postpone or alter exam times, but where were we to hold it, were we to make them shelter? The strain on the children would be great, for no one could get much refreshing sleep as night was the great time for them now."

In the middle of the night a doodlebug fell perilously close. She was woken by the screams of a child in the street below.

"I raked out my uniform, put on old thick shoes for fear of glass and was out of the house in about three minutes. The street was in a haze of dust, people were sweeping piles of glass from the roadway. Before we had gone far the back of my shoe gave way, so that I had to 'dot and carry one', putting on belt and tie the while. The plane had fallen on the Woodward's tennis court in Bosdyke, and one could hardly see down there for the dust. As we entered the First Aid Post we found almost all windows out and ceilings down in the kitchen and surgical pantry. My job was to sterilise instruments, and Mrs Besant had put a pail on the gas ring in the kitchen, where dust and rubble inches thick was scarcely conducive to asepsis!"

BRITAIN'S YOUNGEST
doodlebug spotters,
continuing their lessons
as they scan the skies over
Otham, Kent. Each of
these boys had spotted and
reported 50 doodlebugs.

A HUGE CRATER
at Speakers' Corner,
Hyde Park, caused by a
V-2 bomb.

NATIONAL FIRE SERVICE *workshops destroyed by a V-2 bomb have been blown on to a railway line in Essex, causing disruption to the train service as well as creating yet another pile of mangled wreckage.*

The next secret weapon Hitler had up his sleeve was the rocket-powered V-2. Miss Andrews wrote:

"It is said to be an enormous rocket fired into sub-stratosphere from Germany. There were some twenty odd in the week and we could hear the explosion and feel the concussion from miles away. They make a much deeper crater than the flying bomb but blast damage is not so heavy."

As a Fleet Street journalist, Jory had access to privileged information and recorded the impact that the V-2 rockets were having on the population.

"No mention of them in the Press, by order, though every day evacuees were streaming back, flying bomb danger being apparently over. But even this restarted on Saturday morning when I heard the first alert since my return. No alert can be given for the rockets as they are not seen or heard till the last few seconds. They appear to have set us a pretty problem. They are much more numerous and nearer the centre of the London target than ever before. It is a strange way of living, when quite feasibly one may be dead next minute, next hour, or tomorrow, with no warning and no escape . . . a slaying which is purely a matter of luck. Day and night, light and dark, it is the same. These things fall and the matter is settled – and they may fall anywhere. Yet people show very little fear and except when there is one close enough to shake them or be heard rather louder than usual, take very little notice. Most of us may get, as I do, some consolation from the thought that if we do get a direct hit, we shall know nothing about it and our worries will be over – or we hope they will!"

BRITISH INTELLIGENCE'S *'best guess' at the design of the V-2, December 1944.*

The combined death toll from V-1s and V-2s was 9,000 people. Among those killed by the V-2s were 20 women from the WVS in Lambeth; a further 100 were injured.

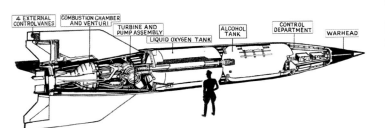

VICTORY AT LAST.
*St Paul's Cathedral was
floodlit as part of the
VE Day celebrations.*

Donald Gulliver was too young to remember playing under a street lamp aglow in the darkness. So when he wrote to his father in early 1945, the news that the lights had come on at last took up most of his letter.

"The light is on at the corner, and I was playing under it last night, and the night before."

Vera Lynn had wished for the lights to come on all over the world, in a popular wartime song, but life is never so clean cut. First of all, the nation and the Allies celebrated Victory in Europe: VE day was on May 8, 1945. Practical difficulties abounded for those on the Home Front and those returning to it. Peg Cotton had spent a large part of the war in North Devon near her husband's munitions factory. When VE day arrived she found the idea of carrying on more of a challenge than before.

"Reality is catching up with us again. There are still the Japs to lick. The war goes on in the East. Casualty lists continue to pour in. Rationing is tight – tighter than ever, with only one ounce of lard instead of two per week. Distribution of food is uneven. Queues are longer. 'Points' [ration units] don't go so far. More articles hibernate beneath the counters. The feeling of anti-climax is so great that everywhere one hears these remarks. 'I think we miss having the War here – the air raids, the bombs, the rockets (V-1's and V-2's). There seems nothing to keep up for now!' I think we miss the war on the Continent. The European War furnished an excitement and an incentive that bolstered morale to high endurance. The war in the Pacific has not the same effect; it's too far away. If this aftermath of the European War is so hard to bear, what will it be like when the Jap War is over – and V-J Day breaks upon us? Dick makes only the gloomiest of predictions. He says the two years following the end of World War II will be more difficult and harder to bear, in England, than the War years themselves. He's been right in his predictions most of the time. So I don't feel too happy."

Added to the hardships of postwar Britain was the challenge that faced couples who had made wartime marriages, sometimes after a brief romance. Mary Hooper (née Ross) had known her husband for a decade before she had married him in the spring of 1941, but as he was away in the army they had spent only brief euphoric 'leave' together. He was still in Germany as part of the army of occupation (the British Army of the Rhine) when the war finally ended. She wrote to him:

> "I've been doing a lot of thinking about life after you do get home pet. It's strange to reflect that although we've known each other ten years we don't really know what sort of people we're like to live with. I mean ordinary everyday sort of life. How you go out to school, how you spend your evenings – when you've years of evenings to spend as you like and things like that. It's going to be difficult at first and we must be intelligent about it."

CROWDS IN WHITEHALL *cheer Prime Minister Winston Churchill on the day that he broadcast the news that the war with Germany had been won, May 8, 1945.*

Munitions worker Louie White had found some comfort through her job at Blackburn's Aircraft Factory in Leeds when her husband Jack and his brother Peter were both shot down within a few weeks of each other. But when victory came, she revealed the cost of 'her' war in her diary.

> "Jack missing 97 weeks. The war is over in Europe. Everyone in suspense. I am not bothered. Worked over. At 9.00 the news was given that it was over in Germany and tomorrow will be VE day. At this moment someone is singing 'None but the weary heart'. How appropriate for me just now. I feel so miserable. There is only one whom I shall miss. Made a Red Flag, but as I won't be at work tomorrow I shan't be able to use it."

It rained in Leeds on VE Day, in empathy with her mood.

> "Had a holiday. In the afternoon went to see Hotel Berlin. Very Good, came home and stayed in."

THE DAILY MAIL BREAKS *the good news to the nation.*

An essential part of the grieving process was taken from many war widows: they did not always know where their husbands' bodies lay. Jack White's brother Peter, who went missing in a bombing raid in 1943, was buried in the Steinhalden Cemetery at Bad Cannstatt. Louie did not record whether her husband Jack had a known grave.

Anne Lee Mitchell never discovered the fate of the Texan, Bill Virgil Evans the 1st, who had brightened up her home in the months before D-Day. She was told by some of his fellow GIs that he had 'left the company'. The war in the Far East did not end until the Japanese surrender on August 14. On August 16 Anne made her final diary entry.

THE WAR MAY BE OVER, *but things didn't get back to normal straight away. Two years later housewives were still having to queue for food.*

OVER 35,000 PRISONERS, *mainly British service people who had been prisoners of the Japanese, had to be returned home. Many were physically frail or mentally damaged.*

"All happy and joyful because of the war being over, and looking forward to getting our POWs back from Japan. But our larders are very bare and there are no houses for the returning soldiers to live in. And many of them are coming back to find small unwelcome black or American babies in their families – not so good. Workhouses and nursery schools crowded with little bastards, and a wave of crime is sweeping Wellington. Boy of 16 has been forging cheques, a young soldier's wife has murdered her baby (not his). Everyone's house needs painting and plastering, our clothes are getting very shabby, and you can not buy a sheet or a blanket unless you have been newly wedded or bombed out. Life is going to be every bit as strenuous."

More than 50,000 British service personnel were taken prisoner by the Japanese; 12,400 of them died in captivity. Those who survived the Japanese POW camps were mentally, as well as physically, maimed by the experience. Miss ME Littleboy had no idea whether the happy, handsome boyfriend who went to fight the Japanese was even alive, until she received a telephone call in 1945.

"The call was from the docks at Southampton. I could hardly believe it, and was not a little perturbed, for I was rather involved with my present boyfriend, and angry to be involved in something I had not bargained for. I was also disturbed by this voice from a long distant past; far too disturbed. It was as if a life had suddenly come back from the dead."

She agreed to see him, with misgivings.

"I felt vulnerable, not in command of the situation. He stood there I couldn't believe my eyes. This was not the young man I had known. I was stunned. Misshapen. Pitted, scarred. Only the eyes were the same. I could have wept. So while we had been fighting, that is what the poor wretch had been turned into. I thought of the handsome boyfriend I was to meet next weekend. Dark, tall, in command of every situation. I looked at this hulk of humanity and my heart bled. It was as if all that was left of my youth was gone in the moment I saw him. He was part of the glamorous pages of my past and now it was there no longer and never would be again."

Her returning POW suffered from bouts of malaria, and she nursed him through. He insisted that the couple marry.

"Here was the challenge given to me for peacetime. Could I meet it? London and the BBC were empty after my wartime activities. Could I keep this man alive and help him get back into life again? I loved the spirit of the man, but could love nothing else. I had to do it. There was no other way. He represented the challenge which was my future, the help I alone could give him."

They married, unhappily, and it was only after his death that she felt able to commit this tragic story to paper.

There were joyful homecomings too, but the relief of victory was a brief respite from the hardships of the war years. The bitter struggle had cost the country dear and Britons were still to endure years of austerity as they witnessed their nation's decline as a world power.

MOST HOMECOMINGS were a cause for celebration. These Glaswegians are preparing to welcome a local man who has been in the Middle East for four years.

INDEX

PICTURE CREDITS